ACCA

PAPER F6

TAXATION (UK)

FA 2012

P
R
A
C
T
I
C
E

&

R
E
V
I
S
I
O
N

K
I
T

BPP Learning Media is the **sole ACCA Platinum Approved Learning Partner – content** for the ACCA qualification. In this, **the only Paper F6 Practice and Revision Kit to be reviewed by the examiner**:

- We discuss the **best strategies** for revising and taking your ACCA exams

- We show you how to be **well prepared** for your exam

- We give you **lots of great guidance** on tackling questions

- We show you how you can **build your own exams**

- We provide you with **three** mock exams including the **December 2012 exam**

Our **Passcard** and **i-Pass** products also support this paper.

FOR EXAMS IN 2013

BPP
LEARNING MEDIA

First edition 2007
Seventh edition January 2013

ISBN 9781 4453 6646 3
(previous ISBN 9781 4453 7995 1)
ebook ISBN 9781 4453 6949 5

British Library Cataloguing-in-Publication Data
A catalogue record for this book
is available from the British Library

Published by

BPP Learning Media Ltd
BPP House, Aldine Place
London W12 8AA

www.bpp.com/learningmedia

Printed in the United Kingdom by

Ricoh
Ricoh House
Ullswater Crescent
Coulsdon
CR5 2HR

We are grateful to the Association of Chartered Certified
Accountants for permission to reproduce past
examination questions. The suggested solutions in the
exam answer bank have been prepared by BPP Learning
Media Ltd, except where otherwise stated.

Contents

A note about copyright

Using your BPP Learning Media products

This Kit gives you the question practice and guidance you need in the exam. Our other products can also help you pass:

- **Learning to Learn Accountancy** gives further valuable advice on revision

- **Passcards** provide you with clear topic summaries and exam tips

- **Success CDs** help you revise on the move

- **i-Pass CDs** offer tests of knowledge against the clock

You can purchase these products by visiting http://www.bpp.com/acca

BPP
LEARNING MEDIA

Question index

The headings in this checklist/index indicate the main topics of questions, but questions often cover several different topics.

Questions set under the old syllabus exam are included in this Kit (labelled BTX) because their style and content are similar to those that appear in the new syllabus exam. The questions have been amended as appropriate to reflect the current syllabus exam format.

BPP
LEARNING MEDIA

Planning your question practice

Our guidance from page xxiii shows you how to organise your question practice, either by attempting questions from each syllabus area or **by building your own exams** – tackling questions as a series of practice exams.

Topic index

Listed below are the key Paper F6 syllabus topics and the numbers of the questions in this Kit covering those topics.

If you need to concentrate your practice and revision on certain topics or if you want to attempt all available questions that refer to a particular subject, you will find this index useful.

Syllabus topic	Question numbers
Administration of tax – individuals	2, 4, 11, 13, 19, 20, ME1 Qu 1, ME3 Qu 1
Administration of tax – companies	31, 35, 37, 43, 46, 49, ME3 Qu2
Capital allowances	17, 31, 32, 33, 36, 37, 41, 43, 45, 48, 49, ME2 Qu 1, ME2 Qu 2, ME3 Qu 1, ME Qu 2
Chargeable gains – reliefs	21, 22, 23, 24, 25, 39, 40, ME1 Qu 3, ME2 Qu 3, ME3 Qu 4
Chargeable gains – companies	32, 38, 39, 40, ME2 Qu 3, ME3 Qu 3
Chargeable gains – individuals	12, 21, 22, 23, 24, 25, 40, ME1 Qu 3, ME3 Qu 4
Companies – calculation of taxable total profits	6, 31, 32, 33, 34, 36, 37, 40, 43, 45, 46, 48, 49, ME1 Qu 2, ME2 Qu 2, ME 3 Qu 2
Companies – calculation of tax	31, 32, 34, 35, 36, 37, 40, 43, 44, 45, 46, 49, ME1 Qu 2, ME2 Qu 2, ME3 Qu 2
Companies – groups	33, 44, 45, 46, 47, 48, 49
Companies – losses	37, 41, 42, 43, 46, ME3 Qu 3
Companies – overseas aspects	32, 44, 45, ME2 Qu 2, ME3 Qu 2
Income tax computation	1, 2, 3, 4, 5, 6, 8, 11, 13, 33, ME1 Qu 1, ME1 Qu 5, ME2 Qu 1, ME2 Qu 4, ME3 Qu 1, M3 Qu 4, ME1 Qu 5
Individuals – employment income	2, 3, 4, 5, 6, 8, 18, ME1 Qu 1, ME2 Qu 1, ME3 Qu 1, M3 Qu 4
Individuals – property income	7, 8, 9, 18, ME1 Qu 1, ME3 Qu 1
Individuals – trading income	2, 3, 5, 11, 12, 13, 14, 17, 18, ME1 Qu 4, ME2 Qu 1, ME3 Qu 1
Individuals – losses	14, 15
Inheritance tax	26, 27, 28, 29, 30, 44, ME1 Qu 3, ME2 Qu 5, ME3 Qu 5
National insurance contributions	3, 6, 8, 12, 13, 17, 18, 33, ME1 Qu 5, ME2 Qu 1, ME3 Qu 4
Partnerships	13, 16, 17, 18
Pensions	2, 3, 10, ME2 Qu 4, ME 3 Qu 5
Value added tax	17, 18, 32, 41, 43, 45, 50, 51, 52, 53, 54, ME1 Qu 2, ME2 Qu 1, ME3 Qu 2

ME1 is Mock Exam 1, ME2 is Mock Exam 2 and ME3 is Mock Exam 3

Helping you with your revision – the ONLY F6 Practice and Revision Kit to be reviewed by the examiner!

BPP Learning Media – the sole Platinum Approved Learning Partner – content

As ACCA's **sole Platinum Approved Learning Partner – content**, BPP Learning Media gives you the **unique opportunity** to use **examiner-reviewed** revision materials for the 2013 exams. By incorporating the examiner's comments and suggestions regarding syllabus coverage, the BPP Learning Media Practice and Revision Kit provides excellent, **ACCA-approved** support for your revision.

Tackling revision and the exam

You can significantly improve your chances of passing by tackling revision and the exam in the right ways. Our advice is based on feedback from ACCA examiners.

- We look at the dos and don'ts of revising for, and taking, ACCA exams
- We focus on Paper F6; we discuss revising the syllabus, what to do (and what not to do) in the exam, how to approach different types of question and ways of obtaining easy marks

Selecting questions

We provide signposts to help you plan your revision.

- A full **question index**
- A **topic index** listing all the questions that cover key topics, so that you can locate the questions that provide practice on these topics, and see the different ways in which they might be examined
- **BPP's question plan** highlighting the most important questions and explaining why you should attempt them
- **Build your own exams**, showing how you can practise questions in a series of exams

Making the most of question practice

At BPP Learning Media we realise that you need more than just questions and model answers to get the most from your question practice.

- Our **Top tips** included for certain questions provide essential advice on tackling questions, presenting answers and the key points that answers need to include
- We show you how you can pick up **Easy marks** on some questions, as we know that picking up all readily available marks often can make the difference between passing and failing
- We include **marking guides** to show you what the examiner rewards
- We include **examiners' comments** to show you where students struggled or performed well in the actual exam
- We refer to the **FA 2012 Study Text** (for exams in 2013) for detailed coverage of the topics covered in questions

There are three mock exams that provide practice at coping with the pressures of the exam day. We strongly recommend that you attempt them under exam conditions. **Mock exams 1** and **2** reflect the question styles and syllabus coverage of the exam and **Mock exam 3** is the December 2012 paper.

Revising F6

Firstly we must emphasise that you will need a good knowledge of the **whole syllabus.**

That said, you must have **sound knowledge in the following fundamental areas** if you are to stand a chance of passing the exam. You should therefore **revise the following areas particularly well.**

- **Income tax computation** including the personal allowance and the tax bands and rates.

- The **calculation of benefits from employment**, such as company car and/or fuel, use of an employer's asset and low cost loans. Make sure you can spot tax free benefits too.

- **Capital allowances proforma** paying particular attention to the availability of annual investment allowance. Note particularly the difference in the calculation rules between individuals (sole traders and partners) and companies.

- **Calculation of taxable total profits**, in relation to companies. Be aware that you may need to calculate the various elements that make up the taxable total profits such as property business income, interest income, gains and so on.

- **Computation of chargeable gains** paying attention to whether the disposal is made by an individual or a company, particularly for aspects such as indexation allowance and annual exempt amount.

- **Inheritance tax computations**, including lifetime transfers and the death estate.

- How to calculate **VAT payable or repayable** depending on the type of supply (ie standard rated, zero rated or exempt).

- The **different classes of NIC** payable by employees and their employers compared to those due from self employed individuals or partners.

Reading articles

The examiner has stressed the importance of reading the technical articles published in *Student Accountant* that relate to F6. The **Finance Act 2012 article** is particularly relevant as it highlights topical aspects which are likely to be tested in the 2013 exams.

Question practice

You should use the Passcards and any brief notes you have to revise the syllabus, but you mustn't spend all your revision time passively reading. **Question practice is vital**; doing as many questions as you can in full will help develop your ability to analyse scenarios and produce relevant discussion and recommendations. The question plan on page xxi tells you what questions cover so that you can choose questions covering a variety of syllabus areas.

Passing the F6 exam

Displaying the right qualities

The examiner expects students to display the following qualities.

Qualities required	
Knowledge development	Questions will test your knowledge of underlying principles and major technical areas of taxation, as they affect the activities of individuals and businesses, across the breadth of the F6 syllabus. You will also be expected to apply this knowledge to the facts of each particular question and also to identify the compliance issues for your client.
Computation skills	Although you will be expected to be able to calculate the tax liability, note that you will also be marked on the methods you use. So, if your numbers are not perfect you will not necessarily lose too many marks so long as your method is correct and you have stated any assumptions you have made.
Ability to explain	Whilst the main focus of the exam is on the computation of tax liabilities, you may also be required to explain rules and conditions, so take care to practise the written elements of the answers also.
Identification capability	You must know who you are calculating tax liabilities for – is the client a company or an individual? Be sure who you are advising as this will seriously impact your answers.

You will not always produce the exact same answer as we have in our answer section. This does not necessarily mean that you have failed the question, but if you do use the suggested proformas and methods you will maximise the number of marks you can achieve.

Avoiding weaknesses

We give details of the examiner's comments and criticisms throughout this Kit. These have hardly varied over the last few years. His reports always emphasise the need for thorough preparation for the exam, but there are various things you can do on the day of the exam to enhance your chances. Although these all sound basic, the examiner has commented that many scripts don't:

- Make the most of the information given in the question
- Follow the question requirements
- Set out workings clearly

Using the reading time

You will have 15 minutes' reading time for Paper F6. Here are some helpful tips on how to best utilise this time.

- Speed read through the question paper, jotting down any ideas that come to you about any of the questions.

- Decide the order which you're likely to tackle questions (probably easiest questions first, most difficult questions last).

- Spend the remainder of reading time reading the question(s) you'll do first in detail jotting down proformas and plans (any plans or proformas written on the question paper should be reproduced in the answer booklet).

- When you can start writing, get straight on with the question(s) you've planned in detail.

If you have looked at all of the questions during the reading time, this should hopefully mean that you will find it easier to answer the more difficult questions when you come to them, as you will have been generating ideas and remembering facts while answering the easier questions.

Choosing which questions to answer first

There are five compulsory questions, with a larger number of marks awarded for the first two questions.

- Many students prefer to answer the questions with the largest number of allocated marks first. Others prefer to answer a question on their most comfortable topic.

- Whatever the order, make sure you leave yourself **sufficient time** to tackle all the questions. Don't get so bogged down in the calculations in the first question you do, especially if it's your favourite topic, that you have to rush the rest of the paper.

- Allocate your time carefully between different question parts. If a question is split into a number of requirements, use the number of marks available for each to allocate your time effectively.

Tackling questions

You'll improve your chances by following a step-by-step approach along the following lines.

Step 1   Read the requirement

Identify the knowledge areas being tested and see precisely what the examiner wants you to do. This will help you focus on what's important in the question.

Step 2   Check the mark allocation

This helps you allocate time.

Step 3   Read the question actively

You will already know which knowledge area(s) are being tested from having read the requirement so whilst you read through the question underline or highlight key words and figures as you read. This will mean you are thinking about the question rather than just looking at the words blankly, and will allow you to identify relevant information for use in your calculations.

Step 4   Plan your answer

You may only spend five minutes planning your answer but it will be five minutes well spent. Identify the calculations you will need to do and whether you have appropriate proformas to assist in these. If there is a written element to the question, determine whether you can you use bullet points or if you need a more formal format.

Step 5   Write your answer

Stick carefully to the time allocation for each question, and for each part of each question.

Gaining the easy marks

There are two main ways to obtain easy marks in the F6 exam.

Proformas

There will always be basic marks available for straightforward tasks such as putting easy figures into proformas, for example putting the cost figure for an addition into a capital allowances proforma. Do not miss out on these easy marks by not learning your proformas properly. Make it easy for yourself to pick up the easy marks.

Deadlines and dates

An important component of your knowledge of the different taxes is the administrative, or compliance, details such as filing deadlines and tax payment dates. This element of the requirement can often be answered even before you make any calculations, for example stating the submission deadline for an individual's self assessment tax return.

Exam information

The exam paper

The syllabus is assessed by a three-hour paper-based examination.

The paper will be predominantly computational and will have five questions, all of which will be compulsory.

- Question one will focus on income tax and question two will focus on corporation tax. The two questions will be for a total of 55 marks, with one of the questions being for 30 marks and the other being for 25 marks.

- Question three will focus on chargeable gains (either personal or corporate) and will be for 15 marks.

- Questions four and five will be on any area of the syllabus, can cover more than one topic, and will be for 15 marks each.

There will always be at a minimum of 10 marks on value added tax. These marks will normally be included within question one or question two, although there might be a separate question on value added tax.

There will always be between 5 and 15 marks on inheritance tax. Inheritance tax can be included within questions three, four or five.

National insurance contributions will not be examined as a separate question, but may be examined in any question involving income tax or corporation tax.

Groups and overseas aspects of corporation tax may be examined in either question two, question four or question five.

A small element of chargeable gains may be included in questions other than question three.

Any of the five questions might include the consideration of issues relating to the minimisation or deferral of tax liabilities.

December 2012

		Question in this Kit
1	Trading income assessment, Employment income, Property business income, investment income. Calculation of income tax payable. Payment of income tax under self-assessment	ME 3 Qu 1
2	Computation of taxable total profits, capital allowances. Submission of corporation tax returns. VAT cash accounting scheme and annual accounting scheme. VAT overseas aspects.	ME 3 Qu 2
3	Chargeable gains for company. Share pool, part disposal and compensation for destruction of asset.	ME 3 Qu 3
4	Extracting profits from company as salary or dividends. Incorporation relief for CGT.	ME 3 Qu 4
5	Pensions. Individual savings accounts. Inheritance tax on lifetime transfers.	ME 3 Qu 5

The December 2012 exam is Mock exam 3 in this kit.

June 2012

Examiner's comments

The vast majority of candidates attempted all five questions, and there was little evidence of time pressure. Where questions were left unanswered by candidates, this appeared to be due to a lack of knowledge or poor exam technique, as opposed to time pressure.

Question 4 was the most difficult of the three 15-mark questions, so it was a sensible strategy to leave this question until last. If time was running out, it would have been much easier and quicker to score marks on question 5.

Candidates performed particularly well on questions 1a, 1b, 1d(i), 2a, 3a, 3b, 3c(i), 4a, 5a and 5b. The questions candidates found most challenging were questions 1c, 1d(ii), 1d(iii) 2b, 3c(ii), 4b and 5c – approximately one-third of the paper. This is mainly due to candidates not covering the entire syllabus as part of their studies

A number of common issues arose in candidate's answers:

- Failing to read the question requirement clearly. For example, calculating the income tax in question 1(a) despite being told that only the taxable income figure was required.

- Poor time management. For example, the 1 mark questions should have been answered with a brief sentence rather than a long paragraph.

- Not learning lessons from earlier examiner's reports and hence making the same mistakes. For example, the necessity of learning basic rules (such as where there is a long corporation tax period of account) has previously been highlighted several times.

- Poor layout of answers. For example, the two sections of question 2 were sometimes combined into one long very confusing answer. The same with question 3(b) where it was often not clear which of the two sections was being answered.

December 2011

Examiner's comments

This was another good performance, although many candidates achieved a pass mark without particularly excelling. There are two aspects that are worth mentioning. The first is that candidates should sometimes stand back and think about their answers to see whether they make sense. For example, for question 5 part (c) it should have been fairly obvious that an answer with six marks attached to it was not simply that no inheritance tax was due. The second aspect is that candidates should give particular attention to the requirements, especially any guidance that is given. In this paper they would have seen that in question 3 there was no need to calculate any CGT liability, in question 4 they were given advice on how to layout their answer, and in question 5 they were told to ignore annual exemptions - making their answer much more straightforward.

June 2011

		Question in this Kit
1	Sole trader; adjustment of profit; income tax computation and administration; national insurance contributions; partnerships	13
2	Company; taxable total profits including trading income; capital allowances; property income; chargeable gain; payment of corporation tax by instalments	31
3	Chargeable gains for individuals; share with takeover.; entrepreneurs' relief; CGT liabilities	21
4	Value added tax; registration; invoices; EU services; penalty for understated tax; annual accounting scheme	51
5	Inheritance tax on lifetime transfers and death estate; payment of tax	29

Examiner's comments

This was a very good performance and it was pleasing to see how well the first Paper F6 inheritance tax question was answered. One particular problem at this sitting was that candidates wasted quite a bit of time where something should have been obvious without having to produce detailed calculations, and also where more calculations were done than was necessary because the requirements were not read properly. This is where the reading time should be put to good use.

December 2010

		Question in this Kit
1	Employment benefits; taxable income; PAYE	4
2	Taxable total profits; calculation of corporation tax; overseas aspects of corporation tax VAT	45
3	Chargeable gains for individual; valuation of deemed proceeds; shares; entrepreneurs' relief; part disposal; chargeable gains for company	40
4	Salary or company car; income tax and NIC aspects for employee and employer	6
5	Losses for individual	n/a

Examiner's comments

This paper continued in the same style as that of the June paper, with the aim of being less predictable and required candidates to think a bit more in order to achieve a pass mark. Although the overall result was satisfactory, the performance was not quite as good as expected. The main problems were that candidates were obviously not expecting a question on PAYE, and question 4, although not being particularly difficult, required some careful planning before doing the computations.

June 2010

		Question in this Kit
1	UK residence for individuals; adjustment of profit; partnerships; national insurance contributions for self employed; VAT tax point; calculation of VAT under normal rules and flat rate scheme	17
2	Property business income for company; taxable total profits; loss relief; capital allowances; income tax and national insurance contributions for director	33
3	Chargeable gains for company; share pool with rights issue; insurance proceeds; rollover relief; part disposal	39
4	Income tax administration; deliberate withholding of information by client; ethics; written information notice; discovery assessment; interest and penalties for overdue tax	20
5	Payment of corporation tax; quarterly instalments	35

Examiner's comments

This style of this paper was slightly different from recent papers, with more smaller sub-parts enabling more of the syllabus to be covered: Some of the other changes were that the VAT information needed for question 1 part (d) was not shown separately (instead being included within the main text), and in question 2 the group relief and capital allowance aspects were in separate sections (requiring explanations instead of straightforward computations) rather than being examined computationally as part of the main corporation tax question. Candidates cannot expect to have an easy income tax or benefits computation in every paper. The pass rate achieved was quite satisfactory.

December 2009

		Question in this Kit
1	Basis periods; adjustment of profit for sole trader; calculation of income tax; administration for self assessment	11
2	Residence of company; capital allowances; calculation of corporation tax; overseas aspects; VAT registration; pre-registration input tax and errors	32
3	CGT for three individuals with incorporation relief; gift relief and principal private residence relief	25
4	Badges of trade; calculation of tax liability if trading or realising capital gain	12
5	Corporate loss relief	42

Examiner's comments

This was another good performance, and well prepared candidates had no difficulty in achieving a pass mark. Questions 3 (capital gains tax (CGT)) and 5 (corporate loss relief) caused the most problems, and the value added tax (VAT) aspects of question 2 were also not particularly well answered.

June 2009

		Question in this Kit
1	Calculation of income tax liabilities; filing dates and record retention	2
2	Calculation of company's adjusted trading profit; corporation tax; interest; capital gains group and use of election	49
3	Calculation of capital gains tax liabilities; use of losses b/f	25
4	Calculation of VAT payable; cash accounting scheme; VAT registration and output VAT on piecemeal sale of fixed assets or TOGC	54
5	Factors indicating employment; income tax and national insurance as employee and self employed	ME1 Qu 5

Examiner's comments

This was another exceptionally good performance with many candidates achieving high marks. The simplification of capital gain tax for individuals, having a separate VAT question, and a fairly straightforward question 5 all contributed to the good pass rate. In addition, candidates seemed very well prepared for this examination. Areas, such as NIC, which a few diets ago were causing problems, are now handled with ease.

December 2008

		Question in this Kit
1	Employment income; property income; calculation of income tax; national insurance	n/a
2	Calculation of loss for company; use of loss; penalties for late submission of return; VAT default surcharge; annual accounting scheme	43
3	Chargeable gains for company; shares; part disposal; relief for replacement of business assets	38
4	Partnership; change of accounting date; cessation of sole trade	16
5	Pension provision	n/a

Examiner's comments

This was an exceptionally good performance with many candidates achieving high marks. None of the questions caused any problems, and even candidates who did not do particularly well with questions 1, 2 and 3, often managed to achieve a pass mark by scoring good marks on questions 4 and 5.

June 2008

		Question in this Kit
1	Employment income; trading income; calculation of income tax; national insurance	5
2	Accounting period for corporation tax; computation of taxable total profits for short period; VAT registration	n/a
3	Chargeable gains for individual; residence and ordinary residence; CGT reliefs, part disposal	n/a
4	Income tax administration	19
5	Corporation tax for long period of account	34

Examiner's comments

This was a reasonable performance. The main problem was caused by question 4, which many candidates found surprisingly difficult. This question was usually left until last, and it was often obvious that insufficient time had been left to attempt it properly.

December 2007

Examiner's comments

This was a very good performance for the first sitting of this paper. Those candidates who marginally failed to achieve a pass mark generally did so because of poor time management. Also, many candidates that were obviously running out of time surprisingly opted to attempt question 5, which was quite the most technically demanding on the paper, rather than question 4 where it was relatively easy to score 9 or 10 marks. Practicing questions under timed, exam-style conditions prior to sitting the examination would have helped as regards time management.

Pilot paper

Analysis of past papers

The table below provides details of when each element of the syllabus has been examined and the question number and section in which each element appeared.

Covered in Text chapter		Dec 2012	June 2012	Dec 2011	June 2011	Dec 2010	June 2010	Dec 2009	June 2009	Dec 2008
	UK TAX SYSTEM									
1	Introduction to the UK tax system		4a							
	INCOME TAX AND NATIONAL INSURANCE CONTRIBUTIONS									
2	The computation of taxable income and the income tax liability	1a, 4a, 5b	1a	1a	1a	1a	1a, 2d	1c, 4b	1a	1a
3	Employment income	1a, 4a		1a		1a			1a, 5	1a
4	Taxable and exempt benefits. The PAYE system	1a	1a	1a		1a, 4			1a	1a
5	Pensions	5a		1c		1a			1a	5
6	Property income	1a	1a	4	2a					1a
7	Computing trading income	1a			1a		1b	1b 4a, 4b	1a	
8	Capital allowances	1a, 2a	2a		2a		2c			
9	Assessable trading income	1a	1c					1a	5	
10	Trading losses		4b			5				
11	Partnerships and limited liability partnerships		1a		1b		1b			4
12	National insurance contributions	4a	1b	1b	1b	4	1c, 2d	4b	5	1b
	CHARGEABLE GAINS FOR INDIVIDUALS									
13	Computing chargeable gains		3b	3	3b	3		3a, 3b, 3c, 4b	3	
14	Chattels and the principal private residence exemption			3				3c	3	
15	Business reliefs	4b	3b	3	3a	3		3a, 3b	3	
16	Shares and securities				3b	3		3b	3	
	TAX ADMINISTRATION FOR INDIVIDUALS									
17	Self assessment and payment of tax for individuals	1b			1a	1a	4	1c, 1d	1b	
	INHERITANCE TAX									
18	Inheritance tax	5c	5a-c	5c	5a-c	n/a	n/a	n/a	n/a	n/a
	CORPORATION TAX									
19	Computing taxable total profits	2a, 4a	2a, 2b	2a, 2b	2a	2a, 4	2a	2a	2a	2a
20	Computing the corporation tax liability	2a, 4a	2a, 2b	5b	2a	2a, 4	5	2a	2b	3a
21	Chargeable gains for companies	3	3a, 3c			3	3a, 3b			3a, 3b
22	Losses			2c			2a	5		2a
23	Groups			5a			2b		2d	
24	Overseas matters for companies	2a		5b		2a		2a		
25	Self assessment and payment of tax by companies	2b			2b				2c	2a
	VALUE ADDED TAX									
26	An introduction to VAT		1d	2d	4a	2b	1d	2b	4	2b
27	Further aspects of VAT	2c	1d	2d	4b-e	2b	1d	2b	4	2b

Useful websites

The websites below provide additional sources of information of relevance to your studies for *Taxation*.

- www.accaglobal.com

    ACCA's website. The students' section of the website is invaluable for detailed information about the qualification, past issues of *Student Accountant* (including technical articles) and even interviews with the examiners.

- www.bpp.com

    Our website provides information about BPP products and services, with a link to the ACCA website.

Planning your question practice

We have already stressed that question practice should be right at the centre of your revision. Whilst you will spend some time looking at your notes and Paper F6 Passcards, you should spend the majority of your revision time practising questions.

We recommend two ways in which you can practise questions.

- Use **BPP Learning Media's question plan** to work systematically through the syllabus and attempt key and other questions on a section-by-section basis

- **Build your own exams** – attempt questions as a series of practice exams

These ways are suggestions and simply following them is no guarantee of success. You or your college may prefer an alternative but equally valid approach.

BPP Learning Media's question plan

The BPP Learning Media plan below requires you to devote a **minimum of 30 hours** to revision of Paper F6. Any time you can spend over and above this should only increase your chances of success.

Step 1   For each section of the syllabus, **review your notes** and the relevant chapter summaries in the Paper F6 **Passcards**.

Step 2   **Answer the key questions** for that section. These questions have boxes round the question number in the table below and you should answer them in full. Even if you are short of time you must attempt these questions if you want to pass the exam. You should complete your answers without referring to our solutions.

Step 3   **Answer the other questions** for that section, if you have time. You must make sure that you attempt a variety of questions from the whole syllabus and not just concentrate on a few aspects.

Step 4   Once you have worked through all of the syllabus sections attempt **Mock exam 1** under strict exam conditions. Then have a go at **Mock exam 2**, again under strict exam conditions. Just before the exam, if you have time, attempt **Mock exam 3**, again under strict exam conditions. This is the December 2012 paper.

Syllabus section	Passcards chapters	Questions in this Kit	Comments	Done ☑
Revision period 1 Introduction to the UK tax system Income tax computations	1, 2	1	Work through this question carefully. It covers the basic income tax computation you will have to do in the exam.	☐
Revision periods 2/3 Employees	3, 4	3,4	Q3 covers some basic aspects of income tax computation and benefits. It also includes an element of tax planning which is becoming more important in the F6 exam. Q4 is a great question on employment income presenting two different jobs with different remuneration packages. It also covers the PAYE system and gives an idea how simple this will be when examined.	☐
			Q2 and Q5 give you extra practice in the type of question set as Q1 in the exam	☐
Revision period 4 Pensions and property income	5	10	Q10 tests the topical area of pensions.	☐
	6	9	Q9 shows how property income can be tested in a full 15 mark question.	☐
		7, 8	Q7 is another full question on property income. Q8 shows how property income can be examined as part of a longer question	☐
Revision periods 5/6 Trading profits and losses for individuals				
Adjustment of profits	7	13	Q13 includes an adjustment of profit computation and also tests employment income. You may want to do part (b) in revision period 7.	☐
Assessable trading income	9	11	Q11 is a good example of a typical Q1 in the exam. It covers basic adjustment of profit and the basis of assessment rules.	☐
Trading losses	10	15	Q15 covers early years loss relief and terminal loss relief. Part (a) is a theory question which is becoming more common in the F6 exam.	☐
		14	Q14 is another question on losses and includes interaction with chargeable gains.	☐

Syllabus section	Passcards chapters	Questions in this Kit	Comments	Done ☑
Revision period 7 Partnerships	11	16, 18	Q16 shows how partnerships can be tested with other rules on basis periods. Q18 has an element of partnerships as part of a longer question – this is common format for the examiner to use.	☐
		17	Q17 is an other example of partnership as part of a longer question.	☐
Revision period 8 National insurance contributions	12	6	Q6 requires you to work out the tax implications of a director leasing a car or being provided with a company car. This type of question is increasingly being asked at F6 so make sure you are prepared.	☐
Revision period 9 Computing chargeable gains	13	12	Gains will be tested in Question 3 in the exam and may also be tested in any of the other questions. The gains rules are therefore key for your exam. Q12 a good question covering both trading income and capital gains. Again, this is making you think about tax planning, not just doing computations.	☐
Revision period 10 Chattels and PPR	14	23	Q23 is great question covering PPR relief and a number of other aspects of CGT.	☐
Revision period 11 Capital gains reliefs	15	22, 25	Q22 deals with CGT liability and the effect of entrepreneurs' relief. Q25 is a good question to practice a number of reliefs.	☐
Revision period 12 Shares and securities	16	21	Q21 covers aspects of disposals of shares and the effect of takeovers.	☐
		24	Q24 covers a number of aspects of CGT.	☐
Revision period 13 Self assessment and payment of tax by individuals	17	20	Don't neglect administrative aspects in your F6 revision. Q20 covers the topical issue of tax evasion and tax avoidance.	☐
		19	Q19 covers some basic administration rules.	☐
Revision period 13/14 Inheritance tax (IHT)			You will be asked between 5 and 15 marks on inheritance tax so this is an important topic to revise.	
	18	27, 29	Q27 tests how to deal with lifetime transfers and a simple death estate. Don't forget the easy administration mark in part (b). Q29 focuses on a more complicated death estate. Note the explanation of the exemption in part (c).	☐
		26, 28, 30	Q26, 28 and 30 give you extra practice in IHT.	☐

Syllabus section	Passcards chapters	Questions in this Kit	Comments	Done ☑
Revision periods 14/15 Computing corporation tax				
Capital allowances	8		These are usually tested in detail in the corporation tax question. But you also need to make sure you understand the rules for unincorporated businesses.	
Computation of taxable total profits and corporation tax liability	19, 20	31, 33, 36	Q31 gives you practice in the style of question which is usually set as Q2 in the exam. Q33 is a slightly unusual style of question which covers basic corporation tax and also requires you to give tax advice on a number of matters. Q36 includes a long period of account.	☐
		34, 37	Q34 deals with a long period of account. Q37 gives you extra practice in a long question with capital allowances.	
Revision period 16 Chargeable gains for companies	21	39, 40	Q39 shows how company gains may be tested in Q3. Q40 is a typical of a question testing a mixture of company and individual gains.	☐
		38	Q38 is another example of a whole question on company gains.	☐
Revision period 17 Corporation tax losses	22	41, 42	Q41 shows how trading losses may be examined in Q2 in the exam. Q42 is an example of a shorter losses question.	☐
		43	Q43 is another example of a longer question include losses.	☐
Revision period 18 Groups	23	48, 49	Q48 covers group relief. Q49 includes capital gains groups.	☐
		46, 47	Q46 is a short question giving you more practice on group relief. Q47 similarly is a short question on capital gains groups.	
Revision period 19 Overseas aspects of corporation tax	24	44, 45	Q44 shows how a number of aspects of tax can be examined in one question. Q45 includes the topical aspect of overseas branches.	☐
Revision period 20 Self assessment and payment of tax by companies	25	35	Q35 is a useful reminder about the payment of corporation tax in instalments.	☐

Syllabus section	Passcards chapters	Questions in this Kit	Comments	Done ☑
Revision periods 21/22 Valued added tax (VAT)			There will be at least 10 marks for VAT in your paper so be prepared.	
	26, 27	32, 51, 54	Q32 shows how VAT may be tested as part of a longer question. Q51 and Q54 are 15 mark questions on VAT.	☐
		50, 52, 53	Q50, Q52 and Q53 give you extra practice on VAT topics.	

Build your own exams

Having revised your notes and the BPP Passcards, you can attempt the questions in the Kit as a series of practice exams. You can organise the questions in the following ways.

- Either you can attempt complete past exam papers; recent papers are listed below:

	June 12 Questions in Kit	December 11 Questions in Kit	June 11 Questions in Kit	December 10 Question in Kit	June 10 Question in Kit
1	18	3	13	4	17
2	36	41	31	45	33
3	22	23	21	40	39
4	15	9	51	6	20
5	27	44	29	n/a	35

- Or you can make up practice exams, either yourself or using the suggestions we have listed below.

	Practice Exam					
	1	2	3	4	5	6
1	3	18	11	13	5	2
2	32	33	41	37	45	49
3	38	21	40	22	23	24
4	30	27	20	28	16	29
5	47	19	26	51	44	50

Questions

TAXATION OF INDIVIDUALS

Questions 1 to 18 cover the taxation of individuals and their income from employment and self-employment, the subject of Part B of the BPP Study Text for Paper F6. Questions 19 and 20 cover tax administration for individuals, the subject of Part D of the BPP Study Text for Paper F6.

1 Brad, Lauren, Tom and Sarah

36 mins

(a)   Brad, an advertising executive, and his wife Lauren, an IT consultant, have one son. Having made a large gain on the sale of a property when they got married, they have acquired a considerable number of investments. They now require assistance in preparing their taxation returns for tax year 2012/13 and have listed out their income and expenditure:

Brad

	£
Salary (before deduction of PAYE)	104,500
Premium Bond prize	5,000
Interest received on National Savings & Investments Certificates	300
Building society interest (Joint account – total net interest credited)	4,400 (net)

Lauren

	£
Salary (before deduction of PAYE)	47,000
Interest received on ISA account	350
Dividend received on Virgin plc shares	2,250
Building society interest (Joint account – total net interest credited)	4,400 (net)
Interest received on 2025 5% Treasury Stock (received gross)	2,000
Gift Aid payment to Dogs Trust (actual amount paid)	1,000

Required

Calculate Brad and Lauren's income tax liability for tax year 2012/13. You should indicate by the use of zero any items that are non-taxable/exempt from tax.   **(10 marks)**

(b)   Lauren's father, Tom, a widower, who is 69, has the following income for tax year 2012/13.

	£
State retirement pension	4,226
Pension from former employer (before deduction of PAYE)	7,890
Building society interest (net interest credited)	14,320

Tom gave £3,200 to Oxfam (a registered charity) on 21 September 2012 under Gift Aid. This was the actual amount paid.

Required

Calculate Tom's income tax liability for tax year 2012/13.   **(5 marks)**

(c)   Sarah, Brad's sister, is self-employed and has the following income for tax year 2012/13:

	£
Trading profits	164,000
Bank interest received from Santander (net interest credited)	8,000
Dividends from BP plc (actual amount received)	4,950

Sarah paid £16,000 (net) into her personal pension scheme during 2012/13.

Required

Calculate Sarah's income tax liability for tax year 2012/13.   **(5 marks)**

                                                                                                    (Total = 20 marks)

2 Domingo, Erigo and Fargo (TX 06/09)   45 mins

Domingo, Erigo and Fargo Gomez are three brothers. The following information is available for the tax year 2012/13:

Domingo Gomez

(1)   Domingo is aged 67.

(2)   During the tax year 2012/13 he received the state pension of £4,500 and a private pension of £3,400

(3)   In addition to his pension income Domingo received building society interest of £15,520 and interest of £600 on the maturity of a savings certificate from National Savings and Investments during the tax year 2012/13. These were the actual cash amounts received.

(4)   During the tax year 2012/13 Domingo made donations of £300 (gross) to local charities. These were not made under the gift aid scheme.

Erigo Gomez

(1)   Erigo is aged 56.

(2)   He is employed as a business journalist by Economical plc, a magazine publishing company. During the tax year 2012/13 Erigo was paid a gross annual salary of £36,000.

(3)   During the tax year 2012/13 Erigo used his private motor car for business purposes. He drove 18,000 miles in the performance of his duties for Economical plc, for which the company paid an allowance of 25 pence per mile.

(4)   During June 2012 Economical plc paid £11,400 towards the cost of Erigo's relocation when he was required to move his place of employment. Erigo's previous main residence was 140 miles from his new place of employment with the company. The £11,400 covered the cost of disposing of Erigo's old property and of acquiring a new property.

(5)   Erigo contributed 6% of his gross salary of £36,000 into Economical plc's HM Revenue and Customs' registered occupational pension scheme.

(6)   During the tax year 2012/13 Erigo donated £100 (gross) per month to charity under the payroll deduction scheme.

Fargo Gomez

(1)   Fargo is aged 53.

(2)   He commenced self-employment as a business consultant on 6 July 2012. Fargo's tax adjusted trading profit based on his draft accounts for the nine-month period ended 5 April 2013 is £65,800. This figure is before making any adjustments required for:

    (i)   Advertising expenditure of £2,600 incurred during May 2012. This expenditure has not been deducted in calculating the profit of £65,800.

    (ii)   Capital allowances.

(3)   The only item of plant and machinery owned by Fargo is his motor car. This cost £11,000 on 6 July 2012 and had CO_2 emissions of 150g/km. During the nine-month period ended 5 April 2013 Fargo drove a total of 24,000 miles, of which 8,000 were for private journeys.

(4)   During the tax year 2012/13 Fargo contributed £5,200 (gross) into a personal pension scheme, and made gift aid donations totalling £2,400 (net) to national charities.

Tax returns

For the tax year 2012/13 Domingo wants to file a paper self-assessment tax return and have HM Revenue and Customs prepare a self-assessment on his behalf. Erigo also wants to file a paper tax return but will prepare his own self-assessment. Fargo wants to file his tax return online.

Required

(a)   Calculate the respective income tax liabilities for the tax year 2012/13 of:

    (i)   Domingo Gomez;   **(6 marks)**
    (ii)   Erigo Gomez;   **(6 marks)**
    (iii)   Fargo Gomez.   **(7 marks)**

(b)   Advise Domingo, Erigo and Fargo Gomez of the latest dates by which their respective self-assessment tax returns for the tax year 2012/13 will have to be submitted given their stated filing preferences.   **(3 marks)**

(c)   Advise Domingo, Erigo and Fargo Gomez as to how long they must retain the records used in preparing their respective tax returns for the tax year 2012/13, and the potential consequences of not retaining the records for the required period.   **(3 marks)**

(Total = 25 marks)

3 The Wind Family (TX 12/11)   45 mins

Philip, Charles and William Wind are grandfather, father and son. The following information is available for the tax year 2012/13:

Philip Wind

Philip is aged 78. During the tax year 2012/13 he received pensions of £13,140.

In addition to his pension income, Philip received building society interest of £13,280 during the tax year 2012/13.

This was the actual cash amount received.

Charles Wind

Charles is aged 49. He is self-employed as an architect, and his tax adjusted trading profit for the year ended 31 December 2012 was £111,400.

During the tax year 2012/13 Charles made a gift aid donation of £800 (gross) to a national charity.

William Wind

William is aged 23. He is employed as a security consultant by Crown plc, a company that supplies security services.

During the tax year 2012/13 William was paid a gross annual salary of £181,335.

During the tax year 2012/13 William contributed £7,300 into Crown plc's HM Revenue and Customs' registered occupational pension scheme. The company contributed a further £10,950 on his behalf.

Throughout the tax year 2012/13 Crown plc provided William with a petrol-powered motor car which has a list price of £83,100. The motor car cost Crown plc £78,800, and it has an official CO_2 emission rate of 227 grams per kilometre. Crown plc also provided William with fuel for private journeys. During the tax year 2012/13 William made contributions of £8,000 to Crown plc in respect of the motor car. This consisted of £4,800 for the use of the motor car, and £3,200 towards the cost of fuel for private journeys. The total cost of the fuel for private journeys was £4,400.

Required

(a)   Calculate the respective income tax liabilities for the tax year 2012/13 of:

    (i)   Philip Wind;   **(4 marks)**
    (ii)   Charles Wind;   **(4 marks)**
    (iii)   William Wind.   **(7 marks)**

(b)   Calculate the respective national insurance contributions, if any, suffered by Philip, Charles and William Wind for the tax year 2012/13.   **(4 marks)**

(c) Explain to Charles and William Wind, with supporting calculations, how their respective income tax liabilities for the tax year 2012/13 would have been reduced if:

(i) Charles Wind had contributed £10,600 (gross) into a personal pension scheme during the tax year 2012/13; **(3 marks)**

(ii) William Wind's contributions of £8,000 to Crown plc in respect of the company motor car for the tax year 2012/13 had been allocated on a more beneficial basis. **(3 marks)**

(Total = 25 marks)

4 Joe Jones (TX 12/10) 45 mins

On 31 December 2012 Joe Jones resigned as an employee of Firstly plc, and on 1 January 2013 commenced employment with Secondly plc. Joe was employed by both companies as a financial analyst. The following information is available for the tax year 2012/13:

Employment with Firstly plc

(1) From 6 April 2012 to 31 December 2012 Joe was paid a salary of £6,360 per month. In addition to his salary, Joe was paid a bonus of £12,000 on 12 May 2012. He had become entitled to this bonus on 22 March 2012.

(2) Joe contributed 6% of his monthly gross salary of £6,360 into Firstly plc's HM Revenue and Customs' registered occupational pension scheme.

(3) On 1 May 2012 Firstly plc provided Joe with an interest free loan of £120,000 so that he could purchase a holiday cottage. Joe repaid £50,000 of the loan on 31 July 2012, and repaid the balance of the loan of £70,000 when he ceased employment with Firstly plc on 31 December 2012.

(4) During the period from 6 April 2012 to 31 December 2012 Joe's three-year-old daughter was provided with a place at Firstly plc's workplace nursery. The total cost to the company of providing this nursery place was £11,400 (190 days at £60 per day).

(5) During the period 6 April 2012 to 31 December 2012 Firstly plc paid gym membership fees of £1,650 for Joe.

(6) Firstly plc provided Joe with a home entertainment system for his personal use costing £4,400 on 6 April 2012. The company gave the home entertainment system to Joe for free, when he left the company on 31 December 2012, although its market value at that time was £3,860.

Employment with Secondly plc

(1) From 1 January 2013 to 5 April 2013 Joe was paid a salary of £6,120 per month.

(2) During the period 1 January 2013 to 5 April 2013 Joe contributed a total of £3,000 (gross) into a personal pension scheme.

(3) From 1 January 2013 to 5 April 2013 Secondly plc provided Joe with living accommodation. The property has an annual value of £10,400 and is rented by Secondly plc at a cost of £2,250 per month. On 1 January 2013 Secondly plc purchased furniture for the property at a cost of £16,320. The company pays for all of the running costs relating to the property, and for the period 1 January 2013 to 5 April 2013 these amounted to £1,900.

(4) During the period 1 January 2013 to 5 April 2013 Secondly plc provided Joe with 13 weeks of childcare vouchers costing £100 per week. Joe used the vouchers to provide childcare for his three-year-old daughter at a registered nursery near to his workplace.

(5) During the period 1 January 2013 to 5 April 2013 Joe used Secondly plc's company gym which is only open to employees of the company. The cost to Secondly plc of providing this benefit to Joe was £340.

(6) During the period 1 January 2013 to 5 April 2013 Secondly plc provided Joe with a mobile telephone costing £560. The company paid for all of Joe's business and private telephone calls.

Required

(a) Calculate Joe Jones' taxable income for the tax year 2012/13. **(17 marks)**

(b) (i) Briefly explain the basis of calculating Joe Jones' PAYE tax code for the tax year 2012/13, and the purpose of this code; **(2 marks)**

(ii) For each of the PAYE forms P45, P60 and P11D, briefly describe the circumstances in which the form will be completed, state who will provide it, the information to be included, and the dates by which they should have been provided to Joe Jones for the tax year 2012/13. **(6 marks)**

Note: your answer to both sub-parts (i) and (ii) should be confined to the details that are relevant to Joe Jones. **(Total = 25 marks)**

5 Sam and Kim White (TX 06/08) 45 mins

Sam and Kim White are a married couple. Sam is aged 36 and Kim is aged 38. The following information is available for the tax year 2012/13:

Sam White

(1) Sam is self-employed running a retail clothing shop. His statement of profit or loss for the year ended 5 April 2013 is as follows:

	Note	£	£
Gross profit			138,823
Depreciation		6,123	
Motor expenses	2	8,800	
Patent royalties	3	700	
Professional fees	4	1,860	
Other expenses	5	71,340	
			(88,823)
Net profit			50,000

(2) During the year ended 5 April 2013 Sam drove a total of 25,000 miles, of which 5,000 miles were driven when he visited his suppliers in Europe. The balance of the mileage is 25% for private journeys and 75% for business journeys in the United Kingdom.

(3) During the year ended 5 April 2013 Sam paid patent royalties of £700 (gross) in respect of specialized technology that he uses when altering clothes for customers.

(4) The figure for professional fees consists of £1,050 for legal fees in connection with an action brought against a supplier for breach of contract and £810 for accountancy. Included in the figure for accountancy is £320 in respect of personal capital gains tax advice for the tax year 2011/12.

(5) The figure for other expenses of £71,340 includes £560 for gifts to customers of food hampers costing £35 each and £420 for gifts to customers of pens carrying an advertisement for the clothing shop costing £60 each.

(6) Sam uses one of the eight rooms in the couple's private house as an office for when he works at home. The total running costs of the house for the year ended 5 April 2013 were £5,120. This cost is not included in the statement of profit or loss expenses of £88,823.

(7) Sam uses his private telephone to make business telephone calls. The total cost of the private telephone for the year ended 5 April 2013 was £1,600, and 25% of this related to business telephone calls. The cost of the private telephone is not included in the statement of profit or loss expenses of £88,823.

(8) During the year ended 5 April 2013 Sam took goods out of the clothing shop for his personal use without paying for them and no entry has been made in the accounts to record this. The goods cost £820 (an amount which has been deducted when calculating gross profit), and had a selling price of £1,480.

(9)   The tax written down values for capital allowance purposes at 6 April 2012 were as follows:

	£
Main pool	18,500
Motor car	20,200

The motor car has CO_2 emissions of 175 g/km and is used by Sam.

Kim White

(1)   Kim is employed as a sales person by Sharp-Suit plc, a clothing manufacturing company. During the tax year 2012/13 she was paid a gross annual salary of £23,730.

(2)   On 1 June 2012 Sharp-Suit plc provided Kim with an interest free loan of £12,000 so that she could purchase a new motor car.

(3)   During the period from 1 June 2012 to 5 April 2013 Kim used her private motor car for business and private purposes. She received no reimbursement from Sharp-Suit plc for any of the expenditure incurred. Kim's mileage during this period included the following:

	Miles
Normal daily travel between home and permanent workplace	3,400
Travel between permanent workplace and Sharp-Suit plc's customers	11,200
Travel between home and a temporary workplace for a period of one month	1,300

(4)   During the tax year 2012/13 Kim paid interest of £140 (gross) on a personal loan taken out on 1 January 2011 to purchase a laptop computer for use in her employment with Sharp-Suit plc.

Joint income – Building society deposit account

The couple have savings of £25,000 in a building society deposit account which is in their joint names.

During the tax year 2012/13 Sam and Kim received building society interest of £1,200 in total from this joint account.

This was the actual cash amount received.

Required

(a)   Calculate Sam's tax adjusted trading profit for the year ended 5 April 2013.

Note: Your computation should start with net profit for the period of £50,000 and should list all of the items in the statement of profit or loss indicating by the use of a zero (0) any items that do not require adjustment.

(11 marks)

(b)   Calculate Sam and Kim's respective income tax liabilities for the tax year 2012/13.

Note: you should ignore any capital allowances that Kim might be entitled to.   **(10 marks)**

(c)   Explain to Sam and Kim how their overall income tax liability could be reduced if they were to either:
(i)   transfer their joint building society deposit account into individual savings accounts (ISAs); or

(2 marks)

(ii)   transfer their joint building society deposit account into Kim's sole name.   **(2 marks)**

(Total = 25 marks)

6 Sammi Smith (TX 12/10)   27 mins

You should assume that today's date is 20 March 2012.

Sammi Smith is a director of Smark Ltd. The company has given her the choice of being provided with a leased company motor car or alternatively being paid additional director's remuneration and then privately leasing the same motor car herself.

Company motor car

The motor car will be provided throughout the tax year 2012/13, and will be leased by Smark Ltd at an annual cost of £26,480. The motor car will be petrol powered, will have a list price of £80,000, and will have an official CO_2 emission rate of 305 grams per kilometre.

The lease payments will cover all the costs of running the motor car except for fuel. Smark Ltd will not provide Sammi with any fuel for private journeys.

Additional director's remuneration

As an alternative to having a company motor car, Sammi will be paid additional gross director's remuneration of £26,000 during the tax year 2012/13. She will then privately lease the motor car at an annual cost of £26,480.

Other information

The amount of business journeys that will be driven by Sammi will be immaterial and can therefore be ignored.

Sammi's current level of director's remuneration is over £150,000 which means that she will pay income tax at the additional rate of 50% in 2012/13. Smark Ltd prepares its accounts to 5 April, and pays corporation tax at the main rate of 24%. The lease of the motor car will commence on 6 April 2012.

Required

(a) Advise Sammi Smith of the income tax and national insurance contribution implications for the tax year 2012/13 if she (1) is provided with the company motor car, and (2) receives additional director's remuneration of £26,000. **(5 marks)**

(b) Advise Smark Ltd of the corporation tax and national insurance contribution implications for the year ended 5 April 2013 if the company (1) provides Sammi Smith with the company motor car, and (2) pays Sammi Smith additional director's remuneration of £26,000.

Note: you should ignore value added tax (VAT). **(5 marks)**

(c) Determine which of the two alternatives is the most beneficial from each of the respective points of view of Sammi Smith and Smark Ltd. **(5 marks)**

(Total = 15 marks)

7 Edmond Brick (TX 12/07)   27 mins

Edmond Brick owns four properties which are let out. The following information relates to the tax year 2012/13:

Property one

This is a freehold house that qualifies as a trade under the furnished holiday letting rules. The property was purchased on 6 April 2012. During the tax year 2012/13 the property was let for eighteen weeks at £370 per week. Edmond spent £5,700 on furniture and kitchen equipment during April 2012. Due to a serious flood £7,400 was spent on repairs during November 2012. The damage was not covered by insurance. The other expenditure on this property for the tax year 2012/13 amounted to £2,710, and this is all allowable.

Property two

This is a freehold house that is let out furnished. The property was let throughout the tax year 2012/13 at a monthly rent of £575, payable in advance. During the tax year 2012/13 Edmond paid council tax of £1,200 and insurance of £340 in respect of this property. He claims the wear and tear allowance for this property.

Property three

This is a freehold house that is let out unfurnished. The property was purchased on 6 April 2012, and it was empty until 30 June 2012. It was then let from 1 July 2012 to 31 January 2013 at a monthly rent of £710, payable in advance. On 31 January 2013 the tenant left owing three months rent which Edmond was unable to recover. The property was not re-let before 5 April 2013. During the tax year 2012/13 Edmond paid insurance of £290 for this property and spent £670 on advertising for tenants. He also paid loan interest of £6,700 in respect of a loan that was taken out to purchase this property.

Property four

This is a leasehold office building that is let out unfurnished. Edmond pays an annual rent of £6,800 for this property, but did not pay a premium when he acquired it. On 6 April 2012 the property was sub-let to a tenant, with Edmond receiving a premium of £15,000 for the grant of a five-year lease. He also received the annual rent of

£4,600 which was payable in advance. During the tax year 2012/13 Edmond paid insurance of £360 in respect of this property.

Furnished room

During the tax year 2012/13 Edmond rented out one furnished room of his main residence. During the year he received rent of £5,040, and incurred allowable expenditure of £1,140 in respect of the room. Edmond always computes the taxable income for the furnished room on the most favourable basis.

Required

(a) State the tax advantages of property one being treated as a trade under the furnished holiday letting rules.

(3 marks)

(b) Calculate Edmond's furnished holiday letting loss in respect of property one for the tax year 2012/13.

(3 marks)

(c) Calculate Edmond's property business profit in respect of the other three properties and the furnished room for the tax year 2012/13.

(9 marks)

(Total = 15 marks)

8 Peter Chic (TX 12/08) 45 mins

Peter Chic is employed by Haute-Couture Ltd as a fashion designer. The following information is available for the tax year 2012/13:

Employment

(1) During the tax year 2012/13 Peter was paid a gross annual salary of £45,600 by Haute-Couture Ltd. Income tax of £14,670 was deducted from this figure under PAYE.

(2) In addition to his salary, Peter received two bonus payments from Haute-Couture Ltd during the tax year 2012/13. The first bonus of £4,300 was paid on 30 April 2012 and was in respect of the year ended 31 December 2011. Peter became entitled to this first bonus on 10 April 2012. The second bonus of £3,600 was paid on 31 March 2013 and was in respect of the year ended 31 December 2012. Peter became entitled to this second bonus on 25 March 2013.

(3) Throughout the tax year 2012/13 Haute-Couture Ltd provided Peter with a diesel powered motor car which has a list price of £22,500. The motor car cost Haute-Couture Ltd £21,200, and it has an official CO_2 emission rate of 212 grams per kilometre. Peter made a capital contribution of £2,000 towards the cost of the motor car when it was first provided to him. Haute-Couture Ltd also provided Peter with fuel for private journeys.

(4) Haute-Couture Ltd has provided Peter with living accommodation since 1 January 2010. The company had purchased the property in 2008 for £160,000, and it was valued at £185,000 on 1 January 2010. Improvements costing £13,000 were made to the property during June 2011. The annual value of the property is £8,225.

(5) Throughout the tax year 2012/13 Haute-Couture Ltd provided Peter with two mobile telephones. The telephones had each cost £250 when purchased by the company in January 2012.

(6) On 5 January 2013 Haute-Couture Ltd paid a health club membership fee of £510 for the benefit of Peter.

(7) During February 2013 Peter spent five nights overseas on company business. Haute-Couture Ltd paid Peter a daily allowance of £10 to cover the cost of personal expenses such as telephone calls to his family.

Property income

(1) Peter owns two properties, which are let out. Both properties are freehold houses, with the first property being let out furnished and the second property being let out unfurnished.

(2) The first property was let from 6 April 2012 to 31 August 2012 at a monthly rent of £500, payable in advance. On 31 August 2012 the tenant left owing two months' rent which Peter was unable to recover. The property was not re-let before 5 April 2013. During March 2013 Peter spent £600 repairing the roof of this property.

(3)   The second property was purchased on 1 July 2012, and was then let from 1 August 2012 to 5 April 2013 at a monthly rent of £820, payable in advance. During July 2012 Peter spent £875 on advertising for tenants. For the period 1 July 2012 to 5 April 2013 he paid loan interest of £1,800 in respect of a loan that was taken out to purchase this property.

(4)   Peter insured both of his rental properties at a total cost of £660 for the year ended 30 June 2012, and £1,080 for the year ended 30 June 2013. The insurance is payable annually in advance.

(5)   Where possible, Peter claims the wear and tear allowance.

Other information

(1)   During the tax year 2012/13 Peter received building society interest of £1,760 and dividends of £720. These were the actual cash amounts received.

(2)   On 4 August 2012 Peter received a premium bond prize of £100.

(3)   During the tax year 2012/13 Peter made Gift Aid donations totaling £2,400 (net) to national charities.

Required

(a)   Calculate the income tax payable by Peter Chic for the tax year 2012/13. You should indicate by the use of zero any items that are non-taxable/exempt from tax. **(21 marks)**

(b)   Calculate the total amount of national insurance contributions that will have been paid by Peter Chic and Haute-Couture Ltd in respect of Peter's earnings and benefits for the tax year 2012/13. **(4 marks)**

(Total = 25 marks)

9 Leticia Stone (TX 12/11)   27 mins

Leticia Stone owns three properties which are let out. The following information relates to the tax year 2012/13:

Property one

This is a freehold house that qualifies as a trade under the furnished holiday letting rules. Leticia purchased this property on 1 July 2012 for £282,000. The purchase price included £4,600 for furniture and kitchen equipment.

Leticia borrowed £220,000 to purchase this property. During the period 1 July 2012 to 5 April 2013 she made loan repayments totalling £14,300, of which £12,700 was in respect of loan interest.

The property was let for 22 weeks at £425 per week during the period 1 July 2012 to 5 April 2013.

Due to a fire, £12,200 was spent on replacing the roof of the house during March 2013. Only £10,900 of this was paid for by Leticia's property insurance.

During the tax year 2012/13 Leticia drove 1,170 miles in her motor car in respect of the furnished holiday letting business. She uses HM Revenue and Customs' authorised mileage rates to calculate her expense deduction. The mileage was for the following purposes:

	Miles
Purchase of property	160
Running the business on a weekly basis	880
Property repairs	130

The other expenditure on this property for the period 1 July 2012 to 5 April 2013 amounted to £3,770, and this is all allowable.

Property two

This is a leasehold shop that is let out unfurnished. The property was acquired on 1 May 2012 and was immediately let to a tenant, with Leticia receiving a premium of £45,000 for the grant of a five-year lease. During the period 1 May 2012 to 5 April 2013 Leticia received four quarterly rental payments of £2,160 per quarter, payable in advance.

Leticia pays a monthly rent of £1,360 for this property, but did not pay a premium when she acquired it.

Property three

This is a freehold house that is let out unfurnished. The property was let from 6 April 2012 to 31 January 2013 at a monthly rent of £580. On 31 January 2013 the tenant left, owing three months rent. Leticia recovered two months of the outstanding rent by retaining the tenant's security deposit, but was unable to recover the balance.

On 1 March 2013 a new tenant paid Leticia a security deposit of £1,200, being two months rent, although the new tenancy did not commence until 15 April 2013.

During the tax year 2012/13 Leticia paid loan interest of £9,100 in respect of a loan that was taken out to purchase this property.

Other expenditure

The other expenditure on properties two and three for the tax year 2012/13 amounted to £36,240, and this is all allowable.

Furnished room

During the tax year 2012/13 Leticia rented out one furnished room of her main residence. During the year she received rent of £3,170, and incurred allowable expenditure of £4,840 in respect of the room. Leticia always uses the most favourable basis as regards the tax treatment of the furnished room.

Required

(a) Calculate Leticia Stone's property business loss for the tax year 2012/13.

Note: Your answer should separately identify the furnished holiday letting loss. **(13 marks)**

(b) Advise Leticia Stone as to the possible ways in which her property business loss for the tax year 2012/13 can be relieved. **(2 marks)**

(Total = 15 marks)

10 Peach, Plum and Pear (TX 12/08)   18 mins

You are a trainee accountant and your manager has asked for your help regarding three taxpayers who have all made personal pension contributions during the tax year 2012/13.

Ann Peach

Ann, aged 30, is self-employed as an estate agent. Her trading profit for the year ended 5 April 2013 was £44,730. Ann made contributions of £47,000 (gross) into a personal pension scheme during the tax year 2012/13. This was the first year that she had been a member of a pension scheme.

Basil Plum

Basil, aged 42, is employed by the Banana Bank plc as a fund manager. During the tax year 2012/13 Basil was paid a gross salary of £330,000. Basil made contributions of £60,000 (gross) into a personal pension scheme during the tax year 2012/13. This was the first year that he had been a member of a pension scheme.

Chloe Pear

Chloe, aged 54, lets out unfurnished property. For the tax year 2012/13 her property business profit was £26,630. Chloe made contributions of £8,200 (gross) into a personal pension scheme during the tax year 2012/13. This was the first year that she had been a member of a pension scheme.

Required

For each of the three taxpayers Ann Peach, Basil Plum and Chloe Pear, state, giving reasons, the amount of personal pension contributions that will have qualified for tax relief for the tax year 2012/13, and calculate their income tax liabilities for the year, assuming that they have no other income.

Note: marks are allocated: Ann Peach 3 marks; Basil Plum 5 marks; and Chloe Pear 2 marks. **(Total = 10 marks)**

11 Na Style (TX 12/09)

45 mins

Na Style commenced self-employment as a hairdresser on 1 January 2010. She had tax adjusted trading profits of £25,200 for the six-month period ended 30 June 2010 and £21,600 for the year ended 30 June 2011.

The following information is available for the tax year 2012/13:

Trading profit for the year ended 30 June 2012

(1)   Na's statement of profit or loss for the year ended 30 June 2012 is as follows:

	Note	£	£
Income			62,300
Expenses			
Depreciation		1,300	
Motor expenses	2	2,200	
Professional fees	3	1,650	
Property expenses	4	12,900	
Purchases	5	4,700	
Other expenses	6	16,550	
			(39,300)
Net profit			23,000

(2)   Na charges all the running expenses for her motor car to the business. During the year ended 30 June 2012 Na drove a total of 8,000 miles, of which 7,000 were for private journeys.

(3)   The figure for professional fees consists of £390 for accountancy and £1,260 for legal fees in connection with the grant of a new five-year lease of parking spaces for customers' motor cars.

(4)   Na lives in a flat that is situated above her hairdressing studio, and one-third of the total property expenses of £12,900 relate to this flat.

(5)   During the year ended 30 June 2012 Na took goods out of the hairdressing business for her personal use without paying for them, and no entry has been made in the accounts to record this. The goods cost £250 (an amount that has been deducted under 'purchases') and had a selling price of £450.

(6)   The figure for other expenses of £16,550 includes £400 for a fine in respect of health and safety regulations, £80 for a donation to a political party and £160 for a trade subscription to the Guild of Small Hairdressers.

(7)   Na uses her private telephone to make business telephone calls. The total cost of the private telephone for the year ended 30 June 2012 was £1,200, and 20% of this related to business telephone calls. The cost of the private telephone is not included in the statement of profit or loss expenses of £39,300.

(8)   Capital allowances for the year ended 30 June 2012 are £810.

Other information

(1)   During the tax year 2012/13 Na received dividends of £1,080, building society interest of £560, interest of £310 from an individual savings account (ISA), interest of £1,100 on the maturity of a savings certificate from the National Savings & Investments Bank and interest of £1,440 from government stocks (gilts). These were the actual cash amounts received in each case.

(2)   Na's payments on account of income tax in respect of the tax year 2012/13 totalled £3,200

Required

(a)   Calculate the amount of trading profits that will have been assessed on Na Style for the tax years 2009/10, 2010/11 and 2011/12 respectively, clearly identifying the amount of any overlap profits.   **(5 marks)**

(b)   Calculate Na Style's tax adjusted trading profit for the year ended 30 June 2012.

Note: your computation should commence with the net profit figure of £23,000, and should list all of the items referred to in notes (1) to (8) indicating by the use of zero (0) any items that do not require adjustment.   **(8 marks)**

(c)   (i)   Calculate the income tax payable by Na Style for the tax year 2012/13.

       Note: you should indicate by the use of zero any items that are non-taxable/exempt from tax.   **(6 marks)**

       (ii)   Calculate Na Style's balancing payment for the tax year 2012/13 and her payments on account for the
              tax year 2013/14, stating the relevant due dates.

       Note: you should ignore national insurance contributions.   **(3 marks)**

(d)   Advise Na Style of the consequences of not making the balancing payment for the tax year 2012/13 until
       31 May 2014.

       Note: your answer should include calculations as appropriate.   **(3 marks)**

       (Total = 25 marks)

12 Simon House (TX 12/09)   27 mins

On 27 April 2012 Simon House purchased a derelict freehold house for £127,000. Legal fees of £1,800 were paid in
respect of the purchase.

Simon then renovated the house at a cost of £50,600, with the renovation being completed on 7 August 2012. He
immediately put the house up for sale, and it was sold on 27 August 2012 for £260,000. Legal fees of £2,600 were
paid in respect of the sale.

Simon financed the transaction by a bank loan of £150,000 that was taken out on 27 April 2012 at an annual
interest rate of 6%. The bank loan was repaid on 27 August 2012.

Simon had no other income or capital gains for the tax year 2012/13 except as indicated above.

Simon has been advised that whether or not he is treated as carrying on a trade will be determined according to the
six following 'badges of trade':

(1)   Subject matter of the transaction.
(2)   Length of ownership.
(3)   Frequency of similar transactions.
(4)   Work done on the property.
(5)   Circumstances responsible for the realisation.
(6)   Motive.

Required

(a)   Briefly explain the meaning of each of the six 'badges of trade' listed in the question.
       Note: you are not expected to quote from decided cases.   **(3 marks)**

(b)   Calculate Simon House's income tax liability and his Class 2 and Class 4 national insurance contributions for
       the tax year 2012/13, if he is treated as carrying on a trade in respect of the disposal of the freehold house.
       (8 marks)

(c)   Calculate Simon House's capital gains tax liability for the tax year 2012/13, if he is not treated as carrying on
       a trade in respect of the disposal of the freehold house.   **(4 marks)**

       (Total = 15 marks)

13 Bayle Defender (TX 06/11)

54 mins

(a) **You should assume that today's date is 20 November 2012.**

Bayle Defender is self-employed as a lawyer. She is also a director of Acquit & Appeal Ltd. The following information is available for the tax year 2012/13:

Self-employment

(1) Bayle's statement of profit or loss for the year ended 30 September 2012 is as follows:

	Note	£	£
Revenue	2		324,100
Expenses			
Gifts and donations	3	8,680	
Lease of motor car	4	10,360	
Professional fees	5	3,240	
Property expenses	6	46,240	
Travel expenses	7	16,770	
Other expenses	8	66,410	
			(151,700)
Net profit			172,400

(2) Revenue includes £2,800 received during May 2012 in respect of an impairment loss that Bayle had written off when calculating her trading profit for the year ended 30 September 2010.

(3) Gifts and donations are as follows:

	£
Gifts to customers (clocks costing £110 each and displaying Bayle's name)	3,300
Gifts to customers (bottles of champagne costing £40 each and displaying Bayle's name)	2,480
Donations to political parties	2,900
	8,680

(4) The lease commenced on 1 October 2011, and is in respect of a motor car with CO_2 emissions of 244 grams per kilometre. There is no private use of the motor car.

(5) The figure of £3,240 for professional fees is in respect of accountancy services, of which £600 is for inheritance tax planning advice.

(6) Bayle lives in an apartment that is situated above her office, and two-fifths of the total property expenses of £46,240 relate to this apartment.

(7) The figure of £16,770 for travel expenses includes £520 for parking fines incurred by Bayle.

(8) The figure for other expenses of £66,410 includes £670 for Bayle's professional subscription to the Law Society, and £960 for her golf club membership fee.

Director's remuneration

(9) Bayle will be paid gross director's remuneration of £42,000 by Acquit & Appeal Ltd during the tax year 2012/13.

(10) In addition to her director's remuneration, Bayle received two bonus payments of £6,000 from Acquit & Appeal Ltd during June 2012, both of which were in respect of the year ended 31 December 2011. Bayle became entitled to the first bonus payment of £6,000 on 10 March 2012, and to the second bonus payment of £6,000 on 20 April 2012.

(11) Acquit & Appeal Ltd deducts PAYE at a flat rate of 50% from all of Bayle's earnings.

Other information

(12) During the tax year 2012/13 Bayle will receive dividends of £9,900, interest of £5,240 on the maturity of a savings certificate issued by National Savings & Investments (NS&I), and interest of £3,600 from government stocks (gilts). These are the actual cash amounts that will be received.

(13) Bayle's payments on account of income tax in respect of the tax year 2012/13 will total £53,526.

Required

(i) Calculate Bayle Defender's tax adjusted trading profit for the year ended 30 September 2012;

Note: Your computation should commence with the net profit figure of £172,400, and you should also list all of the items referred to in notes (2) to (8) indicating by the use of zero (0) any items that do not require adjustment. **(6 marks)**

(ii) Calculate the income tax payable by Bayle Defender for the tax year 2012/13; **(8 marks)**

(iii) Calculate the amount of income tax that will be due for payment by Bayle Defender on 31 January 2014, and advise her of the consequences if this amount is not paid until 31 August 2014.

Note: You should ignore national insurance contributions. **(5 marks)**

(b) On 1 December 2012 Bayle Defender is planning to bring a newly qualified lawyer, Fyle Guardian, into her business. Fyle will either be taken on as an employee, being paid a gross monthly salary of £3,300, or join Bayle as a partner, receiving a 20% share of the new partnership's profits.

Bayle has forecast that her tax adjusted trading profit will be £216,000 for the year ended 30 September 2013, and £240,000 for the year ended 30 September 2014.

Fyle does not have any other income for the tax year 2012/13.

Required

(i) Assuming that Fyle Guardian is employed from 1 December 2012, calculate the total amount of national insurance contributions that will be paid by Bayle Defender and Fyle Guardian, if any, in respect of his earnings for the tax year 2012/13;

Note: You are not expected to calculate the national insurance contributions that will be paid in respect of Bayle Defender's earnings. **(4 marks)**

(ii) Assuming that Fyle Guardian becomes a partner from 1 December 2012:

(1) Calculate his trading income assessments for the tax years 2012/13 and 2013/14.

Note: You are not expected to calculate any overlap profits. **(4 marks)**

(2) Calculate the total amount of national insurance contributions that will be paid by Bayle Defender and Fyle Guardian, if any, in respect of his trading income assessment for the tax year 2012/13.

Note: You are not expected to calculate the national insurance contributions that will be paid in respect of Bayle Defender's trading income assessment. **(3 marks)**

(Total = 30 marks)

14 Samantha Fabrique (TX 12/07)   18 mins

Samantha Fabrique has been a self-employed manufacturer of clothing since 2000. She has the following gross income and chargeable gains for the tax years 2010/11 to 2013/14:

	2010/11 £	2011/12 £	2012/13 £	2013/14 £
Trading profit/(loss)	7,290	52,600	(85,000)	13,390
Building society interest	–	2,100	3,800	2,130
Chargeable gains/(loss)	20,600	23,300	(3,400)	14,000

The chargeable gains are stated before taking account of loss relief and the annual exempt amount.

Required

(a)   State the factors that will influence an individual's choice of loss relief claims.   **(3 marks)**

(b)   Calculate Samantha's taxable income and taxable gains for each of the tax years 2010/11, 2011/12, 2012/13 and 2013/14 on the assumption that she relieves the trading loss of £85,000 for the tax year 2012/13 on the most favourable basis.

You should assume that the tax rates and allowances for the tax year 2012/13 apply throughout.   **(7 marks)**

(Total = 10 marks)

15 Michael and Sean (TX 06/12)   27 mins

(a)   The UK Government uses tax policies to encourage certain types of activity.

Required

Briefly explain how the UK Government's tax policies encourage:

(i)   Individuals to save;   **(1 mark)**
(ii)   Individuals to support charities;   **(1 mark)**
(iii)   Entrepreneurs to build their own businesses and to invest in plant and machinery.   **(2 marks)**

(b)   You are a trainee chartered certified accountant and your manager has asked for your help regarding two taxpayers who have both made trading losses.

Michael

Michael commenced in self-employment on 1 July 2011, preparing accounts to 5 April. His results for the first two periods of trading were as follows:

		£
Nine-month period ended 5 April 2012	– Trading loss	(25,230)
Year ended 5 April 2013	– Trading profit	7,730

For the tax years 2007/08 to 2009/10 Michael had the following income from employment:

	£
2007/08	44,500
2008/09	17,430
2009/10	50,600

Michael did not have any income during the period 6 April 2010 to 30 June 2011.

Sean

Sean has been in self-employment since 2002, but ceased trading on 31 December 2012. He has always prepared accounts to 31 December. His results for the final five years of trading were as follows:

		£
Year ended 31 December 2008	– Trading profit	21,300
Year ended 31 December 2009	– Trading profit	14,400
Year ended 31 December 2010	– Trading profit	18,900
Year ended 31 December 2011	– Trading profit	3,700
Year ended 31 December 2012	– Trading loss	(23,100)

For each of the tax years 2008/09 to 2012/13 Sean has property business profits of £8,430.

Sean has unused overlap profits brought forward of £3,600.

Required

For each of the two taxpayers Michael and Sean, identify the loss relief claims that are available to them, and explain which of the available claims would be the most beneficial.

Notes

1. You should clearly state the amount of any reliefs claimed and the rates of income tax saved. However, you are not expected to calculate any income tax liabilities.

2. You should assume that the tax rates and allowances for the tax year 2012/13 apply throughout.

3. The following mark allocation is provided as guidance for this requirement:

Michael (5 marks)
Sean (6 marks)

(11 marks)

(Total = 15 marks)

16 Ae, Bee, Cae, Dee and Eu (TX 12/08)   27 mins

(a) Ae and Bee commenced in partnership on 1 July 2010 preparing accounts to 30 June. Cae joined as a partner on 1 July 2012. Profits have always been shared equally. The partnership's trading profits since the commencement of trading have been as follows:

	£
Year ended 30 June 2011	54,000
Year ended 30 June 2012	66,000
Year ended 30 June 2013	87,000

Required

Calculate the trading income assessments of Ae, Bee and Cae for each of the tax years 2010/11, 2011/12 and 2012/13. **(5 marks)**

(b) Dee commenced in self-employment on 6 April 2009. She initially prepared accounts to 5 April, but changed her accounting date to 31 July by preparing accounts for the four-month period to 31 July 2011. Dee's trading profits since she commenced trading have been as follows:

	£
Year ended 5 April 2010	35,160
Year ended 5 April 2011	32,880
Four-month period ended 31 July 2011	16,240
Year ended 31 July 2012	54,120

Required

(i) Calculate the amount of trading profits that will have been assessed on Dee for each of the tax years 2010/11, 2011/12 and 2012/13. **(4 marks)**

(ii) State the amount of Dee's unrelieved overlap profits as at 5 April 2013. **(1 mark)**

(c) Eu ceased trading on 30 September 2014, having been self-employed since 1 July 2004.

(1) Eu's trading profits for the final three periods of trading were as follows:

	£
Year ended 30 June 2013	62,775
Year ended 30 June 2014	57,600
Three-month period ended 30 September 2014	14,400

These figures are before taking account of capital allowances.

(2) The tax written-down value of the capital allowances main pool at 1 July 2012 was £8,750. On 15 September 2014 Eu purchased office furniture for £2,400. All of the items included in the main pool were sold for £5,175 on 30 September 2014.

(3) Until the final period of trading Eu had always prepared accounts to 30 June. Her overlap profits for the period 1 July 2004 to 5 April 2005 were £19,800.

Required

Calculate the amount of trading profits that will have been assessed on Eu for each of the tax years 2013/14 and 2014/15. Assume that the rates of capital allowances in 2012/13 apply in future years. **(5 marks)**

(Total = 15 marks)

17 Auy Man and Bim Men (TX 06/10)   54 mins

Auy Man and Bim Men have been in partnership since 6 April 2003 as management consultants. The following information is available for the tax year 2012/13:

Personal information

Auy is aged 32. During the tax year 2012/13 she spent 190 days in the United Kingdom. Bim is aged 56. During the tax year 2012/13 she spent 100 days in the United Kingdom. Bim has spent the same amount of time in the United Kingdom for each of the previous five tax years.

Statement of profit or loss for the year ended 5 April 2013

The partnership's summarised statement of profit or loss for the year ended 5 April 2013 is as follows:

	Note	£	£
Sales revenue	1		140,762
Expenses	2		
Depreciation		3,400	
Motor expenses	3	4,100	
Other expenses	4	1,800	
Wages and salaries	5	50,900	
			(60,200)
Profit before taxation			80,562

(1) The sales figure of £140,762 is exclusive of output value added tax (VAT) of £25,600.

(2) The expenses figures are exclusive of recoverable input VAT of:

Motor expenses £180

Other expenses £140

(3) The figure of £4,100 for motor expenses includes £2,600 in respect of the partners' motor cars, with 30% of this amount being in respect of private journeys.

(4) The figure of £1,800 for other expenses includes £720 for entertaining employees. The remaining expenses are all allowable.

(5) The figure of £50,900 for wages and salaries includes the annual salary of £4,000 paid to Bim (see the profit sharing note below), and the annual salary of £15,000 paid to Auy's husband, who works part-time for the partnership. Another part-time employee doing the same job is paid a salary of £10,000 per annum.

Plant and machinery

On 6 April 2012 the tax written down values of the partnership's plant and machinery were as follows:

	£
Main pool	3,100
Motor car [1]	18,000
Motor car [2]	14,000

The following transactions took place during the year ended 5 April 2013:

		Cost/(proceeds) £
8 May 2012	Sold motor car [2]	(13,100)
8 May 2012	Purchased motor car [3]	11,600
21 November 2012	Purchased motor car [4]	14,200
14 January 2013	Purchased motor car [5]	10,875

Motor car [1] has a CO_2 emission rate of 185 grams per kilometre. It is used by Auy and 70% of the mileage is for business journeys.

Motor car [2] had a CO_2 emission rate of 145 grams per kilometre. It was used by Bim and 70% of the mileage was for business journeys.

Motor car [3] purchased on 8 May 2012 has a CO_2 emission rate of 105 grams per kilometre. It is used by Bim and 70% of the mileage is for business journeys.

Motor car [4] purchased on 21 November 2012 has a CO_2 emission rate of 135 grams per kilometre. Motor car [5] purchased on 14 January 2013 has a CO_2 emission rate of 200 grams per kilometre. These two motor cars are used by employees of the business.

Profit sharing

Profits are shared 80% to Auy and 20% to Bim. This is after paying an annual salary of £4,000 to Bim, and interest at the rate of 5% on the partners' capital account balances. The capital account balances are:

	£
Auy Man	56,000
Bim Men	34,000

VAT

The partnership has been registered for VAT since 6 April 2003. However, the partnership has recently started invoicing for its services on new payment terms, and the partners are concerned about output VAT being accounted for at the appropriate time.

Required

(a) Explain why both Auy Man and Bim Men will each be treated for tax purposes as resident in the United Kingdom for the tax year 2012/13. **(2 marks)**

(b) Calculate the partnership's tax adjusted trading profit for the year ended 5 April 2013 and the trading income assessments of Auy Man and Bim Men for the tax year 2012/13.

Note: Your computation should commence with the profit before taxation figure of £80,562, and should also list all of the items referred to in notes (2) to (5) indicating by the use of zero (0) any items that do not require adjustment. **(15 marks)**

(c) Calculate the Class 4 national insurance contributions payable by Auy Man and Bim Men for the tax year 2012/13. **(3 marks)**

(d) (i) Advise the partnership of the VAT rules that determine the tax point in respect of a supply of services; **(3 marks)**

(ii) Calculate the amount of VAT paid by the partnership to HM Revenue & Customs throughout the year ended 5 April 2013;

Note: you should ignore the output VAT scale charges due in respect of fuel for private journeys. **(2 marks)**

(iii) Advise the partnership of the conditions that it must satisfy in order to join and continue to use the VAT flat rate scheme, and calculate the tax saving if the partnership had used the flat rate scheme to calculate the amount of VAT payable throughout the year ended 5 April 2013. The relevant flat rate scheme percentage for the partnership's trade is 14%.

(5 marks)

(Total = 30 marks)

18 Flick Pick (TX 06/12)

On 6 April 2012 Flick Pick, aged 23, commenced employment with 3D Ltd as a film critic. On 1 January 2013 she commenced in partnership with Art Reel running a small cinema, preparing accounts to 30 April. The following information is available for the tax year 2012/13:

Employment

(1) During the tax year 2012/13 Flick was paid a gross annual salary of £24,330.

(2) Throughout the tax year 2012/13 3D Ltd provided Flick with living accommodation. The company had purchased the property in 2003 for £89,000, and it was valued at £144,000 on 6 April 2012. The annual value of the property is £4,600. The property was furnished by 3D Ltd during March 2012 at a cost of £9,400.

Partnership

(1) The partnership's tax adjusted trading profit for the four-month period ended 30 April 2013 is £29,700. This figure is before taking account of capital allowances.

(2) The only item of plant and machinery owned by the partnership is a motor car that cost £18,750 on 1 February 2013. The motor car has a CO_2 emission rate of 190 grams per kilometre. It is used by Art, and 40% of the mileage is for private journeys.

(3) Profits are shared 40% to Flick and 60% to Art. This is after paying an annual salary of £6,000 to Art.

Property income

(1) Flick owns a freehold house which is let out furnished. The property was let throughout the tax year 2012/13 at a monthly rent of £660.

(2) During the tax year 2012/13 Flick paid council tax of £1,320 in respect of the property, and also spent £2,560 on replacing damaged furniture.

(3) Flick claims the wear and tear allowance.

Value added tax (VAT)

(1) The partnership voluntarily registered for VAT on 1 January 2013, and immediately began using the flat rate scheme to calculate the amount of VAT payable. The relevant flat rate scheme percentage for the partnership's trade is 12%.

(2) For the quarter ended 31 March 2013 the partnership had standard rated sales of £59,700, and these were all made to members of the general public. For the same period standard rated expenses amounted to £27,300. Both figures are stated inclusive of VAT.

(3) The partnership has two private boxes in its cinema that can be booked on a special basis by privileged customers. Such customers can book the boxes up to two months in advance, at which time they have to pay a 25% deposit. An invoice is then given to the customer on the day of the screening of the film, with payment of the balance of 75% required within seven days. For VAT purposes, the renting out of the cinema boxes is a supply of services.

Required

(a) Calculate Flick Pick's taxable income for the tax year 2012/13.   **(12 marks)**

(b) State what classes of national insurance contribution will be paid in respect of Flick Pick's income for the tax year 2012/13, and in each case who is responsible for paying them.

Note: You are not required to calculate the actual national insurance contributions.   **(4 marks)**

(c) List the advantages and disadvantages for the partnership of choosing 30 April as its accounting date rather than 5 April.   **(4 marks)**

(d) (i) Explain whether or not it was beneficial for the partnership to have used the VAT flat rate scheme for the quarter ended 31 March 2013;

Notes

1. Your answer should be supported by appropriate calculations.

2. You should ignore the 1% reduction from the flat rate that is available during the first year of VAT registration. **(3 marks)**

(ii) Explain whether or not it was financially beneficial for the partnership to have voluntarily registered for VAT from 1 January 2013;

Note: Your answer should be supported by appropriate calculations. **(3 marks)**

(iii) Advise the partnership as to when it should account for output VAT on the renting out of its private boxes to privileged customers. **(4 marks)**

(Total = 30 marks)

19 Pi Casso (TX 06/08) 27 mins

Pi Casso has been a self-employed artist since 1993, making up her accounts to 30 June. Pi's tax liabilities for the tax years 2010/11, 2011/12 and 2012/13 are as follows:

	2010/11 £	2011/12 £	2012/13 £
Income tax liability	3,240	4,100	2,730
Class 2 national insurance contributions	125	130	138
Class 4 national insurance contributions	1,240	990	990
Capital gains tax liability	–	4,880	–

No income tax has been deducted at source.

Required

(a) Prepare a schedule showing the payments on account and balancing payments that Pi will have made or will have to make during the period from 1 July 2012 to 31 March 2014 if Pi makes any appropriate claims to reduce her payments on account, clearly identifying the relevant due date of each payment. **(8 marks)**

(b) State the implications if Pi had made a claim to reduce her payments on account for 2012/13 to nil.

(2 marks)

(c) Advise Pi of the latest submission date for her 2012/13 self-assessment tax return. **(2 marks)**

(d) State the date by which HMRC will have to notify Pi if they intend to make a compliance check enquiry into her self-assessment tax return for 2012/13 and the possible reasons why such an enquiry would be made.

(3 marks)

(Total = 15 marks)

20 Ernest Vader (TX 06/10)

27 mins

You should assume that today's date is 30 June 2014.

You are a trainee Chartered Certified Accountant and are dealing with the tax affairs of Ernest Vader.

Ernest's self-assessment tax return for the tax year 2012/13 was submitted to HM Revenue & Customs (HMRC) on 15 May 2013 and Ernest paid the resulting income tax liability by the due date of 31 January 2014. However, you have just discovered that during the tax year 2012/13 Ernest disposed of a freehold property, the details of which were omitted from his self-assessment tax return. The capital gains tax liability in respect of this disposal is £18,000 and this amount has not been paid.

Ernest has suggested that since HMRC's right to make a compliance check enquiry into his self-assessment tax return for the tax year 2012/13 expired on 15 May 2014, no disclosure should be made to HMRC of the capital gain.

Required

(a)   Briefly explain the difference between tax evasion and tax avoidance, and how HMRC would view the situation if Ernest Vader does not disclose his capital gain.   **(3 marks)**

(b)   Briefly explain from an ethical viewpoint how you, as a trainee Chartered Certified Accountant, should deal with the suggestion from Ernest Vader that no disclosure is made to HMRC of his capital gain.   **(3 marks)**

(c)   State the action HMRC will take should they wish to obtain information from Ernest Vader regarding his capital gain.   **(1 mark)**

(d)   Explain why, even though the right to make a compliance check enquiry has expired, HMRC will still be entitled to raise an assessment should they discover that Ernest Vader has not disclosed his capital gain.

(2 marks)

(e)   Assuming that HMRC discover the capital gain and raise an assessment in respect of Ernest Vader's capital gains tax liability of £18,000 for the tax year 2012/13, and that this amount is then paid on 31 July 2014:

(i)   Calculate the amount of interest that will be payable;

Note: you should assume that the rates for the tax year 2012/13 continue to apply.   **(2 marks)**

(ii)   Advise Ernest Vader as to the amount of penalty that is likely to be charged as a result of the failure to notify HMRC and how this could have been reduced if the capital gain had been disclosed.

(4 marks)

(Total = 15 marks)

CHARGEABLE GAINS FOR INDIVIDUALS

Questions 21 to 25 cover the taxation of chargeable gains for individuals, the subject of Part C of the BPP Study Text for Paper F6.

21 Aloi, Bon, Cherry and Dinah (TX 06/11)   27 mins

On 15 October 2012 Alphabet Ltd, an unquoted trading company, was taken over by XYZ plc. Prior to the takeover Alphabet Ltd's share capital consisted of 100,000 £1 ordinary shares, and under the terms of the takeover the shareholders received either cash of £6 per share or one £1 ordinary share in XYZ plc for each £1 ordinary share in Alphabet Ltd. The following information is available regarding the four shareholders of Alphabet Ltd:

Aloi

Aloi has been the managing director of Alphabet Ltd since the company's incorporation on 1 January 2002, and she accepted XYZ plc's cash alternative of £6 per share in respect of her shareholding of 60,000 £1 ordinary shares in Alphabet Ltd. Aloi had originally subscribed for 50,000 shares in Alphabet Ltd on 1 January 2002 at their par value, and purchased a further 10,000 shares on 20 May 2004 for £18,600.

On 6 February 2013 Aloi sold an investment property, and this disposal resulted in a chargeable gain of £22,600.

For the tax year 2012/13 Aloi has taxable income of £60,000.

Bon

Bon has been the sales director of Alphabet Ltd since 1 February 2012, having not previously been an employee of the company. She accepted XYZ plc's share alternative of one £1 ordinary share for each of her 25,000 £1 ordinary shares in Alphabet Ltd. Bon had purchased her shareholding on 1 February 2012 for £92,200.

On 4 March 2013 Bon made a gift of 10,000 of her £1 ordinary shares in XYZ plc to her brother. On that date the shares were quoted on the Stock Exchange at £7.10 – £7.18. There were no recorded bargains. Holdover relief is not available in respect of this disposal.

For the tax year 2012/13 Bon has taxable income of £55,000.

Cherry

Cherry has never been an employee or a director of Alphabet Ltd. She accepted XYZ plc's cash alternative of £6 per share in respect of her shareholding of 12,000 £1 ordinary shares in Alphabet Ltd. Cherry had purchased her shareholding on 27 July 2005 for £23,900.

For the tax year 2012/13 Cherry has taxable income of £30,370, and during the year she contributed £3,400 (gross) into a personal pension scheme.

Dinah

Dinah has been an employee of Alphabet Ltd since 1 May 2003. She accepted XYZ plc's share alternative of one £1 ordinary share for each of her 3,000 £1 ordinary shares in Alphabet Ltd. Dinah had purchased her shareholding on 20 June 2004 for £4,800.

On 13 November 2012 Dinah sold 1,000 of her £1 ordinary shares in XYZ plc for £6,600.

Dinah died on 5 April 2013, and her remaining 2,000 £1 ordinary shares in XYZ plc were inherited by her daughter. On that date these shares were valued at £15,600.

For the tax year 2012/13 Dinah had taxable income of £12,000.

Required

(a)   State why Bon, Cherry and Dinah did not meet the qualifying conditions for entrepreneurs' relief as regards their shareholdings in Alphabet Ltd.   **(3 marks)**

(b)   Calculate the capital gains tax liabilities of Aloi, Bon, Cherry and Dinah for the tax year 2012/13.

Note: In each case, the taxable income is stated after the deduction of the personal allowance.

(12 marks)

(Total = 15 marks)

22 Winston King (TX 06/12)   27 mins

(a)   'Tax is charged when there is a chargeable disposal of a chargeable asset by a chargeable person.'

Required

(i)   State which individuals are subject to capital gains tax on the disposal of chargeable assets situated in the United Kingdom;   **(1 mark)**

(ii)   State which companies are subject to corporation tax on the disposal of chargeable assets situated in the United Kingdom.   **(1 mark)**

(b)   On 19 May 2012 Winston King disposed of a painting, and this resulted in a chargeable gain of £45,860. For the tax year 2012/13 Winston has taxable income of £21,770 after the deduction of the personal allowance.

Winston is considering the sale of a business that he has run as a sole trader since 1 July 2005. The business will be sold for £260,000, and this figure, along with the respective cost of each asset, is made up as follows:

| | Sale proceeds | Cost |
	£	£
Freehold shop	140,000	80,000
Freehold warehouse	88,000	102,000
Net current assets	32,000	32,000
	260,000	

The freehold warehouse has never been used by Winston for business purposes.

Required

(i)   Assuming that Winston King does not sell his sole tradership business, calculate his capital gains tax liability for the tax year 2012/13;   **(3 marks)**

(ii)   Calculate Winston King's capital gains tax liability for the tax year 2012/13 if he sold his sole tradership business on 25 March 2013.   **(4 marks)**

(c)   Wiki Ltd sold a freehold warehouse on 3 February 2013 for £312,000. The warehouse had been purchased on 12 November 2002 for £171,000. Wiki Ltd incurred legal fees of £2,200 in connection with the purchase of the warehouse, and legal fees of £3,400 in connection with the disposal. The relevant retail price indexes (RPIs) are as follows:

| November 2002 | 178.2 |
| February 2013 | 247.1 |

Wiki Ltd is unsure as to how to reinvest the proceeds from the sale of the warehouse. The company can either purchase a freehold factory for £166,000, or it can purchase a freehold office building for £296,000. The reinvestment will take place during July 2013.

All of the above buildings have been, or will be, used for business purposes by Wiki Ltd.

Required

(i)   Before taking account of any available rollover relief, calculate Wiki Ltd's chargeable gain in respect of the disposal of the warehouse;   **(3 marks)**

(ii)   Advise Wiki Ltd of the rollover relief that will be available in respect of each of the two alternative reinvestments.

Note: Your answer should include details of the base cost of the replacement asset for each alternative.   **(3 marks)**

(Total = 15 marks)

23 Jorge Jung (TX 12/11)

27 mins

Jorge Jung disposed of the following assets during the tax year 2012/13:

(1) On 30 June 2012 Jorge sold a house for £308,000. The house had been purchased on 1 January 1995 for £98,000, and throughout the 210 months of ownership had been occupied by Jorge as follows:

Months	
16	Occupied
10	Unoccupied – Travelling overseas
24	Unoccupied – Required to work overseas by his employer
11	Occupied
30	Unoccupied – Required to work elsewhere in the United Kingdom by his employer
22	Unoccupied – Travelling overseas
26	Unoccupied – Required to work elsewhere in the United Kingdom by his employer
17	Occupied
12	Unoccupied – Required to work overseas by his employer
13	Unoccupied –Travelling overseas
<u>21</u>	Unoccupied –Lived with sister
<u>210</u>	

Jorge let the house out during all of the periods when he did not occupy it personally. Throughout the period 1 January 1995 to 30 June 2012 Jorge did not have any other main residence.

(2) On 30 September 2012 Jorge sold a copyright for £8,200. The copyright had been purchased on 1 October 2010 for £7,000 when it had an unexpired life of 10 years.

(3) On 6 October 2012 Jorge sold a painting for £5,400. The painting had been purchased on 18 May 2008 for £2,200.

(4) On 29 October 2012 Jorge sold a motor car for £10,700. The motor car had been purchased on 21 December 2010 for £14,600.

(5) On 3 December 2012 Jorge sold two acres of land for £92,000. Jorge's father-in-law had originally purchased three acres of land on 4 August 2000 for £19,500. The father-in-law died on 17 June 2007, and the land was inherited by Jorge's wife. On that date the three acres of land were valued at £28,600. Jorge's wife transferred the land to him on 14 November 2010. On that date the three acres of land were valued at £39,000. The market value of the unsold acre of land as at 3 December 2012 was £38,000.

(6) On 14 January 2013 Jorge sold 5,000 £1 ordinary shares in Futuristic Ltd, an unquoted trading company, to his sister for £40,000. The market value of the shares on that date was £64,800. The shares had been purchased on 21 March 2008 for £26,300. Jorge and his sister have elected to hold over the gain as a gift of a business asset.

Required

Calculate Jorge Jung's taxable gains for the tax year 2012/13.

(15 marks)

24 Nim and Mae (TX 06/09)

36 mins

Nim and Mae Lom are a married couple. They disposed of the following assets during the tax year 2012/13:

Nim Lom

(1) On 20 July 2012 Nim made a gift of 10,000 £1 ordinary shares in Kapook plc to his daughter. On that date the shares were quoted on the Stock Exchange at £3.70 – £3.90, with recorded bargains of £3.60, £3.75 and £3.80. Nim has made the following purchases of shares in Kapook plc:

19 February 2002	8,000 shares for £16,200
6 June 2007	6,000 shares for £14,600
24 July 2012	2,000 shares for £5,800

Nim's total shareholding was less than 5% of Kapook plc, and so holdover relief is not available.

(2) On 13 August 2012 Nim transferred his entire shareholding of 5,000 £1 ordinary shares in Jooba Ltd, an unquoted company, to his wife, Mae. On that date the shares were valued at £28,200. Nim's shareholding had been purchased on 11 January 2008 for £16,000.

(3) On 26 November 2012 Nim sold an antique table for £8,700. The antique table had been purchased for £5,200.

(4) On 2 April 2013 Nim sold UK Government securities (Gilts) for £12,400. The securities had been purchased for £10,100.

Mae Lom

(1) On 28 August 2012 Mae sold 2,000 of the 5,000 £1 ordinary shares in Jooba Ltd that had been transferred to her from Nim (see (2) above). The sale proceeds were £30,400. Entrepreneurs' relief is not available in respect of this disposal.

(2) On 30 September 2012 Mae sold a house for £186,000. The house had been purchased on 1 October 2002 for £122,000. Throughout the period of ownership the house was occupied by Nim and Mae as their main residence, but one of the house's eight rooms was always used exclusively for business purposes by Mae. Entrepreneurs' relief is not available in respect of this disposal.

(3) On 30 November 2012 Mae sold a business that she had run as a sole trader since 1 December 2004. The sale resulted in the following capital gains:

	£
Goodwill	80,000
Freehold office building	136,000
Investment property	34,000

The investment property has always been rented out.

Mae claimed entrepreneurs' relief in respect of this disposal. This is her first claim for entrepreneurs' relief.

(4) On 31 March 2013 Mae sold a copyright for £9,600. The copyright had been purchased on 1 April 2008 for £10,000 when it had an unexpired life of 20 years.

Other information

Nim has unused capital losses of £16,200 brought forward from the tax year 2011/12.

Mae has unused capital losses of £8,500 brought forward from the tax year 2011/12.

Nim has taxable income of £10,000 in tax year 2012/13.

Mae has taxable income of £25,000 in tax year 2012/13.

Required

Compute Nim and Mae Lom's respective capital gains tax liabilities, if any, for the tax year 2012/13. In each case, the amount of unused capital losses carried forward to future tax years, if any, should be clearly identified.

(20 marks)

25 Amanda, Bo and Charles (TX 12/09)   36 mins

You are a trainee accountant and your manager has asked for your help regarding three taxpayers who have all disposed of assets during the tax year 2012/13.

(a) **Amanda Moon**

On 30 June 2012 Amanda incorporated a business. She had run the business as a sole trader since 1 July 2006.

The market value of the business assets on 30 June 2012 was £300,000. This figure, along with the respective cost of each asset, is made up as follows:

	Market value £	Cost £
Goodwill	90,000	Nil
Freehold shop	165,000	120,000
Net current assets	45,000	45,000
	300,000	

The freehold shop has always been used by Amanda for business purposes. All of the business assets were transferred to a new limited company, Ammoon Ltd, with the consideration consisting of 300,000 £1 ordinary shares valued at £300,000. Amanda took full advantage of the available incorporation relief.

Required

(i) Calculate Amanda Moon's chargeable gains, if any, for the tax year 2012/13, and the base cost of her 300,000 £1 ordinary shares in Ammoon Ltd. **(4 marks)**

(ii) Explain how your answer to (i) above would have differed if the consideration for the transfer of Amanda Moon's business had instead consisted of 200,000 £1 ordinary shares and £100,000 in cash. **(3 marks)**

Note: You should ignore entrepreneurs' relief.

(b) **Bo Neptune**

On 31 July 2012 Bo made a gift of his entire holding of 50,000 £1 ordinary shares (a 100% holding) in Botune Ltd, an unquoted trading company, to his son. The market value of the shares on that date was £210,000. The shares had been purchased by Bo on 22 January 2006 for £94,000. Bo and his son have elected to hold over the gain as a gift of a business asset.

Required

(i) Calculate Bo Neptune's chargeable gain, if any, for the tax year 2012/13, and the base cost of his son's 50,000 £1 ordinary shares in Botune Ltd. **(3 marks)**

(ii) Explain how your answer to (i) above would have differed if the shares in Botune Ltd had instead been sold to Bo Neptune's son for £160,000. **(2 marks)**

Note: You should ignore entrepreneurs' relief.

(c) **Charles Orion**

On 30 September 2012 Charles sold a house for £282,000. The house had been purchased on 1 October 2000 for £110,000.

He occupied the house as his main residence from the date of purchase until 31 March 2002. The house was then unoccupied between 1 April 2002 and 31 December 2010 when Charles went to live with his parents due to his father's illness. From 1 January 2011 until 30 September 2012 Charles again occupied the house as his main residence.

Throughout the period 1 October 2000 to 30 September 2012 Charles did not have any other main residence.

Required

(i) Calculate Charles Orion's chargeable gain, if any, for the tax year 2012/13. **(5 marks)**

(ii) Explain how your answer to (i) above would have differed if Charles Orion had rented out his house during the period 1 April 2002 to 31 December 2010. **(3 marks)**

(Total = 20 marks)

INHERITANCE TAX

Questions 26 to 30 cover inheritance tax, the subject of Part E of the BPP Study Text for Paper F6.

26 Naomi

27 mins

On 6 May each year, Naomi gave quoted shares worth £3,000 to her son Marcus.

She also made the following gifts in her lifetime:

Date	Gift	Donee
15 August 2004	Cash of £313,000	Trust (Trustees paid the IHT due)
12 September 2008	3,000 shares in BCD Ltd (see below)	Marcus
14 February 2011	House valued at £82,000	Trust (Naomi paid the IHT due)

BCD Ltd was an investment company owned by Naomi and her brother and sister. Naomi had owned 5,000 shares in the company since its incorporation. These shares had a market value of £50,000 immediately before the gift to Marcus. At 12 September 2008, the 3,000 shares gifted had a market value of £18,000 and the remaining 2,000 shares retained by Naomi had a market value of £4,000. In April 2012, Naomi sold the remainder of her shares to an outside investor.

Naomi died on 12 October 2012. At her death, the value of the house gifted in 2011 was £110,000.

Naomi left a net estate of £550,000 at her death. In her Will, she left a legacy of £250,000 to her husband, Robert, and the residue of her estate to Marcus.

Required

(a) Describe the inheritance tax implications of the gifts made during Naomi's lifetime whilst Naomi was still alive and calculate any inheritance due during Naomi's lifetime. **(7 marks)**

Nil rate bands for previous years
2004/05	£263,000
2008/09	£312,000
2010/11	£325,000

(b) Describe the inheritance tax implications of Naomi's death on the gifts made during her lifetime. Calculate any inheritance tax due on these gifts as the result of her death. **(6 marks)**

(c) Describe the inheritance tax implications of the terms of Naomi's Will. Compute any inheritance tax due on the death estate. **(2 marks)**

(Total = 15 marks)

27 Ning Gao (TX 06/12)

27 mins

You should assume that today's date is 15 March 2013.

Ning Gao, aged 71, owns the following assets:

(1) Two properties respectively valued at £674,000 and £442,000. The first property has an outstanding repayment mortgage of £160,000, and the second property has an outstanding endowment mortgage of £92,000.

(2) Vintage motor cars valued at £172,000.

(3) Investments in individual savings accounts valued at £47,000, National Savings & Investments savings certificates valued at £36,000, and government stocks (gilts) valued at £69,000.

Ning owes £22,400 in respect of a personal loan from a bank, and she has also verbally promised to pay legal fees of £4,600 incurred by her nephew.

Under the terms of her will Ning has left all of her estate to her children.

Ning's husband died on 12 March 2003, and 70% of his inheritance tax nil rate band was not used.

On 14 August 2002 Ning had made a gift of £100,000 to her daughter, and on 7 November 2012 she made a gift of £220,000 to her son. Both these figures are after deducting all available exemptions.

The nil rate band for the tax year 2002/03 is £250,000.

Required

(a) Advise Ning Gao as to how much nil rate band will be available when calculating the inheritance tax payable in respect of her estate were she to die on 20 March 2013.   **(4 marks)**

(b) (i)   Calculate the inheritance tax that would be payable in respect of Ning Gao's estate were she to die on 20 March 2013, and state who will be responsible for paying the tax;   **(7 marks)**

     (ii) Advise Ning Gao as to whether the inheritance tax payable in respect of her estate would alter if she were to live for either another six or another seven years after 20 March 2013, and if so by how much.

           Note: You should assume that both the value of Ning Gao's estate and the nil rate band will remain unchanged.   **(2 marks)**

(c) State what conditions would have to be met if Ning Gao wanted to make gifts out of her income to her children so that these gifts are exempt from inheritance tax.   **(2 marks)**

                                                                                                    (Total = 15 marks)

28 Artem   **27 mins**

Artem died on 15 December 2012. During his lifetime he made the following cash gifts:

Date	Donee	£
10 December 2004	Daughter	65,000
17 January 2009	Trust	323,000
	(Artem paid the IHT)	
15 February 2009	Nephew	200
18 August 2009	Sister	46,000
17 June 2010	Trust	103,000
	(Trustees paid the IHT)	
1 August 2011	Grandson on the occasion of his marriage	66,000
5 September 2011	Wife	40,000

Required

(a) Explain the inheritance tax implications of these gifts during Artem's lifetime and compute any lifetime inheritance tax payable.   **(9 marks)**

     Nil rate bands
2004/05	£263,000
2008/09	£312,000
2009/10 onwards	£325,000

(b) Explain the inheritance tax implications of these gifts as a result of Artem's death on 15 December 2012 and compute the resulting inheritance tax payable.   **(6 marks)**

                                                                                                    (Total = 15 marks)

29 Jimmy (TX 06/11)

27 mins

Jimmy died on 14 February 2013. He had made the following gifts during his lifetime:

(1)   On 2 August 2011 Jimmy made a cash gift of £50,000 to his grandson as a wedding gift when he got married.

(2)   On 14 November 2011 Jimmy made a cash gift of £800,000 to a trust. Jimmy paid the inheritance tax arising from this gift.

At the date of his death Jimmy owned the following assets:

(1)   His main residence valued at £260,000.

(2)   Building society deposits of £515,600.

(3)   A life assurance policy on his own life. On 14 February 2013 the policy had an open market value of £182,000, and proceeds of £210,000 were received following Jimmy's death.

The cost of Jimmy's funeral amounted to £5,600.

Under the terms of his will Jimmy left £300,000 to his wife, with the residue of his estate to his daughter.

The nil rate band for the tax year 2011/12 is £325,000.

Required:

(a)   Explain why it is important to differentiate between potentially exempt transfers and chargeable lifetime transfers for inheritance tax purposes.   **(2 marks)**

(b)   Calculate the inheritance tax that will be payable as a result of Jimmy's death.   **(12 marks)**

(c)   State by when the personal representatives must pay the inheritance tax due on Jimmy's estate.   **(1 mark)**

(Total = 15 marks)

30 IHT transfers

27 mins

Describe the inheritance tax effects of the following events:

(a)   Bilal gives his daughter £20,000 on her marriage in June 2012 (his first lifetime gift).   **(3 marks)**

(b)   Sammy gives her grandson and granddaughter £200 each in August 2012.   **(1 mark)**

(c)   Terry sells a vase to his friend Alan for £1,000 which both Terry and Alan believe to be the market value of the vase. The vase is valued by an antiques expert and it is, in fact, worth £20,000.   **(3 marks)**

(d)   Lucas gives 2,000 shares (a 20% holding) in A Ltd, an investment company, to a trust for his children in December 2012. Before the transfer, Lucas owned 8,000 shares in A Ltd (an 80% holding). The following values per share applied at the date of the transfer:

%shareholding	Value per share
	£
80%	37.50
60%	18.75
20%	7.50

The only other lifetime gift that Lucas has made is a gift of quoted shares worth £3,000 each year to his son on 30 April each year.   **(3 marks)**

(e)   Donald decides to give his grandson £1,000 each month to pay university living expenses for at least four years. Donald will use income surplus to his living requirements to make these payments.   **(2 marks)**

(f)   Jas wants to make a gift to his son in November 2012. He can either give the son £100,000 in cash or shares in a newly incorporated investment company worth £100,000. These are the only shares Jas owns in the company. Jas thinks that the shares in the company will be worth five times their current value in three years' time. Jas gives £3,000 to his sister in June each year. He made a lifetime chargeable transfer of £500,000 in July 2012.   **(3 marks)**

(Total = 15 marks)

TAXATION OF COMPANIES

Questions 31 to 49 cover corporate businesses, the subject of Part F of the BPP Study Text for Paper F6.

31 Molten-Metal plc (TX 06/11)   45 mins

Molten-Metal plc is a manufacturer of machine tools. The following information is available for the year ended 31 March 2013:

Trading profit

The tax adjusted trading profit for the year ended 31 March 2013 is £2,138,415. This figure is before making any deductions required for:

(1)   Interest payable.
(2)   Capital allowances.
(3)   Any revenue expenditure that may have been debited to the company's capital expenditure account in error.

Interest payable

During the year ended 31 March 2013 Molten-Metal plc paid loan stock interest of £22,500. Loan stock interest of £3,700 was accrued at 31 March 2013, with the corresponding accrual at 1 April 2012 being £4,200. The loan is used for trading purposes.

The company also incurred a loan interest expense of £6,800 in respect of a loan that is used for non-trading purposes.

Capital expenditure account

The following items of expenditure have been debited to the capital expenditure account during the year ended 31 March 2013:

1 May 2012	Purchase of a second-hand freehold office building for £378,000. This figure included £11,000 for a ventilation system and £12,000 for a lift. Both the ventilation system and the lift are integral to the office building. During May 2012 Molten-Metal plc spent a further £97,400 on repairs. The office building was not usable until these repairs were carried out, and this fact was represented by a reduced purchase price.
26 June 2012	Purchase of machinery for £61,600. During June 2012 a further £7,700 was spent on building alterations that were necessary for the installation of the machinery.
8 August 2012	A payment of £41,200 for the construction of a new decorative wall around the company's premises.
27 August 2012	Purchase of movable partition walls for £22,900. Molten-Metal plc uses these to divide up its open plan offices, and the partition walls are moved around on a regular basis.
18 November 2012	Purchase of a motor car costing £24,000. This motor car has a CO_2 emission rate of 175 grams per kilometre. This car is used only for business purposes.
28 January 2013	Purchase of a computer costing £2,500. This computer has an expected working life of 5 years. Any relevant election will be made in respect of this asset.
11 March 2013	Purchase of two motor cars each costing £17,300. Each motor car has a CO_2 emission rate of 140 grams per kilometre. One motor car is used by the factory manager, and 60% of the mileage is for private journeys. The other motor car is used as a pool car.

Written down value

On 1 April 2012 the tax written down value of plant and machinery in Molten-Metal plc's main pool was £87,800.

Property income

Since 1 February 2013 Molten-Metal plc has let out an unfurnished freehold office building that is surplus to requirements. On that date the tenant paid the company £78,800, consisting of a premium of £68,000 for the grant of a six-year lease, and the advance payment of three months' rent.

Interest receivable

Molten-Metal plc made a loan for non-trading purposes on 1 August 2012. Loan interest of £9,800 was received on 31 January 2013, and £3,100 was accrued at 31 March 2013.

The company also received bank interest of £2,600 during the year ended 31 March 2013. The bank deposits are held for non-trading purposes.

Disposal of office building

On 20 May 2012 Molten-Metal plc sold a freehold office building for £872,000. The office building had been purchased on 13 June 2004 for £396,200 (including legal fees). During June 2008 the office building was extended at a cost of £146,000, and during the same month the company spent £48,000 replacing part of the office building roof following a fire. Molten-Metal plc incurred legal fees of £28,400 in connection with the disposal. Indexation factors are as follows:

June 2004 to May 2012   0.302

June 2008 to May 2012   0.123

Quarterly instalment payments

Molten-Metal plc makes quarterly instalment payments in respect of its corporation tax liability. The first three instalment payments for the year ended 31 March 2013 totalled £398,200.

Required

(a)   Calculate Molten-Metal plc's corporation tax liability for the year ended 31 March 2013.

Note: You should ignore any chargeable gain arising from the grant of the lease and also ignore rollover relief.   **(23 marks)**

(b)   Calculate the final quarterly instalment payment that will have to be made by Molten-Metal plc for the year ended 31 March 2013, and state when this will be due.   **(2 marks)**

(Total = 25 marks)

32 Crash-Bash Ltd (TX 12/09)   54 mins

(a)   Crash-Bash Ltd commenced trading on 1 July 2012 as a manufacturer of motor cycle crash helmets in the United Kingdom. The company is incorporated overseas, although its directors are based in the United Kingdom and hold their board meetings in the United Kingdom.

Crash-Bash Ltd prepared its first accounts for the nine-month period ended 31 March 2013. The following information is available:

UK trading profit

The tax adjusted UK trading profit based on the draft accounts for the nine-month period ended 31 March 2013 is £365,148. This figure is **before** making any adjustments required for:

(1)   Capital allowances.

(2)   Advertising expenditure of £12,840 incurred during June 2012. This expenditure has not been deducted in arriving at the tax adjusted trading profit for the period ended 31 March 2013 of £365,148.

Plant and machinery

The accounts for the nine-month period ended 31 March 2013 showed the following additions and disposals of plant and machinery:

		Cost/(Proceeds) £
2 October 2012	Purchased machinery	25,000
28 November 2012	Purchased a motor car	13,200
12 February 2013	Sold machinery	(3,600)

The motor car purchased on 28 November 2012 for £13,200 has a CO_2 emission rate of 108 grams per kilometre. The machinery sold on 12 February 2013 for £3,600 originally cost £5,300 and is part of the machinery purchased on 2 October 2012 for £25,000.

Capital gain

On 30 November 2012, Crash-Bash Ltd sold a warehouse for £500,000. The indexed cost was £375,000. Crash-Bash Ltd bought another warehouse for £480,000 on 10 September 2012.

Overseas branch profits

Crash-Bash Ltd also had overseas trading profits of £20,000 (gross) for the nine-month period ended 31 March 2013 from its sales through an overseas branch. Overseas tax was payable on these profits at the rate of 25%. No election had been made in relation to the overseas branch.

Overseas dividend received

On 31 March 2013 Crash-Bash Ltd received a dividend of £14,250 from a 100% owned subsidiary company, Safety Inc, that is resident overseas.

UK dividends received

During the period ended 31 March 2013 Crash-Bash Ltd received dividends of £36,000 from Flat-Out plc, an unconnected United Kingdom company. This figure was the actual cash amount received.

Export of crash helmets to Safety Inc

Safety Inc, Crash-Bash Ltd's 100% owned overseas subsidiary company, sells crash helmets that have been manufactured by Crash-Bash Ltd. Crash-Bash Ltd is a large company for the purposes of transfer pricing legislation.

Other information

With the exception of Safety Inc, Crash-Bash Ltd does not have any associated companies.

Required

(i) Explain why Crash-Bash Ltd is treated as being resident in the United Kingdom. **(2 marks)**

(ii) Calculate Crash-Bash Ltd's corporation tax liability for the nine-month period ended 31 March 2013 after taking account of double taxation relief. **(14 marks)**

(iii) Explain the corporation tax implications if Crash-Bash Ltd were to invoice Safety Inc for the exported crash helmets at a price that was less than the market price. **(4 marks)**

(b) Note that in answering this part of the question you are not expected to take account of any of the information provided in part (a) above.

Crash-Bash Ltd's outputs and inputs for the first two months of trading from 1 July 2012 to 31 August 2012 were as follows:

	July £	August £
Outputs		
Sales	13,200	18,800
Inputs		
Goods purchased	94,600	193,100
Services incurred	22,300	32,700

The above figures are stated exclusive of value added tax (VAT). On 1 September 2012 Crash-Bash Ltd realised that its sales for September 2012 were going to exceed £100,000, and therefore immediately registered for VAT. On that date the company had inventory that had cost £108,600 (exclusive of VAT).

During February 2013 Crash-Bash Ltd discovered that a number of errors had been made when completing its VAT return for the quarter ended 30 November 2012. As a result of these errors the company will have to make an additional payment of VAT to HM Revenue and Customs (HMRC).

Required

(i)   Explain why Crash-Bash Ltd was required to compulsorily register for VAT from 1 September 2012, and state what action the company then had to take as regards notifying HM Revenue and Customs of the registration. **(3 marks)**

(ii)   Calculate the amount of input VAT that Crash-Bash Ltd was able to recover in respect of inputs incurred prior to registering for VAT on 1 September 2012. Your answer should include an explanation as to why the input VAT is recoverable. **(4 marks)**

(iii) Explain how Crash-Bash Ltd could have voluntarily disclosed the errors relating to the VAT return for the quarter ended 30 November 2012, and state the circumstances in which default interest would have been due. **(3 marks)**

(Total = 30 marks)

33 Mice Ltd (TX 06/10)   45 mins

(a)   **You should assume that today's date is 28 March 2013.**

Mice Ltd commenced trading on 1 July 2009 as a manufacturer of computer peripherals. The company prepares accounts to 31 March, and its results for the first three periods of trading were as follows:

	Period ended 31 March 2010 £	Year ended 31 March 2011 £	Year ended 31 March 2012 £
Trading profit	83,200	24,700	51,200
Property business profit	2,800	7,100	12,200
Qualifying charitable donations	(1,000)	(1,500)	-

The following information is available in respect of the year ended 31 March 2013:

Trading loss

Mice Ltd expects to make a trading loss of £180,000.

Property business income

Mice Ltd lets out three freehold office buildings that are surplus to requirements.

The first office building was let throughout the year ended 31 March 2013 at a quarterly rent of £3,200, payable in advance. Mice Ltd paid business rates of £2,200 and insurance of £460 in respect of this property for the year ended 31 March 2013. During June 2012 Mice Ltd repaired the existing car park for this property at a cost of £1,060 and then subsequently enlarged the car park at a cost of £2,640.

The second office building was let on 1 April 2012 to a tenant, with Mice Ltd receiving a premium of £18,000 for the grant of an eight-year lease. The company also received the annual rent of £6,000 which was payable in advance. Mice Ltd paid insurance of £310 in respect of this property for the year ended 31 March 2013.

The third office building was purchased by Mice Ltd on 1 January 2013 and it will be empty until 31 March 2013. The building is to be let from 1 April 2013 at a monthly rent of £640, and on 15 March 2013 Mice Ltd received three months rent in advance. On 1 January 2013 Mice Ltd paid insurance of £480 in respect of this property for the year ended 31 December 2013, and during February 2013 spent £680 on advertising for tenants. Mice Ltd paid loan interest of £1,800 in respect of the period 1 January 2013 to 31 March 2013 on a loan that was taken out to purchase this property.

Loan interest received

On 1 July 2012 Mice Ltd made a loan for non-trading purposes. Loan interest of £6,400 was received on 31 December 2012 and £3,200 will be accrued at 31 March 2013.

Overseas dividend

On 15 October 2012 Mice Ltd received a dividend of £7,400 (net) from a 3% shareholding in USB Inc, a company that is resident overseas. Withholding tax was withheld from this dividend at the rate of 7.5%.

Chargeable gain

On 20 December 2012 Mice Ltd sold its 3% shareholding in USB Inc. The disposal resulted in a chargeable gain of £2,750, after taking account of indexation.

Required

(i)   Calculate Mice Ltd's property business profit for the year ended 31 March 2013;   **(8 marks)**

(ii)   Assuming that Mice Ltd claims relief for its trading loss as early as possible, calculate the company's taxable total profits for the nine-month period ended 31 March 2010, and each of the years ended 31 March 2011, 2012 and 2013.   **(7 marks)**

(b)   Mice Ltd has owned 100% of the ordinary share capital of Web-Cam Ltd since it began trading on 1 April 2012. For the three-month period ended 30 June 2012 Web-Cam Ltd made a trading profit of £28,000 and is expected to make a trading profit of £224,000 for the year ended 30 June 2013. Web-Cam Ltd has no other taxable profits or allowable losses.

Required

Assuming that Mice Ltd does not make any loss relief claim against its own profits, advise Web-Cam Ltd as to the maximum amount of group relief that can be claimed from Mice Ltd in respect of the trading loss of £180,000 for the year ended 31 March 2013.   **(3 marks)**

(c)   Mice Ltd has surplus funds of £125,000 which it is planning to spend before 31 March 2013. The company will either purchase new equipment for £125,000, or alternatively it will purchase a new ventilation system for £125,000, which will be installed as part of its factory.

Required

Explain the maximum amount of capital allowances that Mice Ltd will be able to claim for the year ended 31 March 2013 in respect of each of the two alternative purchases of assets.

Note: you are not expected to recalculate Mice Ltd's trading loss for the year ended 31 March 2013, or redo any of the calculations made in parts (a) and (b) above.   **(4 marks)**

(d)   Mice Ltd is planning to pay its managing director a bonus of £40,000 on 31 March 2013. The managing director has already been paid gross director's remuneration of £50,000 during the tax year 2012/13 and the bonus of £40,000 will be paid as additional director's remuneration. The managing director has no other income in 2012/13.

Required

Advise the managing director as to the additional amount of income tax and national insurance contributions (both employee's and employer's) that will be payable as a result of the payment of the additional director's remuneration of £40,000.

Note: you are not expected to recalculate Mice Ltd's trading loss for the year ended 31 March 2013, or redo any of the calculations made in parts (a) and (b) above.   **(3 marks)**

(Total = 25 marks)

34 Do-Not-Panic Ltd (TX 06/08)
18 mins

Do-Not-Panic Ltd is a United Kingdom resident company that installs burglar alarms. The company commenced trading on 1 January 2012 and its results for the fifteen-month period ended 31 March 2013 are summarised as follows:

(1) The trading profit as adjusted for tax purposes is £285,000. This figure is before taking account of capital allowances.

(2) Do-Not-Panic Ltd purchased equipment for £5,000 on 20 February 2013.

(3) Do-Not-Panic Ltd bought some loan stock on 1 January 2013 as an investment. Interest of £7,500 was received on 31 March 2013 which was also the amount accrued to that date.

(4) On 21 December 2012 Do-Not-Panic Ltd disposed of some investments and this resulted in a capital loss of £4,250. On 28 March 2013 the company made a further disposal and this resulted in a chargeable gain of £39,000.

(5) Franked investment income of £25,000 was received on 22 February 2013.

Do-Not-Panic Ltd has no associated companies.

Required

Calculate Do-Not-Panic Ltd's corporation tax liabilities in respect of the fifteen-month period ended 31 March 2013 and advise the company by when these should be paid. **(10 marks)**

35 Quagmire plc (TX 06/10)
18 mins

For the year ended 31 March 2013 Quagmire plc had taxable total profits of £1,200,000 and franked investment income of £200,000. For the year ended 31 March 2012 the company had taxable total profits of £1,600,000 and franked investment income of £120,000.

Quagmire plc's profits accrue evenly throughout the year.

Quagmire plc has one associated company.

Required

(a) Explain why Quagmire plc will have been required to make quarterly instalment payments in respect of its corporation tax liability for the year ended 31 March 2013. **(3 marks)**

(b) Calculate Quagmire plc's corporation tax liability for the year ended 31 March 2013 and explain how and when this will have been paid. **(3 marks)**

(c) Explain how your answer to part (b) above would differ if Quagmire plc did not have an associated company. Your answer should include a calculation of the revised corporation tax liability for the year ended 31 March 2013. **(4 marks)**

(Total = 10 marks)

36 Heavy Ltd and Soft Ltd (TX 06/12)
45 mins

Heavy Ltd runs a music publishing business. On 1 September 2012 Heavy Ltd acquired 100% of the ordinary share capital of Soft Ltd, a company that runs a music recording studio. Neither company has any other associated companies.

Heavy Ltd has prepared accounts for the year ended 31 December 2012, whilst Soft Ltd has prepared accounts for the 16-month period ended 31 December 2013 so as to make its accounting date coterminous with that of Heavy Ltd. The following information is available:

Heavy Ltd

(1) The operating profit for the year ended 31 December 2012 is £417,340. Depreciation of £12,880 and amortisation of leasehold property of £9,000 (see note (2) below) have been deducted in arriving at this figure.

(2) On 1 January 2012 Heavy Ltd acquired a leasehold office building, paying a premium of £90,000 for the grant of a ten-year lease. The office building was used for business purposes by Heavy Ltd throughout the year ended 31 December 2012.

(3) On 1 January 2012 the tax written down values of Heavy Ltd's plant and machinery were as follows:

	£
Main pool	900
Special rate pool	21,700
Short life asset (acquired July 2011)	3,200

The following purchases and disposals of plant and machinery took place during the year ended 31 December 2012:

		Cost/ (proceeds) £
23 March 2012	Purchased office equipment	22,400
15 June 2012	Sold the short life asset	(4,600)
28 July 2012	Sold all the items included in the special rate pool	(9,950)

(4) On 1 August 2012 Heavy Ltd acquired loan stock as an investment. Interest of £8,800 was received on 30 November 2012, and £1,500 was accrued at 31 December 2012.

(5) During the year ended 31 December 2012 Heavy Ltd received bank interest of £1,600, which was the amount accrued during the year. The bank deposits are held for non-trading purposes.

(6) On 31 March 2012 Heavy Ltd repaid a bank loan taken out for non-trading purposes. The final interest payment on that date amounted to £900 which was the amount accrued since 1 January 2012.

(7) On 18 October 2012 Heavy Ltd sold a freehold office building to Soft Ltd for £113,600. The indexed cost of the office building on that date was £102,800.

(8) During the year ended 31 December 2012 Heavy Ltd received the following dividends:

	£
Company paying the dividend	
An unconnected United Kingdom company	18,000
Soft Ltd	6,300
An unconnected overseas company	9,000

Soft Ltd

(1) The tax adjusted trading profit for the 16-month period ended 31 December 2013 is £120,200. This figure is before taking account of capital allowances.

(2) On 1 September 2012 the tax written down value of Soft Ltd's plant and machinery in the main pool was £24,000. On 15 December 2013 Soft Ltd sold an item of plant for £3,900. The plant had originally cost £5,200.

(3) On 4 August 2013 Soft Ltd disposed of some investments and this resulted in a chargeable gain of £16,170. On 3 September 2013 the company made a further disposal and this resulted in a capital loss of £2,900.

Required

(a) Calculate Heavy Ltd's corporation tax liability for the year ended 31 December 2012. **(18 marks)**

(b) Calculate Soft Ltd's corporation tax liabilities in respect of the 16-month period ended 31 December 2013.

(7 marks)

Note: Assume that the rates of capital allowances and the small profits rate for Financial Year 2012 also apply in Financial Year 2013.

(Total = 25 marks)

37 Thai Curry Ltd (BTX)   47 mins

Thai Curry Ltd is a manufacturer of ready to cook food. The following information is available in respect of the year ended 31 March 2013:

Trading loss

The trading loss is £55,036. This figure is before taking account of capital allowances.

Plant and machinery

On 1 April 2012 the tax written down values of plant and machinery were as follows:

	£
Main pool	10,600
Special rate pool	16,400

The special rate pool consists of one motor car which has CO_2 emissions of 180 g/km and was acquired in July 2010.

The following transactions took place during the year ended 31 March 2013:

		Cost/ (Proceeds) £
1 May 2012	Sold equipment	(12,800)
8 July 2012	Purchased equipment	9,460
14 July 2012	Sold the special rate pool motor car	(9,700)
26 August 2012	Purchased motor car (1) CO_2 emissions 149g/km	15,800
19 November 2012	Purchased motor car (2) CO_2 emissions 103g/km	9,700
20 March 2013	Purchased a new freehold office building	220,000

The equipment sold on 1 May 2012 for £12,800 originally cost £27,400.

The cost of the new freehold office building purchased on 20 March 2013 included £5,500 for the central heating system, £2,200 for sprinkler equipment and the fire alarm system and £5,050 for the ventilation system.

Income from property

Thai Curry Ltd lets out two warehouses that are surplus to requirements.

The first warehouse was let from 1 April 2012 until 30 November 2012 at a monthly rent of £2,200. On that date the tenant left owing two months rent which Thai Curry Ltd was not able to recover. During February 2013 £8,800 was spent on painting the warehouse. The warehouse was not re-let until 1 April 2013.

The second warehouse was empty from 1 April 2012 until 31 July 2012, but was let from 1 August 2012. On that date Thai Curry Ltd received a premium of £60,000 for the grant of a four-year lease, and the annual rent of £18,000 which is payable in advance.

Loan interest received

Loan interest of £8,000 was received on 30 September 2012 relating to the period from 1 April 2012 and £3,500 was accrued at 31 March 2013. The loan was made for non-trading purposes.

Dividends received

During the year ended 31 March 2013 Thai Curry Ltd received dividends of £36,000 from African Spice plc, an unconnected UK company. This figure was the actual cash amount received.

Profit on disposal of shares

On 28 July 2012 Thai Curry Ltd sold 10,000 £1 ordinary shares in investment company African Spice plc, making a capital gain of £152,300 on the disposal.

Other information

Thai Curry Ltd has three associated companies.

Required

(a) Calculate Thai Curry Ltd's tax adjusted trading loss for the year ended 31 March 2013. You should assume that the company claims the maximum available capital allowances. **(9 marks)**

(b) Assuming that Thai Curry Ltd claims relief for its trading loss against total profits, calculate the company's corporation tax liability for the year ended 31 March 2013. **(11 marks)**

(c) (i) State the date by which Thai Curry Ltd's self-assessment corporation tax return for the year ended 31 March 2013 should be submitted, and advise the company of the penalties that will be due if the return is not submitted until 30 November 2014. **(3 marks)**

(ii) State the date by which Thai Curry Ltd's corporation tax liability for the year ended 31 March 2013 should be paid, and advise the company of the interest that will be due if the liability is not paid until 30 November 2014. **(3 marks)**

(Total = 26 marks)

38 Hawk Ltd (TX 12/08)   36 mins

Hawk Ltd sold the following assets during the year ended 31 March 2013:

(1) On 30 April 2012 a freehold office building was sold for £270,000. The office building had been purchased on 2 July 2004 for £81,000, and had been extended at a cost of £43,000 during May 2006. Hawk Ltd incurred legal fees of £3,200 in connection with the purchase of the office building, and legal fees of £5,726 in connection with the disposal. The office building has always been used by Hawk Ltd for business purposes. The relevant retail prices indexes (RPIs) are as follows:

July 2004	186.8
May 2006	197.7
April 2012	242.6

(2) On 29 August 2012 5,000 £1 ordinary shares in Albatross plc were sold for £42,500. Hawk Ltd had purchased 6,000 shares in Albatross plc on 1 August 2012 for £18,600, and purchased a further 2,000 shares on 17 August 2012 for £9,400.

(3) On 27 October 2012 10,000 £1 preference shares in Cuckoo plc were sold for £32,000. Hawk Ltd had originally purchased 5,000 £1 ordinary shares in Cuckoo plc on 2 October 2012 for £60,000. On 18 October 2012 Cuckoo plc had a reorganisation whereby each £1 ordinary share was exchanged for three new £1 ordinary shares and two £1 preference shares. Immediately after the reorganisation each new £1 ordinary share was quoted at £4.50 and each £1 preference share was quoted at £2.25.

(4) On 28 March 2013 two acres of land were sold for £120,000. Hawk Ltd had originally purchased three acres of land on 1 March 2013 for £203,500. The market value of the unsold acre of land as at 28 March 2013 was £65,000. The land has never been used by Hawk Ltd for business purposes.

Hawk Ltd's only other income for the year ended 31 March 2013 was a trading profit of £125,000. Hawk Ltd does not have any associated companies.

Required

(a) Calculate Hawk Ltd's corporation tax liability for the year ended 31 March 2013. **(16 marks)**

(b) Advise Hawk Ltd of:

(i) The minimum amount that will have to be reinvested in qualifying replacement business assets in order for the company to claim the maximum possible amount of rollover relief in respect of its chargeable gains for the year ended 31 March 2013. **(2 marks)**

(ii) The period during which the reinvestment must take place. **(1 mark)**

(iii) The amount of corporation tax that will be deferred if the maximum possible amount of rollover relief is claimed for the year ended 31 March 2013. **(1 mark)**

(Total = 20 marks)

39 Problematic Ltd (TX 06/10)

36 mins

Problematic Ltd sold the following assets during the year ended 31 March 2013:

(1) On 14 June 2012 16,000 £1 ordinary shares in Easy plc were sold for £54,400. Problematic Ltd had originally purchased 15,000 shares in Easy plc on 26 June 2005 for £12,600. On 28 September 2008 Easy plc made a 1 for 3 rights issue. Problematic Ltd took up its allocation under the rights issue in full, paying £2.20 for each new share issued. The relevant retail prices indexes (RPIs) are as follows:

June 2005	192.2
September 2008	218.4
June 2012	242.3

(2) On 1 October 2012 an office building owned by Problematic Ltd was damaged by a fire. The indexed cost of the office building on that date was £169,000. The company received insurance proceeds of £36,000 on 10 October 2012 and spent a total of £41,000 during October 2012 on restoring the office building. Problematic Ltd has made a claim to defer the gain arising from the receipt of the insurance proceeds. The office building has never been used for business purposes.

(3) On 28 January 2013 a freehold factory was sold for £171,000. The indexed cost of the factory on that date was £127,000. Problematic Ltd has made a claim to holdover the gain on the factory against the cost of a replacement leasehold factory under the rollover relief (replacement of business assets) rules. The leasehold factory has a lease period of 20 years, and was purchased on 10 December 2012 for £154,800. The two factory buildings have always been used entirely for business purposes.

(4) On 20 February 2013 an acre of land was sold for £130,000. Problematic Ltd had originally purchased four acres of land, and the indexed cost of the four acres on 20 February 2013 was £300,000. The market value of the unsold three acres of land as at 20 February 2013 was £350,000. Problematic Ltd incurred legal fees of £3,200 in connection with the disposal. The land has never been used for business purposes.

Problematic Ltd's only other income for the year ended 31 March 2013 is a tax adjusted trading profit of £106,321.

Required

(a) Calculate Problematic Ltd's taxable total profits for the year ended 31 March 2013. **(16 marks)**

(b) Advise Problematic Ltd of the carried forward indexed base costs for capital gains purposes of any assets included in (1) to (4) above that are still retained at 31 March 2013. **(4 marks)**

(Total = 20 marks)

40 Lim Lam (TX 12/10)

27 mins

Lim Lam is the controlling shareholder and managing director of Mal-Mil Ltd, an unquoted trading company that provides support services to the oil industry.

Lim Lam

Lim disposed of the following assets during the tax year 2012/13:

(1) On 8 July 2012 Lim sold five acres of land to Mal-Mil Ltd for £260,000, which was the market value of the land on that date. The land had been inherited by Lim upon the death of her mother on 17 January 2006, when the land was valued at £182,000. Lim's mother had originally purchased the land for £137,000.

(2) On 13 August 2012 Lim made a gift of 5,000 £1 ordinary shares in Oily plc, a quoted trading company, to her sister. On that date the shares were quoted on the Stock Exchange at £7.40–£7.56, with recorded bargains of £7.36, £7.38 and £7.60. Lim had originally purchased her 5,000 shares in the company on 23 November 2006 for £15,925.

Entrepreneurs' relief and holdover relief are not available in respect of this disposal.

(3) On 22 March 2013 Lim sold 40,000 £1 ordinary shares in Mal-Mil Ltd for £280,000. She had originally purchased 125,000 shares in the company on 8 June 2005 for £142,000, and had purchased a further 60,000 shares on 23 May 2007 for £117,000. Mal-Mil Ltd has a total share capital of 250,000 £1 ordinary shares.

Entrepreneurs' relief is available in respect of this disposal. Lim has made no previous disposals eligible for entrepreneurs' relief.

Lim had taxable income of £28,000 in 2012/13.

Mal-Mil Ltd

On 20 December 2012 Mal-Mil Ltd sold two of the five acres of land that had been purchased from Lim on 8 July 2012. The sale proceeds were £162,000 and legal fees of £3,800 were incurred in connection with the disposal. The market value of the unsold three acres of land as at 20 December 2012 was £254,000. During July 2012 Mal-Mil Ltd had spent £31,200 levelling the five acres of land. The relevant retail price indexes (RPIs) are as follows:

July 2012   241.7
December 2012   246.6

Mal-Mil Ltd's only other income for the year ended 31 December 2012 was a trading profit of £163,000.

Required

(a) Calculate Lim Lam's capital gains tax liability for the tax year 2012/13, and state by when this should be paid. **(8 marks)**

(b) Calculate Mal-Mil Ltd's corporation tax liability for the year ended 31 December 2012, and state by when this should be paid. **(7 marks)**

(Total = 15 marks)

41 Starfish Ltd (TX 12/11)   **54 mins**

Starfish Ltd, a retailer of scuba diving equipment, was incorporated on 15 October 2008, and commenced trading on 1 December 2008. The company initially prepared accounts to 31 March, but changed its accounting date to 31 December by preparing accounts for the nine-month period ended 31 December 2012. Starfish Ltd ceased trading on 31 March 2013, and a resolution was subsequently passed to commence winding up procedures.

Starfish Ltd's results for each of its periods of account up to 31 December 2012 are as follows:

	Tax adjusted trading profit/(loss)	Bank interest	Qualifying charitable donations
	£	£	£
Four-month period ended 31 March 2009	(12,600)	600	(800)
Year ended 31 March 2010	64,200	1,400	(1,000)
Year ended 31 March 2011	53,900	1,700	(900)
Year ended 31 March 2012	14,700	0	(700)
Nine-month period ended 31 December 2012	49,900	0	(600)

The company's summarised statement of profit or loss for its final three-month period of trading ended 31 March 2013 is as follows:

	Note	£	£
Gross profit			16,100
Expenses			
Depreciation		25,030	
Donations	1	1,650	
Impairment loss	2	2,000	
Legal fees	3	9,370	
Other expenses	4	168,050	
			(206,100)
Loss before taxation			(190,000)

Note 1 – Donations

Donations were made to the following:

	£
A political party	300
A charity (not qualifying charitable donation)	600
A national charity (qualifying charitable donation)	750
	1,650

Note 2 – Impairment loss

On 31 March 2013 Starfish Ltd wrote off an impairment loss of £2,000 in respect of a trade debt.

Note 3 – Legal fees

Legal fees were in connection with the following:

	£
Defence of the company's internet domain name	3,490
Court action for a misleading advertisement	2,020
Issue of 6% loan notes that was subsequently cancelled	3,860
	9,370

Note 4 – Other expenses

Other expenses are as follows:

	£
Entertaining customers	3,600
Entertaining employees	1,840
Counselling services provided to employees who were made redundant	8,400
Balance of expenditure (all allowable)	154,210
	168,050

Note 5 – Plant and machinery

On 1 January 2013 the tax written down values of the company's plant and machinery were as follows:

	£
Main pool	23,600
Special rate pool	13,200

The special rate pool consists of a motor car that was purchased on 18 June 2009, and which has CO_2 emissions of 190 grams per kilometre.

On 10 January 2013 Starfish Ltd purchased a laptop computer for £3,120. This figure is inclusive of value added tax (VAT).

On 31 March 2013 the company sold all of the items included in the main pool for £31,200, the laptop computer for £1,800, and the motor car for £9,600. These figures are inclusive of VAT where applicable. None of the items included in the main pool was sold for more than its original cost, and all of the items were standard rated.

Note 6 – Final VAT return

Starfish Ltd deregistered from VAT on 31 March 2013. The following information relates to the company's final VAT return for the quarter ended 31 March 2013:

(i)   Cash sales revenue amounted to £41,160, of which £38,520 was in respect of standard rated sales and £2,640 was in respect of zero-rated sales.

(ii)   Sales invoices totalling £2,000 were issued in respect of credit sales revenue. This figure is exclusive of VAT, and the sales were all standard rated. Starfish Ltd offered all of its credit sale customers a 4% discount for payment within 14 days of the date of the sales invoice, and 60% of the customers paid within this period.

(iii)   In addition to the above sales revenue, Starfish Ltd sold its remaining inventory of scuba diving equipment on 31 March 2013 for £28,800. The inventory had originally cost £32,400.

(iv)   There were no purchases of inventory during the period.

(v)   Standard rated expenses amounted to £69,960, of which £4,320 was in respect of entertaining UK customers.

(vi)   The impairment loss which Starfish Ltd wrote off on 31 March 2013 (as per note (2) above) was in respect of a sales invoice (exclusive of VAT) that was due for payment on 8 August 2012. Output VAT of £384 was originally paid in respect of this sale.

(vii)   Purchases and sales of non-current assets during the period are as per note (5) above. Unless otherwise stated, all of the above figures are inclusive of VAT where applicable.

Starfish Ltd did not use the cash accounting scheme.

Required

(a)   State when an accounting period starts and when an accounting period finishes for corporation tax purposes.   **(4 marks)**

(b)   Calculate Starfish Ltd's tax adjusted trading loss for the three-month period ended 31 March 2013.

        Notes:

        1.   Your computation should commence with the loss before taxation figure of £190,000, and should also list all of the items referred to in notes (1) to (4) indicating by the use of zero (0) any items that do not require adjustment.

        2.   In answering this part of the question you are not expected to take account of any of the information provided in note (6) above regarding the final VAT return.   **(12 marks)**

(c)   Assuming that Starfish Ltd claims relief for its trading losses on the most beneficial basis, calculate the company's taxable total profits for the four-month period ended 31 March 2009, the years ended 31 March 2010, 2011 and 2012 and the nine-month period ended 31 December 2012.   **(5 marks)**

(d)   (i)   Calculate the amount of VAT payable by Starfish Ltd in respect of its final VAT return for the quarter ended 31 March 2013;

                Notes:

                1.   In answering this part of the question you are not expected to take account of any of the information provided in notes (1), (3) or (4) above.

                2.   You should ignore the output VAT scale charge due in respect of fuel for private journeys.
                                                                                        (7 marks)

        (ii)   Explain, with supporting calculations, how your answer to part (d)(i) above would differ if Starfish Ltd had instead sold its entire business as a going concern to a single VAT registered purchaser.
                                                                                        (2 marks)

                                                                                (Total = 30 marks)

42 Volatile Ltd (TX 12/09)   **18 mins**

Volatile Ltd commenced trading on 1 July 2008. The company's results for its first five periods of trading are as follows:

	Period ended 31 December 2008	Year ended 31 December 2009	Year ended 31 December 2010	Period ended 30 September 2011	Year ended 30 September 2012
	£	£	£	£	£
Trading profit/(loss)	44,000	(73,800)	95,200	78,700	(186,800)
Property business profit	9,400	6,600	6,500	–	–
Chargeable gains	5,100	–	–	9,700	–
Qualifying charitable donations	(800)	(1,000)	(1,200)	–	–

Required

(a) State the factors that will influence a company's choice of loss relief claims.

Note: You are not expected to consider group relief. **(3 marks)**

(b) Assuming that Volatile Ltd claims relief for its trading losses as early as possible, calculate the company's taxable total profits for the six-month period ended 31 December 2008, each of the years ended 31 December 2009 and 2010 and the nine-month period ended 30 September 2011. Your answer should also clearly identify the amount of any unrelieved trading losses as at 30 September 2012. **(7 marks)**

(Total = 10 marks)

43 Jogger Limited (TX 12/08) 54 mins

(a) Jogger Ltd is a manufacturer of running shoes. The company's summarised statement of profit or loss for the year ended 31 March 2013 is as follows:

	Note	£	£
Operating loss	1		(81,518)
Income from investments			
Bank interest	3	8,460	
Loan interest	4	24,600	
Income from property	5	144,000	
Dividends	6	45,000	
			222,060
Profit from sale of non-current assets			
Disposal of shares	7		102,340
Profit before taxation			237,882

Note 1 – Operating loss

Depreciation of £58,840 has been deducted in arriving at the operating loss of £81,518.

Note 2 – Plant and machinery

On 1 April 2012 the tax written down values of plant and machinery were as follows:

	£
Main pool	26,600
Special rate pool	18,800

The following transactions took place during the year ended 31 March 2013:

		Cost/(proceeds) £
20 July 2012	Sold a special rate pool motor car	(11,700)
31 July 2012	Purchased motor car	11,800
	CO$_2$ emissions 135g/km	
30 September 2012	Purchased machinery	20,000
15 December 2012	Purchased computer system	12,500
14 March 2013	Sold a lorry	(8,600)

The motor car sold on 20 July 2012 for £11,700 originally cost more than this amount. The computer system purchased on 15 December 2012 has a predicted working life of six years and any relevant election has been made. The lorry sold on 14 March 2013 for £8,600 originally cost £16,600.

Note 3 – Bank interest received

The bank interest was received on 31 March 2013. The bank deposits are held for non-trading purposes.

Note 4 – Loan interest receivable

The loan was made for non-trading purposes on 1 July 2012. Loan interest of £16,400 was received on 31 December 2012, and interest of £8,200 was accrued at 31 March 2013.

Note 5 – Income from property

Jogger Ltd lets out an unfurnished freehold office building that is surplus to requirements. The office building was let throughout the year ended 31 March 2013. On 1 April 2012 Jogger Ltd received a premium of £100,000 for the grant of a ten-year lease, and the annual rent of £44,000 which is payable in advance.

Note 6 – Dividends received

During the year ended 31 March 2013 Jogger Ltd received dividends of £45,000 from Sprinter plc, an unconnected UK company. This figure was the actual cash amount received.

Note 7 – Profit on disposal of shares

The profit on disposal of shares is in respect of a shareholding that was sold on 5 December 2012. The disposal resulted in a chargeable gain of £98,300. This figure is after taking account of indexation.

Note 8 – Other information

Jogger Ltd has two associated companies.

Required

Ignore VAT throughout part (a).

(i)   Calculate Jogger Ltd's tax adjusted trading loss for the year ended 31 March 2013.

Notes: (1)   Your computation should start with the operating loss of £(81,518).
      (2)   You should assume that the company claims the maximum available capital allowances.

(7 marks)

(ii)   Assuming that Jogger Ltd claims relief for its trading loss against total profits, calculate the company's corporation tax liability for the year ended 31 March 2013.   **(8 marks)**

(iii)   State the date by which Jogger Ltd's self-assessment corporation tax return for the year ended 31 March 2013 should be submitted, and advise the company of the penalties that will be due if the return is submitted eight months late.

Note: you should assume that the company pays its corporation tax liability at the same time that the self-assessment tax return is submitted.   **(4 marks)**

(b)   *Note:* In answering this part of the question you are not expected to take account of any of the information provided in part (a) above.

Jogger Ltd has been registered for value added tax (VAT) since 1 April 2006. From that date until 30 June 2011 the company's VAT returns were all submitted on time. Since 1 July 2011 the company's VAT returns have been submitted as follows:

Quarter ended	VAT paid £	Submitted
30 September 2011	42,700	One month late
31 December 2011	41,200	On time
31 March 2012	38,900	One month late
30 June 2012	28,300	On time
30 September 2012	49,100	On time
31 December 2012	63,800	On time
31 March 2013	89,100	Two months late

Jogger Ltd always pays any VAT that is due at the same time as the related return is submitted.

Required

(i)   State, giving appropriate reasons, the default surcharge consequences arising from Jogger Ltd's submission of its VAT returns for the quarter ended 30 September 2011 to the quarter ended 31 March 2013 inclusive, at the times stated.   **(6 marks)**

(ii)   Advise Jogger Ltd why it might be beneficial to use the VAT annual accounting scheme, and state the conditions that it will have to satisfy before being permitted to do so.   **(5 marks)**

(Total = 30 marks)

44 Black Ltd, Brown Ltd and Blu Reddy (TX 12/11)   27 mins

(a)   Black Ltd owns 100% of the ordinary share capital of White Ltd. The results of Black Ltd and White Ltd for the year ended 31 March 2013 are as follows:

	Black Ltd	White Ltd
	£	£
Trading profit/(loss)	396,800	(351,300)
Property business profit	21,100	26,700
Capital loss	–	(17,200)
Qualifying charitable donations	(4,400)	(5,600)

As at 1 April 2012 Black Ltd had unused trading losses of £57,900, and unused capital losses of £12,600, whilst White Ltd had unused trading losses of £21,800.

Required

Advise Black Ltd as to the maximum amount of group relief that can be claimed from White Ltd in respect of its losses for the year ended 31 March 2013. Clearly identify any losses that cannot be surrendered by White Ltd as part of the group relief claim.

Note: You are not expected to calculate either company's corporation tax liability.   **(5 marks)**

(b)   Brown Ltd is a UK resident company with two overseas branches. For the year ended 31 March 2013 the company made a trading profit of £30,000 (excluding the results of its two overseas branches).

The first overseas branch made a trading profit of £200,000 for the year ended 31 March 2013. Overseas corporation tax of £32,000 was paid in respect of this profit.

The second overseas branch made a trading loss of £(22,000) for the year ended 31 March 2013.

Required

(i)   Calculate Brown Ltd's corporation tax liability for the year ended 31 March 2013 after taking account of double taxation relief, assuming that no election was made in respect of the overseas branches before 1 April 2012.   **(3 marks)**

(ii)   Calculate Brown Ltd's corporation tax liability for the year ended 31 March 2013, assuming that an election was made in respect of the overseas branches before 1 April 2012.   **(1 mark)**

(c)   On 15 January 2013 Blu Reddy made a gift of 200,000 £1 ordinary shares in Purple Ltd, an unquoted investment company, to a trust. Blu paid the inheritance tax arising from this gift.

Before the transfer Blu owned 300,000 shares out of Purple Ltd's issued share capital of 500,000 £1 ordinary shares. On 15 January 2013 Purple Ltd's shares were worth £2 each for a holding of 20%, £3 each for a holding of 40%, and £4 each for a holding of 60%.

Blu has not made any previous gifts.

Required

Calculate the inheritance tax that will be payable as a result of Blu Reddy's gift to the trust, and the additional inheritance tax that would be payable if Blu were to die on 31 May 2017.

Note: You should ignore annual exemptions, and should assume that the nil rate band for the tax year 2012/13 remains unchanged.   **(6 marks)**

(Total = 15 marks)

45 Neung Ltd (TX 12/10)   54 mins

(a)   Neung Ltd is a UK resident company that runs a business providing financial services. The company's business is mainly based in the UK, but Neung Ltd also has two overseas branches. The company's summarised statement of profit or loss for the year ended 31 March 2013 is as follows:

	Note	£
Operating profit	1 & 2	289,694
Income from investments		
Loan interest	3	37,800
Dividends	4	54,000
Profit before taxation		381,494

Note 1 – Operating profit

The operating profit does not include the results from either of Neung Ltd's two overseas branches (see note 2 below).

Depreciation of £18,830 has been deducted in arriving at the operating profit of £289,694.

Note 2 – Overseas branches

Neung Ltd's first overseas branch made a trading profit of £41,000 for the year ended 31 March 2013. No overseas corporation tax was paid on this profit.

The second overseas branch made a trading loss of £15,700 for the year ended 31 March 2013.

No election has been made in respect of overseas branches.

Note 3 – Loan interest receivable

The loan was made for non-trading purposes on 1 July 2012. Loan interest of £25,200 was received on 31 December 2012, and interest of £12,600 was accrued at 31 March 2013.

Note 4 – Dividends received

Neung Ltd holds shares in four UK resident companies as follows:

	Percentage shareholding	Status
Second Ltd	25%	Trading
Third Ltd	60%	Trading
Fourth Ltd	100%	Dormant
Fifth Ltd	100%	Trading

During the year ended 31 March 2013 Neung Ltd received a dividend of £37,800 from Second Ltd, and a dividend of £16,200 from Third Ltd. These figures were the actual cash amounts received.

Additional information

Leasehold property

On 1 April 2012 Neung Ltd acquired a leasehold office building, paying a premium of £140,000 for the grant of a 20-year lease. The office building was used for business purposes by Neung Ltd throughout the year ended 31 March 2013.

Plant and machinery

On 1 April 2012 the tax written down values of Neung Ltd's plant and machinery were as follows:

	£
Main pool	4,800
Special rate pool	25,500

The company purchased the following assets during the year ended 31 March 2013:

		£
19 July 2012	Motor car [1]	15,400
12 December 2012	Motor car [2]	28,600
20 December 2012	Ventilation system	20,000

Motor car [1] purchased on 19 July 2012 has a CO_2 emission rate of 242 grams per kilometre. Motor car [2] purchased on 12 December 2012 has a CO_2 emission rate of 148 grams per kilometre.

The ventilation system purchased on 20 December 2012 for £20,000 is integral to the freehold office building in which it was installed.

Required

(i) State, giving reasons, which companies will be treated as being associated with Neung Ltd for corporation tax purposes; **(2 marks)**

(ii) Calculate Neung Ltd's corporation tax liability for the year ended 31 March 2013;

Note: you should assume that the whole of the annual investment allowance is available to Neung Ltd, and that the company wishes to maximise its capital allowances claim. **(13 marks)**

(iii) Advise Neung Ltd of the taxation disadvantages of converting its two overseas branches (see note 2) into 100% overseas subsidiary companies **(3 marks)**

(iv) Advise Neung Ltd of the taxation disadvantage of making an election in relation to its overseas branches. State when the election would take effect. **(2 marks)**

(b) Note that in answering this part of the question you are not expected to take account of any of the information provided in part (a) above.

The following information is available in respect of Neung Ltd's value added tax (VAT) for the quarter ended 31 March 2013:

(1) Invoices were issued for sales of £44,600 to VAT registered customers. Of this figure, £35,200 was in respect of exempt sales and the balance in respect of standard rated sales. The standard rated sales figure is exclusive of VAT.

(2) In addition to the above, on 1 March 2013 Neung Ltd issued a VAT invoice for £8,000 plus VAT of £1,600 to a VAT registered customer. This was in respect of a contract for standard rated financial services that will be completed on 15 April 2013. The customer paid for the contracted services in two instalments of £4,800 on 31 March 2013 and 30 April 2013 respectively.

(3) Invoices were issued for sales of £289,300 to non-VAT registered customers. Of this figure, £242,300 was in respect of exempt sales and the balance in respect of standard rated sales. The standard rated sales figure is inclusive of VAT.

(4) The managing director of Neung Ltd is provided with free fuel for private mileage driven in her company motor car. During the quarter ended 31 March 2013 this fuel cost Neung Ltd £270. The relevant quarterly scale charge is £467. Both these figures are inclusive of VAT.

For the quarters ended 30 September 2011 and 30 June 2012 Neung Ltd was one month late in submitting its VAT returns and in paying the related VAT liabilities. All of the company's other VAT returns have been submitted on time.

Required

(i) Calculate the amount of output VAT payable by Neung Ltd for the quarter ended 31 March 2013; **(4 marks)**

(ii) Advise Neung Ltd of the default surcharge implications if it is one month late in submitting its VAT return for the quarter ended 31 March 2013 and in paying the related VAT liability; **(3 marks)**

(iii) State the circumstances in which Neung Ltd is and is not required to issue a VAT invoice, and the period during which such an invoice should be issued. **(3 marks)**

(Total = 30 marks)

46 A Ltd

18 mins

On 1 July 2012 A Ltd, a manufacturing company resident in the United Kingdom, acquired 100% of the share capital of B Ltd, also a manufacturing company.

B Ltd makes up accounts each year to 30 June. For its year ended 30 June 2013, it sustained a trading loss of £68,000 and had no other profits.

A Ltd produced the following information in relation to its nine-month period of accounts to 31 December 2012.

Income

	£
Trading income	342,000
Property income	10,000
Loan interest receivable (received gross) (including £2,000 accrued at 31 December 2012)	16,000
Franked investment income (FII) (including tax credit; received August 2012)	1,000
Payments	
Qualifying charitable donation (paid September 2012)	17,000

A Ltd wishes to claim maximum group relief in respect of B Ltd's trading loss.

Required

(a) Compute the corporation tax payable by A Ltd for the nine-month period to 31 December 2012. **(8 marks)**

(b) State the due date for payment of the corporation tax payable by A Ltd for the nine-month period to 31 December 2012. **(1 mark)**

(c) State the date by which A Ltd must file the corporation tax return for the nine-month period to 31 December 2012. **(1 mark)**

(Total = 10 marks)

47 Apple Ltd

27 mins

You should assume that today's date is 30 November 2012.

Apple Ltd has owned 80% of the ordinary share capital of Bramley Ltd and 85% of the ordinary share capital of Cox Ltd since these two companies were incorporated on 1 April 2010. Cox Ltd acquired 80% of the ordinary share capital of Delicious Ltd on 1 April 2011, the date of its incorporation.

The tax adjusted trading profits/(losses) of each company for the years 31 March 2011, 2012 and 2013 are as follows.

	Year ended 31 March		
	2011	2012	2013 (forecast)
	£	£	£
Apple Ltd	620,000	250,000	585,000
Bramley Ltd	(64,000)	52,000	70,000
Cox Ltd	83,000	(58,000)	40,000
Delicious Ltd	n/a	90,000	(15,000)

The following information is also available.

(1) Apple Ltd sold a freehold office building on 10 March 2012 for £380,000, and this resulted in a capital gain of £120,000.

(2) Apple Ltd sold a freehold warehouse on 5 October 2012 for £365,000, and this resulted in a capital gain of £80,000.

(3) Cox Ltd purchased a freehold factory on 20 September 2012 for £360,000.

(4) Delicious Ltd is planning to sell a leasehold factory building on 15 February 2013 for £180,000, and this will result in a capital loss of £44,000.

Because each of the subsidiary companies has minority shareholders, the managing director of Apple Ltd has proposed that:

(1)   Trading losses should initially be carried back and relieved against profits of the loss making company, with any unrelieved amount then being carried forward.

(2)   Chargeable gains and allowable losses should not be transferred between group companies, and rollover relief should only be claimed where reinvestment is made by the company that incurred the chargeable gain.

Required

(a)   Assuming that the managing director's proposals are followed, calculate the taxable total profits for each of the companies in the Apple Ltd group for the years ended 31 March 2011, 2012 and 2013 respectively.

(5 marks)

(b)   Advise the Apple Ltd group of the amount of corporation tax that could be saved for the years ended 31 March 2011, 2012 and 2013 if reliefs were instead claimed in the most beneficial manner.

(10 marks)

Assume that Financial Year 2012 rates apply throughout.

(Total = 15 marks)

48 Sofa Ltd (TX 12/07)   40 mins

(a)   Sofa Ltd is a manufacturer of furniture. The company's summarised statement of profit or loss for the year ended 31 March 2013 is as follows:

	£	£
Gross profit		257,298
Operating expenses		
Depreciation	87,100	
Professional fees (note 1)	19,900	
Repairs and renewals (note 2)	22,800	
Other expenses (note 3)	363,000	(492,800)
Operating loss		(235,502)
Profit from sale of non-current assets		
Disposal of shares (note 4)		3,300
Income from investments		
Bank interest (note 5)		8,400
		(223,802)
Interest payable (note 6)		(31,200)
Loss before taxation		(255,002)

Notes

1   *Professional fees*

Professional fees are as follows:

	£
Accountancy and audit fee	3,400
Legal fees in connection with the issue of share capital	7,800
Legal fees in connection with the renewal of a ten year property lease	2,900
Legal fees in connection with the issue of loan stock (see note 6)	5,800
	19,900

2   *Repairs and renewals*

The figure of £22,800 for repairs and renewals includes £9,700 for constructing a new wall around the company's premises and £3,900 for repairing the wall of an office building after it was damaged by a lorry. The remaining expenses are all fully allowable.

3   *Other expenses*

The figure of £363,000 for other expenses includes £1,360 for entertaining suppliers; £700 for entertaining employees; £370 for counselling services provided to an employee who was made redundant; and a fine of £420 for infringing health and safety regulations. The remaining expenses are all fully allowable.

4   *Profit on disposal of shares*

The profit on the disposal of shares of £3,300 is in respect of a shareholding that was sold on 29 October 2012.

5   *Bank interest received*

The bank interest was received on 31 March 2013. The bank deposits are held for non-trading purposes.

6   *Interest payable*

Sofa Ltd issued loan stock on 1 July 2012, and this was used for trading purposes. Interest of £20,800 was paid on 31 December 2012, and £10,400 was accrued at 31 March 2013.

7   *Plant and machinery*

On 1 April 2012 the tax written down values of plant and machinery were as follows:

	£
Main pool	27,800
Special rate pool	16,400

The following transactions took place during the year ended 31 March 2013:

		Cost/proceeds £
12 May 2012	Purchased equipment	1,400
8 June 2012	Sold motor car from the special rate pool	(17,800)
8 June 2012	Purchased motor car (1) CO_2 emissions 175g/km	22,200
2 August 2012	Purchased motor car (2) CO_2 emissions 125 g/km	10,900
19 October 2012	Purchased motor car (3) CO_2 emissions 105 g/km	13,800
8 January 2013	Sold a lorry	(7,600)
18 January 2013	Sold motor car (2)	(8,800)
10 February 2013	Purchased a second-hand freehold office building	280,000

The motor car sold on 8 June 2012 for £17,800 originally cost £28,400. The lorry sold on 8 January 2013 for £7,600 originally cost £24,400.

The cost of the second-hand office building purchased on 10 February 2013 for £280,000 includes fixtures qualifying as plant and machinery (but not as integral features). These fixtures originally cost £11,200, and at the date of purchase had a market value of £6,200 and a written down value of £3,400. Sofa Ltd and the vendor of the office building have made a joint election regarding the sale price of the fixtures to enable Sofa Ltd to claim the maximum possible amount of capital allowances in respect of them.

Required

Calculate Sofa Ltd's tax adjusted trading loss for the year ended 31 March 2013. Your answer should commence with the loss before taxation figure of £255,002 and should list all of the items in the statement of profit or loss indicating by the use of a zero (0) any items that do not require adjustment. You should assume that the company claims the maximum available capital allowances.   **(17 marks)**

(b)   Sofa Ltd has three subsidiary companies:

Settee Ltd

Sofa Ltd owns 100% of the ordinary share capital of Settee Ltd. For the year ended 30 June 2012 Settee Ltd had taxable total profits of £240,000, and for the year ended 30 June 2013 will have taxable total profits of £90,000.

Couch Ltd

Sofa Ltd owns 60% of the ordinary share capital of Couch Ltd. For the year ended 31 March 2013 Couch Ltd had taxable total profits of £64,000.

Futon Ltd

Sofa Ltd owns 80% of the ordinary share capital of Futon Ltd. Futon Ltd commenced trading on 1 January 2013, and for the three-month period ended 31 March 2013 had taxable total profits of £60,000.

Required

Advise Sofa Ltd as to the maximum amount of group relief that can potentially be claimed by each of its three subsidiary companies in respect of its trading loss for the year ended 31 March 2013.

(5 marks)

(Total = 22 marks)

49 Gastron Ltd (TX 06/09)   54 mins

Gastron Ltd, a United Kingdom resident company, is a luxury food manufacturer. The company's summarised statement of profit or loss for the year ended 31 March 2013 is as follows:

	Note	£	£
Gross profit			844,668
Operating expenses			
Depreciation		85,660	
Amortisation of leasehold property	1	6,000	
Gifts and donations	2	2,700	
Professional fees	3	18,800	
Other expenses	4	220,400	
			(333,560)
Operating profit			511,108
Income from investments			
Income from property	5	20,600	
Bank interest	6	12,400	
Dividends	7	54,000	
			87,000
Profit from sale of non-current assets			
Disposal of shares	8		80,700
			678,808
Interest payable	9		(60,800)
Profit before taxation			618,008

Note 1 – Leasehold property
On 1 April 2012 Gastron Ltd acquired a leasehold office building, paying a premium of £60,000 for the grant of a new ten-year lease. The office building was used for business purposes by Gastron Ltd throughout the year ended 31 March 2013. No legal costs were incurred by Gastron Ltd in respect of this lease.

Note 2 – Gifts and donations
Gifts and donations are as follows:

	£
Gifts to customers (pens costing £60 each and displaying Gastron Ltd's name)	1,200
Gifts to customers (hampers of food costing £25 each)	1,100
Donation to local charity (Gastron Ltd received free advertising in the charity's magazine)	400
	2,700

Note 3 – Professional fees
Professional fees are as follows:

	£
Legal fees in connection with the renewal of a 45-year property lease in respect of a warehouse	3,600
Legal fees in connection with the issue of loan stock (see note 9)	15,200
	18,800

Note 4 – Other expenses
The figure of £220,400 for other expenses includes £1,300 for entertaining suppliers and £900 for entertaining employees.

Note 5 – Income from property
Gastron Ltd lets out the whole of an unfurnished freehold office building that is surplus to requirements. The office building was let from 1 April 2012 to 31 December 2012 at a monthly rent of £1,800, payable in advance. On 31 December 2012 the tenant left owing two months' rent which Gastron Ltd was unable to recover. During January 2013 the company spent £3,700 decorating the property. The office building was then re-let from 1 February 2013 at a monthly rent of £1,950, on which date the new tenant paid six months' rent in advance.

Note 6 – Bank interest received
The bank interest was received on 31 March 2013. The bank deposits are held for non-trading purposes.

Note 7 – Dividends received
During the year ended 31 March 2013 Gastron Ltd received dividends of £36,000 from Tasteless plc, an unconnected UK company, and dividends of £18,000 from Culinary Ltd, a 100% UK subsidiary company (see note 11). Both figures are the actual cash amounts received.

Note 8 – Profit on disposal of shares
The profit on disposal of shares is in respect of a 1% shareholding that was sold on 14 October 2012. The disposal resulted in a chargeable gain of £74,800. This figure is after taking account of indexation.

Note 9 – Interest payable
The interest payable is in respect of the company's 5% loan stock that was issued on 1 April 2012. The proceeds of the issue were used to finance the company's trading activities. Interest of £30,400 was paid on 30 September 2012 and again on 31 March 2013.

Note 10 – Plant and machinery
On 1 April 2012 the tax written down values of plant and machinery were as follows:

	£
Main pool	16,700
Special rate pool	18,400

The following transactions took place during the year ended 31 March 2013:

		Cost/(Proceeds) £
19 May 2012	Purchased equipment	1,600
12 July 2012	Purchased motor car (1)	9,800
	CO_2 emissions 140 g/km	
11 August 2012	Purchased motor car (2)	16,200
	CO_2 emissions 105 g/km	
5 October 2012	Purchased a lorry	17,200
5 March 2013	Sold equipment	(3,300)

The equipment sold on 5 March 2013 for £3,300 was originally purchased in 2008 for £8,900.

Note 11 – Subsidiary company
Gastron Ltd owns 100% of the ordinary share capital of Culinary Ltd. On 13 February 2013 Culinary Ltd sold a freehold factory and this resulted in a capital loss of £66,000. For the year ended 31 March 2013 Culinary Ltd made no other disposals and paid corporation tax at the small profits rate of 20%.

Required

(a) Calculate Gastron Ltd's tax adjusted trading profit for the year ended 31 March 2013, after deducting capital allowances. Your computation should commence with the profit before taxation figure of £618,008, and should list all of the items referred to in notes (1) to (9) indicating by the use of zero (0) any items that do not require adjustment.

(15 marks)

(b) Calculate Gastron Ltd's corporation tax liability for the year ended 31 March 2013, on the basis that no election is made between Gastron Ltd and Culinary Ltd in respect of capital gains. **(7 marks)**

(c) State the date by which Gastron Ltd's corporation tax liability for the year ended 31 March 2013 should be paid, and advise the company of the interest that will be due if the liability is not paid until 31 August 2014.

(3 marks)

(d) Explain the group relationship that must exist in order for two or more companies to form a group for capital gains purposes. **(2 marks)**

(e) State the time limit for Gastron Ltd and Culinary Ltd to make a joint election to transfer the capital gain on Gastron Ltd's disposal of shares (see note 8) to Culinary Ltd, and explain why such an election will be beneficial.

(3 marks)

(Total = 30 marks)

VAT

Questions 50 to 54 cover the VAT rules for both corporate and unincorporated businesses, the subject of Part G of the BPP Study Text for Paper F6.

50 Lithograph Ltd (BTX)

18 mins

Lithograph Ltd runs a printing business, and is registered for VAT. Because its annual taxable turnover is only £250,000, the company uses the annual accounting scheme so that it only has to prepare one VAT return each year. The annual VAT period is the year ended 31 December.

Year ended 31 December 2011

The total amount of VAT payable by Lithograph Ltd for the year ended 31 December 2011 was £10,200.

Year ended 31 December 2012

The following information is available:

(1)   Sales invoices totalling £250,000 were issued to VAT registered customers, of which £160,000 were for standard rated sales and £90,000 were for zero-rated sales.

(2)   Purchase invoices totalling £45,000 were received from VAT registered suppliers, of which £38,000 were for standard rated purchases and £7,000 were for zero-rated purchases.

(3)   Standard rated expenses amounted to £28,000. This includes £3,600 for entertaining UK customers.

(4)   On 1 January 2012 Lithograph Ltd purchased a motor car costing £18,400 for the use of its managing director. The manager director is provided with free petrol for private mileage, and the cost of this is included in the standard rated expenses in note (3). The relevant annual scale charge is £1,400. Both figures are inclusive of VAT.

(5)   During the year ended 31 December 2012 Lithograph Ltd purchased machinery for £24,000, and sold office equipment for £8,000. Input VAT had been claimed when the office equipment was originally purchased.

(6)   On 31 December 2012 Lithograph Ltd wrote off £4,800 due from a customer as an impairment loss. The debt was in respect of an invoice for a standard rated supply that was due for payment on 31 May 2012.

Unless stated otherwise all of the above figures are exclusive of VAT.

Required

(a)   Calculate the monthly payments on account of VAT that Lithograph Ltd will have made in respect of the year ended 31 December 2012, and state in which months these will have been paid.   **(3 marks)**

(b)   (i)   Calculate the total amount of VAT payable by Lithograph Ltd for the year ended 31 December 2012.
                                                                                                                            (5 marks)

        (ii)   Based on your answer to part (i) above, calculate the balancing payment that would have been paid with the annual VAT return, and state the date by which this return was due for submission.
                                                                                                                            (2 marks)

                                                                                                        (Total = 10 marks)

51 Aston Martyn (TX 06/11)

27 mins

Aston Martyn commenced self-employment on 1 August 2012 providing consultancy services to the motor industry.

His sales revenue has been as follows:

		Standard rated £	Zero rated £
2012	August	2,300	–
	September	6,400	–
	October	21,900	4,800
	November	11,700	–
	December	17,100	–
2013	January	13,800	1,200
	February	4,200	–
	March	31,500	3,300
	April	44,600	6,600

Where applicable, the above figures are stated exclusive of value added tax (VAT). Aston only supplies services and all of his supplies are to VAT registered businesses. He does not offer any discount for prompt payment.

The following is a sample of the new sales invoice that Aston is going to issue to his customers:

SALES INVOICE

Aston Martyn
111 Long Road
London W1 9MG
Telephone 0207 123 3456

Customer: Faster Motors plc
Address: 22 Short Lane
Manchester M1 8MB

Invoice Date 6 June 2013
Tax Point 6 June 2013

Description of services
Business advice

	£
Total price (excluding VAT)	12,000.00
Total price (including VAT)	14,400.00

Aston sometimes receives supplies of standard rated services from VAT registered businesses situated elsewhere within the European Union. As business to business services these are treated as being supplied in the United Kingdom. Aston wants to know how he should account for these services for VAT purposes.

Because of the complexity of the VAT legislation, Aston is concerned that despite his best efforts he will incorrectly treat a standard rated supply as zero-rated, thus understating the amount of VAT payable. He wants to know if such an error will result in a penalty, and if so how much the penalty will be.

Aston understands that he is entitled to use the annual accounting scheme so that he would only have to submit one VAT return each year, but wants to know how using the scheme will otherwise affect him as regards the submission of VAT returns and the payment of VAT.

Required

(a) Explain from what date Aston Martyn's business was required to be registered for VAT. **(3 marks)**

(b) State the FOUR additional pieces of information that Aston Martyn will have to show on his new sales invoices in order for them to be valid for VAT purposes. **(2 marks)**

(c) Explain when and how Aston Martyn should account for VAT in respect of the supplies of services he receives from VAT registered businesses situated elsewhere within the European Union. **(2 marks)**

(d) Assuming that Aston Martyn incorrectly treats a standard rated supply as zero-rated with the result that the amount of VAT payable is understated, advise him as to the maximum amount of penalty that is likely to be charged by HM Revenue and Customs, and by how much this penalty would be reduced as a result of a subsequent unprompted disclosure. **(3 marks)**

(e) (i) If Aston Martyn does not use the annual accounting scheme, advise him as to how and when he will have to submit his quarterly VAT returns and pay the related VAT; **(2 marks)**

(ii) If Aston Martyn uses the annual accounting scheme, advise him as to when he will have to pay VAT and submit his annual VAT return. **(2 marks)**

(Total = 15 marks)

52 Ram-Rom Ltd (BTX)   18 mins

Ram-Rom Ltd commenced trading as a manufacturer of computer equipment on 1 January 2012. The company registered for value added tax (VAT) on 1 September 2012. Its inputs for each of the months from January 2012 to August 2012 are as follows:

		Goods purchased	Services incurred	Non-current assets
		£	£	£
2012	January	12,300	1,400	42,000
	February	11,200	5,100	–
	March	12,300	7,400	–
	April	16,400	6,300	14,400
	May	14,500	8,500	–
	June	18,800	9,000	–
	July	18,500	9,200	–
	August	23,400	8,200	66,600

During August 2012 Ram-Rom Ltd sold all of the non-current assets purchased during April 2012 for £12,000.

On 1 September 2012 £92,000 of the goods purchased were still in inventory.

The above figures are all exclusive of VAT. Ram-Rom Ltd's sales are all standard rated.

The following is a sample of the new sales invoice that Ram-Rom Ltd is going to issue to its customers:

SALES INVOICE

Ram-Rom Ltd   **Customer:** XYZ Computers plc
123 The High Street   **Address:** 99 The Low Road
London WC1 2AB   Glasgow G1 2CD
Telephone 0207 100 1234

Invoice Date and Tax Point: 1 September 2012

Item Description	Quantity	Price
		£
Hard Drives	5	220.00
Motherboards	2	100.00
Total Amount Payable (Including VAT)		320.00

Directors: Y Ram & Z Rom
Company Number: 1234567
Registered Office: 123 The High Street, London WC1 2AB

Ram-Rom Ltd pays for all of its inputs one month after receiving the purchase invoice. However, many customers are not paying Ram-Rom Ltd until four months after the date of the sales invoice. In addition, several customers have recently defaulted on the payment of their debts. In order to encourage more prompt payment, Ram-Rom Ltd is considering offering all of its customers a 5% discount if they pay within one month of the date of the sales invoice. No discount is currently offered.

Required

(a) Explain why Ram-Rom Ltd was able to recover input VAT totalling £49,840 in respect of inputs incurred prior to registering for VAT on 1 September 2012. **(5 marks)**

(b) State what alterations Ram-Rom Ltd will have to make to its new sales invoices in order for them to be valid for VAT purposes. **(3 marks)**

(c) Explain the VAT implications of Ram-Rom Ltd offering all of its customers a 5% discount for prompt payment. **(2 marks)**

(Total = 10 marks)

53 Sandy Brick (BTX)   18 mins

Sandy Brick has been a self-employed builder since 2006. He registered for value added tax (VAT) on 1 January 2013, and is in the process of completing his VAT return for the quarter ended 31 March 2013. The following information is relevant to the completion of this VAT return:

(1) Sales invoices totalling £44,000 were issued to VAT registered customers in respect of standard rated sales. Sandy offers his VAT registered customers a 5% discount for prompt payment.

(2) Sales invoices totalling £16,920 were issued to customers that were not registered for VAT. Of this figure, £5,170 was in respect of zero-rated sales with the balance being in respect of standard rated sales. Standard rated sales are inclusive of VAT.

(3) On 10 January 2013 Sandy received a payment on account of £5,000 in respect of a contract that was completed on 28 April 2013. The total value of the contract is £10,000. Both of these figures are inclusive of VAT at the standard rate.

(4) Standard rated materials amounted to £11,200, of which £800 were used in constructing Sandy's private residence.

(5) Since February 2012 Sandy has paid £120 on the 15th of each month for the lease of office equipment. This expense is standard rated.

(6) During the quarter ended 31 March 2013 £400 was spent on mobile telephone calls, of which 30% relates to private calls. This expense is standard rated.

(7) On 20 February 2013 £920 was spent on repairs to a motor car. The motor car is used by Sandy in his business, although 20% of the mileage is for private journeys. This expense is standard rated.

(8) On 15 March 2013 equipment was purchased for £6,000. The purchase was partly financed by a bank loan of £5,000. This purchase is standard rated.

Unless stated otherwise all of the above figures are exclusive of VAT.

Required

Calculate the amount of VAT payable by Sandy for the quarter ended 31 March 2013. **(10 marks)**

54 Anne Attire (TX 06/09)

27 mins

Anne Attire runs a retail clothing shop. She is registered for value added tax (VAT) and is in the process of completing her VAT return for the quarter ended 30 November 2012.

The following information is available (all figures are exclusive of VAT):

(1)   Cash sales amounted to £42,000, of which £28,000 was in respect of standard rated sales and £14,000 was in respect of zero-rated sales

(2)   Sales invoices totalling £12,000 were issued in respect of credit sales. These sales were all standard rated. Anne offers all of her credit sale customers a 5% discount for payment within one month of the date of the sales invoice, and 90% of the customers pay within this period. The sales figure of £12,000 is stated before any deduction for the 5% discount.

(3)   Purchase and expense invoices totalling £19,200 were received from VAT registered suppliers. This figure is made up as follows:

	£
Standard rated purchases and expenses	11,200
Zero rated purchases	6,000
Exempt expenses	2,000
	19,200

Anne pays all of her purchase and expense invoices two months after receiving the invoice.

(4)   On 30 November 2012 Anne wrote off two impairment losses that were in respect of standard rated credit sales. The first impairment loss was for £300, and was in respect of a sales invoice due for payment on 15 July 2012. The second impairment loss was for £800, and was in respect of a sales invoice due for payment on 10 April 2012.

Anne does not use the cash accounting scheme.

Anne will soon be 60 years old and is therefore considering retirement. On the cessation of trading Anne can either sell the non-current assets of her business on a piecemeal basis to individual VAT registered purchasers, or she can sell the entire business as a going concern to a single VAT registered purchaser.

Required

(a)   Calculate the amount of VAT payable by Anne Attire for the quarter ended 30 November 2012 and state the date by which the VAT return for this period was due for submission. **(6 marks)**

(b)   State the conditions that Anne Attire must satisfy before she will be permitted to use the cash accounting scheme and advise her of the implications of using the scheme. **(5 marks)**

(c)   Advise Anne Attire as to what will happen to her VAT registration, and whether output VAT will be due in respect of the non-current assets, if she ceases trading and then:

(i)   Sells these assets on a piecemeal basis to individual VAT registered purchasers; **(2 marks)**

(ii)   Sells her entire business as a going concern to a single VAT registered purchaser. **(2 marks)**

(Total = 15 marks)

Answers

1 Brad, Lauren, Tom and Sarah

> **Text references.** Chapters 2 and 3.
>
> **Top tips.** Note that the question asked for the tax liability and not the tax due – the tax liability is **before** deduction of any tax credits such as PAYE.

			Marks
(a)	**Brad**		
	Employment income	½	
	Building society interest	½	
	Premium bond prize (exempt)	½	
	NS&I interest (exempt)	½	
	PA	1	
	Tax bands	1	
	Tax rates	1	
	Lauren		
	Interest and treasury stock (gross)	½	
	ISA interest (exempt)	½	
	Dividends	½	
	PA	½	
	Gift Aid – increase basic rate limit	1	
	Tax bands	1	
	Tax rates	1	
			10
(b)	**Tom**		
	Pensions	½	
	Building society interest	½	
	Gift Aid	1	
	PAA	1	
	Tax bands	1	
	Tax rates	1	
			5
(c)	**Sarah**		
	Trade profit	½	
	Bank interest	½	
	Dividend	½	
	Pension premiums	1	
	Tax bands	1½	
	Tax rates	1	
			5
			20

(a) **Brad: Income Tax Computation 2012/13**

	Non-savings £	Savings £	Total £
Employment income	104,500		
BSI (2,200 × 100/80)		2,750	
Premium bond prize (exempt)		0	
NS&I certificates interest (exempt)		0	
Net income	104,500	2,750	107,250
Less PA (W)	(4,480)		(4,480)
Taxable income	100,020	2,750	102,770

Tax

	£
On Non-savings income	
£34,370 @ 20%	6,874
£65,650 @ 40%	26,260
On Savings income	
£2,750 @ 40%	1,100
Income tax liability	34,234

Personal allowance

	£	£
PA		8,105
Net income	107,250	
Less limit	(100,000)	
	7,250	
÷ 2		(3,625)
PA		4,480

Lauren: Income Tax Computation 2012/13

	Non-savings £	Savings £	Dividend £	Total £
Employment income	47,000			
BSI (2,200 × 100/80)		2,750		
Treasury stock		2,000		
ISA interest (exempt)		0		
Dividends (2,250 × 100/90)			2,500	
Net income	47,000	4,750	2,500	54,250
Less PA	(8,105)			(8,105)
Taxable income	38,895	4,750	2,500	46,145

Tax

	£
On Non-savings Income	
£35,620 @ 20% (N)	7,124
£3,275 @ 40%	1,310
On Savings Income	
£4,750 @ 40%	1,900
On Dividend Income	
£2,500 @ 32.5%	812
Income tax liability	11,146

Note. The basic rate limit is increased by the gross amount of the Gift Aid payment. £34,370 + (1,000 × 100/80) = £35,620.

(b) **Tom: Income Tax Computation 2012/13**

	Non-savings income £	Savings income £	Total £
State pension	4,226		
Employment pension	7,890		
BSI (14,320 × 100/80)		17,900	
Net income	12,116	17,900	30,016
Less age allowance (W)	(10,192)		(10,192)
Taxable income	1,924	17,900	19,824

Tax

	£
On Non-savings income	
£1,924 @ 20%	385
On Savings income	
(£2,710 − £1,924) = £786 @ 10%	79
(£17,900 − £786) = £17,114 @ 20%	3,423
Income tax liability	3,887

Working

Age enhanced personal allowance

	£	£
PAA > 65		10,500
Net income	30,016	
Less Gift Aid £3,200 × 100/80	(4,000)	
	26,016	
Less limit	(25,400)	
	616	
÷ 2		(308)
PAA		10,192

Note. The grossed up value of the Gift Aid payment is deducted from net income when calculating the age allowance.

(c) **Sarah: Income Tax Computation 2012/13**

	Non-savings £	Savings £	Dividend £	Total £
Trading income	164,000			
BI (8,000 × 100/80)		10,000		
Dividends (4,950 × 100/90)			5,500	
Net/taxable income (no PA)	164,000	10,000	5,500	179,500

Tax

	£
On Non-savings income	
£54,370 @ 20% (N)	10,874
£109,630 @ 40%	43,852
On Savings income	
£6,000 @ 40%	2,400
£4,000 @ 50%	2,000
On Dividend income	
£5,500 @ 42.5%	2,337
Income tax liability	61,463

Note. The basic rate limit and the higher rate limit are extended by the gross amount of the personal pension payments to £34,370 + (16,000 × 100/80) = £54,370 and £150,000 + (16,000 × 100/80) = £170,000 respectively.

2 Domingo, Erigo and Fargo

Text references. Chapters 3 and 4 on employees, Chapter 5 on pensions, Chapter 7 on trading income, Chapter 8 on capital allowances and Chapter 17 on self assessment for individuals.

Top tips. Watch out for the starting rate band for savings income where there is little or no non-savings income.

Easy marks. The administrative aspects in parts (b) and (c) were easy marks.

Examiner's comments. In part (a) many candidates did not appreciate that donations to charity not made under gift aid are simply ignored, and some candidates missed the income limit for the age-related personal allowance. The expense claim in respect of the business mileage driven by the employed brother often caused problems. Either it was incorrectly calculated, or it was treated as a benefit. Part (b) was well answered. In part (c) few candidates appreciated that the period of retention differs between taxpayers in business and those not in business. However, virtually all candidates were aware of the £3,000 penalty.

Marking scheme

				Marks
(a)	(i)	*Domingo Gomez*		
		Pensions	1	
		Building society interest	1	
		Interest from savings certificates	½	
		Donations	½	
		Personal allowance	2	
		Income tax	1	
				6
	(ii)	*Erigo Gomez*		
		Salary	½	
		Pension contributions	1	
		Charitable payroll deductions	1	
		Relocation costs	1	
		Mileage allowance	1½	
		Personal allowance	½	
		Income tax	½	
				6
	(iii)	*Fargo Gomez*		
		Trading profit	½	
		Pre-trading expenditure	1	
		Capital allowances	2	
		Personal allowance	½	
		Increase of basic rate limit	2	
		Income tax	1	
				7
(b)		Paper returns	2	
		Return filed online	1	
				3
(c)		Domingo and Erigo	1	
		Fargo	1	
		Penalty for not keeping records	1	
				3
				25

(a) (i) **Domingo Gomez – Income tax computation 2012/13**

	Non-savings income £	Savings income £	Total £
State pension	4,500		
Occupational pension	3,400		
BSI £15,520 × 100/80		19,400	
NS&I certificate interest - exempt			
Net income	7,900	19,400	27,300
Less: PAA	(7,900)	(1,650)	(9,550)
Taxable income	-	17,750	17,750

Income tax

£		
2,710 @ 10%		271
15,040 @ 20%		3,008
17,750		
Income tax liability		3,279

Note. No tax relief is available in respect of the donations as they were not made under the Gift Aid scheme.

Working

	£
Net income	27,300
Less income limit	(25,400)
Excess	1,900
PAA (65 - 74)	10,500
Less half excess £1,900 × ½	(950)
Revised PAA	9,550

(ii) **Erigo Gomez – Income tax computation 2012/13**

	Non-savings income £
Salary	36,000
Less: pension contributions £36,000 × 6%	(2,160)
charitable payroll deductions £100 × 12	(1,200)
	32,640
Relocation costs (W1)	3,400
	36,040
Less: mileage allowance (W2)	(2,000)
Net income	34,040
Less: personal allowance	(8,105)
Taxable income	25,935

Income tax

£25,935 @ 20%/ Income tax liability	5,187

Workings

1   Only £8,000 of relocation costs are exempt, and so the taxable benefit is £3,400 (11,400 – 8,000).

2   The mileage allowance received will be tax-free, and Erigo can make the following expense claim:

	£
10,000 miles @ 45p	4,500
8,000 miles @ 25p	2,000
	6,500
Mileage allowance 18,000 @ 25p	(4,500)
	2,000

(iii)   **Fargo Gomez – Income tax computation 2012/13**

	Non-savings income
	£
Trading profit £(65,800 – 2,600) (N)	63,200
Less: capital allowances (W1)	(990)
Net income	62,210
Less: personal allowance	(8,105)
Taxable income	54,105

Income tax

£		
42,570 @ 20% (W2)		8,514
11,535 @ 40%		4,614
54,105		
Income tax liability		13,128

Note. The advertising expenditure incurred during May 2012 is pre-trading, and is treated as incurred on 6 July 2012. An adjustment is therefore required.

Workings

1   Fargo's period of account is nine months' long so the capital allowances in respect of his motor car are £11,000 × 18% x 9/12 = 1,485 × 16,000/24,000 = £990.

2   Fargo's basic rate tax limit is increased by £5,200 in respect of the personal pension contribution and £2,400 × 100/80 = £3,000 in respect of the gift aid donations. The basic rate limit is therefore £34,370 + £(5,200 + 3,000) = £42,570.

(b)   (1)   Unless the return is issued late, the latest date that Domingo and Erigo can file paper self-assessment tax returns for 2012/13 is 31 October 2013.

(2)   If Domingo completes a paper tax return by 31 October 2013 then HM Revenue and Customs will prepare a self-assessment tax computation on his behalf.

(3)   Fargo has until 31 January 2014 to file his self-assessment tax return for 2012/13 online.

(c)   (1)   Domingo and Erigo were not in business during 2012/13, so their records must be retained until one year after 31 January following the tax year, which is 31 January 2015.

(2)   Fargo was in business during 2012/13, so all of his records (both business and non-business) must be retained until five years after 31 January following the tax year, which is 31 January 2019.

(3)   A failure to retain records for 2012/13 could result in a maximum penalty of £3,000.

3 The Wind Family

Text references. Chapter 2 deals with the computation of taxable income and the income tax liability. Chapters 3 and 4 cover employment income. The basis of assessment for trading income is dealt with in Chapter 9. National insurance contributions are covered in Chapter 12.

Top tips. You must deal with each member of the Wind family separately – one possible approach to this question might have been to deal with all the parts in relation to one member of the family (leaving an appropriate amount of space to insert the remaining parts of your answer), then go back to the second and then the third. Setting out your computations using the standard layouts would also have been helpful.

Easy marks. There were some easy marks here for basic income tax computations such as the restriction of the personal allowance, the increase in the basic rate limit, and the car and fuel benefits. The national insurance contributions were also straightforward.

Examiner's comments. Part (a) was very well answered, particularly for the second and third taxpayers. The only aspect which sometimes caused problems was the benefit calculations. For the fuel benefit, the contribution towards the cost of fuel was often incorrectly deducted. There were few problems in part (b) as regards the calculation of the national insurance contributions. Part (c) was the most difficult aspect on the paper, and it was pleasing to see several good attempts. For the second taxpayer most candidates appreciated that the basic rate tax band would be extended by the amount of the pension contribution, and several candidates realised that that the amount of contribution was the exact amount required so that the personal allowance was not restricted. For the third taxpayer several candidates stated that tax could be saved if the whole of the contributions were set against just the car benefit, and marks were awarded for this approach. However, the most beneficial basis was to allocate additional contributions towards the fuel benefit so as to cover the full cost of fuel for private journeys – and a few candidates did take this approach.

Marking scheme

			Marks
(a) (i)	**Philip Wind**		
	Pensions	½	
	Building society interest	½	
	Personal allowance	2	
	Income tax	1	
			4
(ii)	**Charles Wind**		
	Trading profit	½	
	Personal allowance	2	
	Increase in basic rate limit	½	
	Income tax	1	
			4
(iii)	**William Wind**		
	Salary	½	
	Pension contributions - employee	½	
	Pension contributions - employer	½	
	Car benefit - List price	½	
	- Relevant percentage	1	
	- Contribution	½	
	- Calculation	½	
	Fuel benefit	1	
	Personal allowance	1	
	Income tax	1	
			7

		Marks
(b)	**Philip Wind**	
	No NICs	½
	Charles Wind	
	Class 2 NICs	½
	Class 4 NICs	1½
	William Wind	
	Class 1 NICs	1½
		1
(c) (i)	**Charles Wind**	
	Personal allowance	1
	Basic rate band	1
	Income tax liability	1
		3
(ii)	**William Wind**	
	Allocation	1
	Contributions for use of motor car	1
	Income tax	1
		3
		25

(a) (i) **Philip Wind – Income tax computation 2012/13**

	Non-savings income £	Savings income £	Total £
Pensions	13,140		
Building society interest £13,280 × 100/80		16,600	
Net income	13,140	16,600	29,740
Less: personal allowance (W)	(8,490)		(8,490)
Taxable income	4,650	16,600	21,250

Working

	£	£
Personal allowance (75+)		10,660
Net income	29,740	
Less: income limit for age related allowances	(25,400)	
Excess income	4,340	
÷ 2		(2,170)
Adjusted personal allowance		8,490

Tax

	£
On non-savings income	
£4,650 @ 20%	930
On savings income	
£16,600 @ 20%	3,320
Income tax liability	4,250

(ii) **Charles Wind – Income tax computation 2012/13**

	Non-savings Income £
Trading income/net income	111,400
Less: personal allowance (W)	(2,805)
Taxable income	108,595

Working

	£	£
Personal allowance (standard)		8,105
Net income	111,400	
Less: gift aid donation	(800)	
Adjusted net income	110,600	
Less: income limit for standard personal allowance	(100,000)	
Excess income	10,600	
÷ 2		(5,300)
Adjusted personal allowance		2,805

Tax

	£
On non-savings income	
£35,170 (W) @ 20%	7,034
£(108,595 – 35,170) = 73,425 @ 40%	29,370
Income tax liability	36,404

Working

	£
Basic rate limit	34,370
Add: gift aid donation (gross)	800
Increased basic rate limit	35,170

(iii) **William Wind – Income tax computation 2012/13**

	Non-savings income £
Employment income	
Salary	181,335
Less: pension contributions (employee)	(7,300)
	174,035
Pension contributions by Crown plc (exempt benefit)	0
Car benefit (W1)	24,285
Fuel benefit (W2)	7,070
Net income	205,390
Less: personal allowance (net income clearly exceeds £116,210)	(0)
Taxable income	205,390

Workings

1   *Car benefit*

Amount by which CO_2 emissions exceed base level: (225 (rounded down) – 100) = 125 ÷ 5 = 25

Add to 11% = 36% – but maximum taxable % is 35%

	£
£83,100 (list price) × 35%	29,085
Less: contribution for private use	(4,800)
Taxable benefit	24,285

2   *Fuel benefit*

£20,200 × 35%	£7,070

Tutorial note

There is no reduction in the taxable benefit for part reimbursement of private fuel.

Tax

	£
On non-savings income	
£34,370 @ 20%	6,874
£(150,000 – 34,370) = 115,630 @ 40%	46,252
£(205,390 – 150,000) = 55,390 @ 50%	27,695
Income tax liability	80,821

(b) **Philip Wind**

There are no national insurance contributions (NICs) suffered by Philip for 2012/13 as he has no income liable for these contributions.

Charles Wind

Class 2 NICs

£2.65 × 52	£138

Class 4 NICs

	£
£(42,475 – 7,605) = 34,870 × 9%	3,138
£(111,400 – 42,475) = 68,925 × 2%	1,378
	4,516

William Wind

Primary Class 1 NICs

	£
£(42,475 – 7,605) = 34,870 × 12%	4,184
£(181,335 – 42,475) = 138,860 × 2%	2,777
	6,961

Tutorial note

Pension contributions are not deductible for Class 1 NICs and taxable benefits are subject to Class 1A NICs payable by Crown plc.

(c) (i) **Charles Wind**

If Charles Wind had contributed £10,600 (gross) into a personal pension scheme during the tax year 2012/13, his adjusted net income would have been £(110,600 – 10,600) = £100,000. This means that his personal allowance will not be restricted.

The personal pension contribution will also increase the basic rate limit by £10,600.

Charles' income tax liability would therefore have been reduced by £4,240 as follows:

	£
Personal allowance £5,300 @ 40%	2,120
Income tax on income now in basic rate band instead of higher rate band	
£10,600 × (40 – 20)%	2,120
Reduction in income tax	4,240

(ii) **William Wind**

William and Crown plc should have allocated £4,400 of the contributions towards the fuel for private use, as there will then be no fuel benefit.

This will then reduce the contributions for the use of the motor car by £(4,400 – 3,200) = £1,200.

William's income tax liability would have been reduced by £2,935 as follows:

	£
Fuel benefit no longer taxable £7,070 @ 50%	3,535
Less: increase in car benefit £1,200 @ 50%	(600)
Reduction in income tax	2,935

4 Joe Jones

Text references. Chapters 3 and 4 deal with employment income, employment benefits and the PAYE system.

Top tips. Read the requirement of the question carefully. Did you remember to deduct the personal allowance from net income to compute Joe Jones' taxable income?

Examiner's comments. Part (a) of this question was reasonably well answered, but part (b) caused problems for virtually all candidates. In part (a) there were no areas that consistently caused difficulty, although a surprising number of candidates did not appreciate that a bonus would have been assessed in the previous tax year as the taxpayer was entitled to it in that year. When calculating the beneficial loan using the average method, many candidates used a nil figure rather than the balance at the date of repayment. Candidates should try not to repeat their answers. For example, exempt benefits were often shown as such in the computation of taxable income, but were then shown again in subsequent notes. There is no need to do this. It was surprising in part (b) that very few candidates knew anything about the PAYE tax code, and not much more about the PAYE forms. This just seems to be an area of the syllabus that was not revised. As regards the PAYE forms, a bit of common sense together with the knowledge that form P45 is given when employment ceases, form P60 is given at the end of the tax year, and form P11D is in respect of the benefits provided to a taxpayer, would have meant that most of the marks were easily obtainable.

Marking scheme

					Marks
(a)	Salary – Firstly plc			½	
	Occupational pension scheme contributions			1	
	Bonus			½	
	Salary – Secondly plc			½	
	Personal pension contributions			½	
	Beneficial loan	– Average method		1½	
		– Strict method		1½	
	Workplace nursery			1	
	Gym membership			½	
	Home entertainment system	– Use		1½	
		– Acquisition		1½	
	Living accommodation			2	
	Furniture			1½	
	Running costs			½	
	Childcare vouchers			1	
	Company gym			½	
	Mobile telephone			½	
	Personal allowance			½	
					17
(b)	(i)	Basic of calculation		1	
		Deduction from salary		1	
					2

		Marks
(ii)	**Form P45**	
	By Firstly plc when employment ceases	½
	Details	1
	Date provided	½
	Form P60	
	By Secondly plc at end of tax year	½
	Details	1½
	Date provided	½
	Form P11D	
	Both employers	½
	Details	½
	Date provided	½
		$\frac{6}{25}$

(a) **Joe Jones – Taxable income 2012/13**

		£
Employment income		
Salary – Firstly plc (6,360 × 9)		57,240
Pension contributions (57,240 × 6%) (N2)		(3,434)
		53,806
Bonus (N1)		Nil
Salary – Secondly plc (6,120 × 3)		18,360
Beneficial loan (W1)		2,367
Workplace nursery (N3)		Nil
Gym membership		1,650
Home entertainment system	– Use (W2)	660
	– Acquisition (W2)	3,860
Living accommodation (W3)		6,750
Furniture (W3)		816
Running costs		1,900
Childcare vouchers (W4)		936
Company gym (N3)		Nil
Mobile telephone (N3)		Nil
Net income		91,105
Less: personal allowance		(8,105)
Taxable income		83,000

Workings

1 *Loan benefit*

The benefit of the beneficial loan using the average method is £2,533 ((120,000 + 70,000)/2 = 95,000 at 4% × 8/12).

Using the strict method the benefit is £2,367 ((120,000 at 4% × 3/12) + (70,000 at 4% × 5/12)).

Joe will therefore elect to have the taxable benefit calculated according to the strict method.

2 *Home entertainment system*

The benefit for the use of the home entertainment system is £660 (4,400 × 20% × 9/12).

The benefit for the acquisition of the home entertainment system is the market value of £3,860, as this is greater than £3,740 (4,400 – 660).

3   *Living accommodation and furniture*

The benefit for the living accommodation is the higher of the annual value of £2,600 (10,400 × 3/12) and the rent paid of £6,750 (2,250 × 3).

The benefit for the use of the furniture is £816 (16,320 × 20% × 3/12).

4   *Childcare vouchers*

The exemption for childcare vouchers is £28 per week since Joe is a higher rate employee. The benefit for the provision of the vouchers is therefore £936 ((100 − 28) = 72 × 13).

Notes

1   The bonus of £12,000 will have been treated as being received during 2011/12 as Joe became entitled to it during that tax year.

2   The personal pension contributions will increase Joe's basic rate tax limit, and are therefore irrelevant as regards the calculation of taxable income.

3   The provision of a place in a workplace nursery, the use of a company gym (sporting facility), and the provision of one mobile telephone do not give rise to taxable benefits.

(b)   (i)   **Joe's tax code**

Joe's tax code will have been calculated by starting with his personal allowance of £8,105, and then reducing it by the value of the taxable benefits.

An employee's tax code is used to adjust their salary when calculating the amount of income tax that has to be paid each week or month under the PAYE system.

(ii)   **Form P45**

Form P45 will be prepared by Firstly plc when Joe's employment ceases. It will show his taxable earnings and income tax deducted up to the date of leaving, together with his tax code at the date of leaving.

Firstly plc should have provided this form to Joe immediately following his cessation of employment with the company.

Form P60

Form P60 will be prepared by Secondly plc at the end of the tax year. It will show Joe's taxable earnings, income tax deducted, final tax code, national insurance contributions, and Secondly plc's name and address.

Secondly plc should have provided this form to Joe by 31 May 2013.

Form P11D

A separate form P11D will be prepared by both Firstly plc and Secondly plc, detailing the cash equivalents of the benefits provided to Joe.

Both companies should have provided a form to Joe by 6 July 2013.

5 Sam and Kim White

Text references. Chapter 2 includes individual savings accounts. Chapter 3 deals with employment income and Chapter 4 covers employment benefits. Chapter 7 is about the computation of trading income and Chapter 8 covers capital allowances.

Top tips. Allocate your time for each part of the question and ensure you attempt every part.

Easy marks. The adjustment to profit in part (a) and Kim's income tax computation in part (b) were easy marks.

Examiner's comments. This question was very well answered by the majority of candidates. In part (a) the adjustments for use of office, business use of a private telephone and own consumption caused the most problems, with a number of candidates being unsure as to whether adjustments should be added or subtracted in order to arrive at the tax adjusted trading profit. Part (b) was also well answered, with only the expense claim for the business mileage causing any difficulty. This was often treated as a benefit rather than as an expense. Part (c) was answered reasonably well, especially the transfer into the spouse's sole name. Many candidates correctly calculated the amount of income tax saving.

Marking scheme

			Marks
(a)	Net profit	½	
	Depreciation	½	
	Motor expenses	1½	
	Patent royalties	1	
	Professional fees: breach of contract	½	
	Professional fees: professional fees	½	
	Gifts to customers	1	
	Own consumption	1	
	Use of office	1	
	Private telephone	1	
	Capital allowances – Main pool	1	
	– Motor car	1½	
			11
(b)	**Sam White**		
	Trading profit	½	
	Building society interest	1	
	Personal allowance	½	
	Income tax	1	
	Kim White		
	Salary	½	
	Beneficial loan	1	
	Expense claim	2	
	Building society interest	½	
	Loan interest	1	
	Personal allowance	½	
	Income tax	1½	
			10

			Marks
(c)	**Individual savings accounts**		
	Limit	1	
	Tax saving	1	
			2
	Transfer to Kim's sole name		
	Tax rates	1	
	Tax saving	1	
			2
			25

(a) **Sam White – Trading profit for the year ended 5 April 2013**

		£	£
Net profit			50,000
Add back:	Depreciation	6,123	
	Motor expenses £8,800 × 20% (N1)	1,760	
	Patent royalties (N2)	0	
	Professional fees: breach of contract	0	
	Professional fees: accountancy personal CGT advice	320	
	Other expenses: gifts to customers £(560 + 420) (N3)	980	
	Goods for own consumption	1,480	10,663
			60,663
Less:	Use of home £5,120 × 1/8	640	
	Private telephone £1,600 × 25%	400	
	Capital allowances (W)	4,623	(5,663)
Trading profit			55,000

Working – Capital allowances

	Main pool £	Motor car £	Allowances £
TWDV brought forward	18,500	20,200	
WDA – 18%	(3,330)		3,330
WDA – 8%		(1,616) × 80%	1,293
WDV carried forward	15,170	18,584	
Allowances			4,623

Notes

1   Of the 25,000 miles driven by Sam during the year ended 5 April 2013, 20,000 (5,000 + 15,000 [(25,000 – 5,000 = 20,000) × 75%]) were for business journeys. The business proportion is therefore 80% (20,000/25,000 × 100).

2   Patent royalties are allowed as a deduction when calculating the trading profit, so no adjustment is required.

3   Gifts to customers are an allowable deduction if they cost less than £50 per recipient per year, are not of food, drink, tobacco or vouchers for exchangeable goods and carry a conspicuous advertisement for the business making the gift.

(b)   **Sam White – Income tax computation 2012/13**

	Non-savings income £	Savings income £	Total £
Trading income (part (a))	55,000		
Building society interest			
£1,200/2 × 100/80 = £1,500/2		750	
Net income	55,000	750	55,750
Less: personal allowance	(8,105)		(8,105)
Taxable income	46,895	750	47,645

Income tax	£
Non-savings income	
£34,370 × 20%	6,874
£12,525 × 40%	5,010
Savings income	
£750 × 40%	300
Income tax liability	12,184

Kim White – Income tax computation 2012/13

	£	Non-savings income £	Saving income £	Total £
Employment income				
Salary	23,730			
Loans (W1)	400			
	24,130			
Less expense claim (W3)	(5,125)	19,005		
BSI £1,200/2 × 100/80 = £1,500 ÷2			750	
Total income		19,005	750	19,755
Less deductible interest (W4)		(140)		(140)
Net income		18,865	750	19,615
Less personal allowance		(8,105)		(8,105)
Taxable income		10,760	750	11,510

Income tax	£
Non-savings income	
£10,760 × 20%	2,152
Savings income	
£750 × 20%	150
Income tax liability	2,302

Workings

(1)   The taxable benefit from the beneficial loan is £12,000 at 4% × 10/12 = £400.

(2)   Ordinary commuting (travel between home and the permanent workplace) does not qualify for relief. The travel to a temporary workplace qualifies as it is for a period lasting less than 24 months.

(3)   Kim can therefore make an expense claim based on 12,500 (11,200 + 1,300) miles as follows:

	£
10,000 miles at 45p	4,500
2,500 miles at 25p	625
	5,125

(4)   The loan interest paid of £140 is eligible for relief since the loan was used by Kim to finance expenditure for a relevant purpose.

(c)   **Individual savings accounts**

(1)   Both Sam and Kim can invest a maximum of £11,280 each tax year into an ISA of which up to £5,640 can be held as cash.

(2)   Interest received from ISAs is exempt from income tax, so Sam will save tax at the rate of 40% whilst Kim will save tax at the rate of 20%, each on gross interest of £338 (£1,500 × 5,640/25,000).

Transfer to Kim's sole name

(1)   Sam pays income tax at the rate of 40%, whilst Kim's basic rate tax band is not fully utilised.

(2)   Transferring the building society deposit account into Kim's sole name would therefore save tax of £150 (£750 × 20% (40% – 20%)).

6 Sammi Smith

Text references. Chapter 4 deals with employment benefits. National insurance contributions are covered in Chapter 12. Computing taxable total profits is in Chapter 19 and computing corporation tax in Chapter 20.

Top tips. Use headings to show the examiner which of two options you are dealing with.

Easy marks. There were easy marks for computing the car benefit and computing the national insurance contributions.

Examiner's comments. This question was generally answered quite badly, with the main problem being that candidates simply did not spend enough time thinking and planning their answers, but just plunged straight in performing every calculation that they could think of. In part (a) the answer was in fact very straightforward, with a fairly simple car benefit calculation and then income tax and NIC calculations at the director's marginal rates of 50% and 2% respectively. Far too many candidates calculated a fuel benefit despite being told that fuel was not provided for private journeys. In part (b) many candidates stated that capital allowances would be available despite the motor car being leased. Candidates often stated that the company's corporation tax liability would be increased rather than reduced as a result of the additional expenditure, and very few candidates appreciated that NIC was a deductible expense. Part (c) was more difficult, although credit was given for any sensible approach such as comparing the tax liabilities under each alternative.

			Marks
(a)	**Company motor car**		
	Car benefit	2	
	Income tax	1	
	NIC implications	½	
	Additional director's remuneration		
	Income tax	½	
	Class 1 NIC	1	
			5
(b)	**Company motor car**		
	Class 1A NIC	1	
	Allowable leasing costs	1	
	Corporation tax saving	1	
	Additional director's remuneration		
	Class 1 NIC	1	
	Corporation tax saving	1	
			5

(c)   **Sammi**

		Marks
Director's remuneration	- Net of tax income	1
	- Overall result	1
Conclusion		1
Smark Ltd		
Director's remuneration		1
Conclusion		<u>1</u>

$$\frac{5}{15}$$

(a)   **Sammi Smith – Company motor car**

The list price used in the car benefit calculation is £80,000. The relevant percentage is restricted to a maximum of 35% (11% + 41% (305 – 100 = 205/5) = 52%).

Sammi will therefore be taxed on a car benefit of £28,000 (80,000 x 35%).

Sammi's marginal rate of income tax is 50%, so her additional income tax liability for 2012/13 will be £14,000 (28,000 at 50%).

There are no national insurance contribution implications for Sammi.

Tutorial note

There is no fuel benefit as fuel is not provided for private journeys.

Sammi Smith – Additional director's remuneration

Sammi's additional income tax liability for 2012/13 will be £13,000 (26,000 at 50%).

The additional employee's Class 1 NIC liability will be £520 (26,000 at 2%).

Tutorial note

Sammi's director's remuneration exceeds the upper earnings limit of £42,475, so her additional class 1 NIC liability is at the rate of 2%.

(b)   **Smark Ltd – Company motor car**

The employer's Class 1A NIC liability in respect of the car benefit will be £3,864 (28,000 at 13.8%).

The motor car has a CO_2 emission rate in excess of 160 grams per kilometre, so only £22,508 (26,480 less 15%) of the leasing costs are allowed for corporation tax purposes.

Smark Ltd's corporation tax liability will be reduced by £6,329 (22,508 + 3,864 = 26,372 at 24%).

Smark Ltd – Additional director's remuneration

The employer's Class 1 NIC liability in respect of the additional director's remuneration will be £3,588 (26,000 at 13.8%).

Smark Ltd's corporation tax liability will be reduced by £7,101 (26,000 + 3,588 = 29,588 at 24%).

(c)   **Most beneficial alternative for Sammi Smith**

Under the director's remuneration alternative, Sammi will receive additional net of tax income of £12,480 (26,000 – 13,000 – 520).

However, she will have to lease the motor car at a cost of £26,480, so the overall result is additional expenditure of £14,000 (26,480 – 12,480).

If Sammi is provided with a company motor car then she will have an additional tax liability of £14,000, so she is in exactly the same financial position.

Most beneficial alternative for Smark Ltd

The net of tax cost of paying additional director's remuneration is £22,487 (26,000 + 3,588 – 7,101).

This is more beneficial than the alternative of providing a company motor car since this has a net of tax cost of £24,015 (26,480 + 3,864 – 6,329).

7 Edmond Brick

Text references. Chapter 6 deals with property income.

Top tips. Remember that property income is pooled to give a single profit or loss. However, if someone has furnished holiday lettings and other lettings, two sets of accounts have to be drawn up as if there were two separate UK property businesses. This is so that profits and losses treated as trade profits and losses can be identified. The examiner has helpfully structured this question so that you were required to make such separate calculations.

Easy marks. Deduction of expenses such as council tax, insurance and advertising were easy marks.

Examiner's comments. This was a very well answered question. In part (a) some candidates discussed the qualifying conditions for a furnished holiday letting rather than the advantages of a property being so treated. Parts (b) and (c) presented few problems. The only aspects that consistently caused difficulty were the capital allowances for the furnished holiday letting (candidates either claimed wear and tear allowance or deducted the full cost of the capital expenditure) and the furnished room (candidates did not appreciate that rent-a-room relief could be claimed).

Marking scheme

			Marks
(a)	Availability of capital allowances	1	
	Capital gains tax business reliefs	1	
	Relevant earnings for pension purposes	<u>1</u>	
			3
(b)	Rent receivable	½	
	Repairs	1	
	Other expenses	½	
	Capital allowances	<u>1</u>	
			3
(c)	**Property two**		
	Rent receivable	½	
	Council tax	½	
	Insurance	½	
	Wear and tear allowance	1	
	Property three		
	Rent receivable	½	
	Insurance	½	
	Advertising	½	
	Impairment loss	½	
	Loan interest	½	
	Property four		
	Lease premium	1	
	Rent receivable	½	
	Insurance	½	
	Rent paid	½	
	Room		
	Rent received	½	
	Rent a room relief	<u>1</u>	
			<u>9</u>
			<u>15</u>

(a)   The tax advantages of property one being treated as a trade under the furnished holiday letting rules are:

(i)   Capital allowances are available on furniture instead of the 10% wear and tear allowance.

(ii)   Capital gains tax reliefs which apply to businesses, apply here ie entrepreneurs' relief, rollover relief, gift relief.

(iii)   The income qualifies as relevant earnings for pension relief purposes.

(b)   **Property one**

	£
Rent receivable £370 × 18	6,660
Less: repairs	(7,400)
other allowable expenditure	(2,710)
capital allowances	
£5,700 (covered by AIA)	(5,700)
Loss	(9,150)

(c)   **Property two**

	£	£
Rent receivable £575 × 12	6,900	
Less: council tax	(1,200)	
insurance	(340)	
wear and tear allowance		
10% × £(6,900 – 1,200)	(570)	
Profit		4,790

Property three

	£	£
Rent receivable £710 × 7	4,970	
Less: insurance	(290)	
advertising	(670)	
impairment loss £710 × 3	(2,130)	
loan interest	(6,700)	
Loss		(4,820)

Property four

	£	£
Premium taxable as property business income (W)	13,800	
Rent receivable	4,600	
	18,400	
Less: insurance	(360)	
rent payable	(6,800)	
		11,240

Furnished Room

	£	£
Rent receivable	5,040	
Less: rent a room relief (note)	(4,250)	
Profit		790

Property business profit		12,000

Working

	£
Premium paid	15,000
Less: 2% × (5 – 1) × £15,000	(1,200)
Taxable as property business income	13,800

Note.   Claiming rent a room relief in respect of the furnished room £(5,040 – 4,250) = £790 is more beneficial than the normal basis of assessment £(5,040 – 1,140) = £3,900.

8 Peter Chic

Text reference. Employment income and benefits are covered in Chapters 3 and 4. Property income is dealt with in Chapter 6. The computation of taxable income and the income tax liability is covered in Chapter 2. National insurance contributions are dealt with in Chapter 12.

Top tips. Set out the computation of taxable income in the standard three column layout. Use workings to show the details rather than putting them directly into the computation.

Easy marks. The calculation of national insurance contributions should have been easy marks.

Examiner's comments. In part (a) a few candidates did not appreciate that both bonuses were to be treated as earnings, whilst the basis of assessing the second mobile telephone was not always known. Some candidates deducted the gift aid donation rather than extending the basic rate tax band. In part (b) the most common mistake was to include taxable benefits when calculating Class 1 national insurance contributions.

Marking scheme

			Marks
(a)	Salary		½
	Bonus payments		1
	Car benefit	– relevant percentage	1
		– capital contribution	½
		– calculation	½
	Fuel benefit		1
	Living accommodation	– annual value	1
		– additional benefit	2
	Mobile telephone		1
	Health club membership		½
	Overseas allowance		½
	Property business profit	– rent receivable	1
		– irrecoverable rent	½
		– repairs	½
		– advertising	½
		– loan interest	1
		– insurance	1
		– wear and tear allowance	1
	Building society interest		½
	Dividends		½
	Premium bond prize (exempt)		½
	Personal allowance		½
	Increase in basic rate limit		1
	Income tax		1½
	Tax suffered at source		1½
			21
(b)	Employee Class 1 NIC		1½
	Employer Class 1 NIC		1½
	Employer Class 1A NIC		1
			4
			25

(a) **Income tax computation 2012/13**

	Non-savings income £	Savings income £	Dividend income £	Total £
Employment income (W1)	80,450			
Property income (W5)	3,660			
BSI £1,760 × 100/80		2,200		
Dividends £720 × 100/90			800	
Premium bond prize (exempt)		0		
Net income	84,110	2,200	800	87,110
Less: personal allowance	(8,105)			
Taxable income	76,005	2,200	800	79,005

	£	£
Tax		
£37,370 × 20%		7,474
£38,635 × 40%		15,454
£2,200 × 40%		880
£800 × 32½%		260
Tax liability		24,068
Less: tax deducted at source		
PAYE	14,670	
BSI £2,200 × 20%	440	
Dividend £800 × 10%	80	(15,190)
Tax payable		8,878

Workings

1 *Employment income*

	£	£
Salary	45,600	
Bonus received 10.4.12	4,300	
Bonus received 25.3.13	3,600	53,500
Car benefit (W2)	7,175	
Fuel benefit (W2)	7,070	
Living accommodation (W3)	12,145	
Mobile phone (W4)	50	
Health club membership	510	
Overseas allowance – exempt up to £10 per night for overseas expenses	nil	26,950
Employment income		80,450

2 *Car benefit*

$$\frac{210-100}{5} = 22 + 11 + 3 \text{ (diesel)} = 36\%$$

Maximum % is 35.

	£
List price	22,500
Less: contribution	(2,000)
	20,500
× 35%	7,175

Fuel benefit

£20,200 × 35%	7,070

3   *Living accommodation*

	£	£
Annual benefit		8,225
Additional benefit		
Cost of property	160,000	
Improvements before start of tax year	13,000	
	173,000	
Less: *de minimis*	(75,000)	
	98,000	
Benefit @ 4%		3,920
Total accommodation benefit		12,145

4   *Mobile phone*

One mobile phone is exempt
Second mobile phone is calculated on private use of asset basis ie £250 × 20%   £50

5   *Property income*

	£	£
Property one – rent receivable £500 × 5		2,500
Property two – rent receivable £820 × 8		6,560
		9,060
Irrecoverable rent £500 × 2	1,000	
Repairs to roof	600	
Advertising	875	
Loan interest	1,800	
Insurance £(660 × 3/12 + 1,080 × 9/12)	975	
Wear and tear £(2,500 – 1,000) × 10% (N)	150	(5,400)
Property income		3,660

Note. It is arguable that the wear and tear allowance should be calculated as 10% of the gross rents receivable as this is more beneficial than 10% of the rents receivable. Credit would be given for either approach in the exam.

6   Basic rate limit increased by gross Gift Aid donations
£34,370 + £(2,400 × 100/80)   £37,370

(b)   **National insurance contributions 2012/13**

Primary Class 1 (paid by Peter)

	£
£(42,475 – 7,605) = 34,870 × 12%	4,184
£(53,500 – 42,475) = 11,025 × 2%	220
	4,404

Secondary Class 1 (paid by Haute-Couture Ltd)
£(53,500 – 7,488) = 46,012 × 13.8%   6,350

Class 1A (paid by Haute-Couture Ltd)
£26,950 × 13.8%   3,719

9 Leticia Stone

Text references. Property income is covered in Chapter 6.

Top tips. You were given a useful instruction in the question to keep the furnished holiday letting loss separate from the general property loss. It was vital that you approached the question in this manner.

Easy marks. There were some easy marks in this question for the computation of the losses provided that you remembered to apply the accruals basis to income and expenses.

Examiner's comments. Part (a) of this question was very well answered, with no aspect causing significant problems. However, several candidates claimed the wear and tear allowance for the furnished holiday letting rather than capital allowances. Although candidates were not penalised if they combined the property losses into just one calculation, not separating out the furnished holiday letting loss invariably meant that marks were then lost in part (b) as marks were not awarded for vague details on loss relief if it was not clearly stated as to which reliefs were available for which type of loss.

Marking scheme

			Marks
(a)	**Furnished holiday letting loss**		
	Rent receivable	½	
	Loan interest	1	
	Repairs	1	
	Mileage allowance	1½	
	Other expenses	½	
	Capital allowances	1	
	Property business loss		
	Lease premium received	1	
	Rent receivable – Property 2	1	
	– Property 3	1	
	– Security deposit	½	
	Rent payable	1	
	Impairment loss	1	
	Loan interest	½	
	Other expenses	½	
	Furnished room	1	
			13
(b)	Furnished holiday letting loss	1	
	Property business loss	1	
			2
			15

(a) **Leticia Stone – Furnished holiday letting loss 2012/13**

	£	£
Income		
Rent receivable £425 × 22		9,350
Expenses		
Loan interest	12,700	
Repairs not covered by insurance £(12,200 – 10,900)	1,300	
Mileage allowance (N1) (880 + 130) = 1,010 × 45p	455	
Other expenses	3,770	
Capital allowances (N2)	4,600	
		(22,825)
Furnished holiday letting loss		(13,475)

Tutorial notes

1   The mileage that Leticia drove in respect of the property purchase is a capital expense and so not deductible.

2   Capital allowances on furniture are available for furnished holiday lettings. The expenditure is covered by the annual investment allowance.

Leticia Stone – Property business loss 2012/13

	£	£
Income		
Premium received for sublease – Property 2	45,000	
Less: £45,000 × (5 – 1) × 2%	(3,600)	
		41,400
Rent receivable – Property 2 £(2,160 × 4) = 8,640 × 11/12		7,920
– Property 3 £580 ×10		5,800
– Property 3 Security deposit (N1)		0
– Room in own residence (N2)		3,170
		58,290
Expenses		
Rent payable – Property 2 £1,360 × 11	14,960	
Impairment loss – Property 3	580	
Loan interest – Property 3	9,100	
Other expenses – Properties 2 and 3	36,240	
Other expenses – Room in own residence	4,840	
		(65,720)
Property business loss		(7,430)

Tutorial notes

1   The security deposit received on 1 March 2013, even if it was treated as rental income, relates to a letting commencing in 2013/14 and is therefore not relevant for 2012/13.

2   Leticia should claim to ignore the rent a room exemption since this allows a loss to be generated.

(b) The furnished holiday letting loss is relieved by carrying it forward and deducting from the first available future profits of the same furnished holiday letting business.

The general property business loss is relieved by carrying it forward and deducting from the first available future profits of the general property business.

10 Peach, Plum and Pear

Marking scheme

		Marks
Ann Peach		
Taxable income	½	
Increase in basic rate limit	1	
Income tax	½	
Amount qualifying for tax relief	1	
		3
Basil Plum		
Taxable income	½	
Increase in basic rate limit	½	
Increase in higher rate limit	½	
Income tax	1½	
Excess contribution charge	1	
Amount qualifying for tax relief	1	
		5
Chloe Pear		
Taxable income	½	
Income tax	½	
Amount qualifying for tax relief	1	2
		10

(a) **Ann Peach**

	Non-savings income £
Trading income	44,730
Less: personal allowance	(8,105)
Taxable income	36,625

Maximum personal pension contribution is higher of (1) £3,600 and (2) Relevant earnings £44,730 ie £44,730. The remaining £2,270 is not given tax relief.

Basic rate limit £(34,370 + 44,730)	£79,100
Tax £36,625 × 20%	£7,325

(b) **Basil Plum**

Basil can make a maximum personal pension contribution of £330,000. Therefore his contribution of £60,000 will be given tax relief. However, the excess charge applies to the contribution over the annual allowance of £50,000 so some of the tax relief given will be clawed back.

	Non-savings income £
Employment income	330,000
Excess pension contribution over annual allowance £(60,000 – 50,000)	10,000
Taxable income (no PA as net adjusted income exceeds £116,210)	340,000

The excess contribution is treated as extra non-savings income.

Basic rate limit £(34,370 + 60,000)	94,370
Higher rate limit £(150,000 + 60,000)	210,000

Tax is therefore calculated as follows:

£94,370 × 20%	18,874
£(210,000 – 94,370) = £115,630 × 40%	46,252
£(340,000 – 210,000) = £130,000 × 50%	65,000
Tax	130,126

(c) **Chloe Pear**

	Non-savings income £
Property income	26,630
Less: personal allowance	(8,105)
Taxable income	18,525

Maximum personal pension contribution is £3,600 since Chloe has no relevant earnings. This will have been given tax relief at source by Chloe paying £3,600 × 80% = £2,880. The remaining £4,600 contribution is not given tax relief.

Tax is therefore £18,525 × 20%	3,705

11 Na Style

Text references. Assessment of trading profits is covered in Chapter 9. Adjustment of trading profit is in Chapter 7. The income tax computation is dealt with in Chapter 2 and administration aspects in Chapter 17.

Top tips. As you deal with each adjustment to profit, tick it off in the question – this method should ensure that you do not miss out any item and thus lose marks.

Easy marks. The administration aspects in part (d) should have been 3 easy marks.

Examiner's comments. This question was very well answered, and there were many high scoring answers. In part (a) some candidates lost marks because they did not show the relevant tax years in which profits were assessable. There were few problems as regards the calculation of the trading profit or the income tax payable, although many candidates did not appreciate that interest from government stocks is received gross and is taxable. As regards the balancing payment and payments on account, candidates were often not aware of the relevant dates. In part (d) many candidates did not appreciate that a 5% penalty would be imposed in addition to the interest charge.

Marks

(a) First tax year trading profits   1
Second tax year trading profits   1½
Third tax year trading profits   ½
Overlap profits   2

      5

(b) Net profit   ½
Depreciation   ½
Motor expenses   1
Accountancy   ½
Legal fees   ½
Property expenses   1
Own consumption   1
Fine   ½
Donation to political party   ½
Trade subscription   ½
Private telephone   1
Capital allowances   ½

      8

(c) (i) *Income tax computation*
Trading profit   ½
Building society interest   ½
Individual savings account interest (exempt)   ½
Interest from NS&I certificates (exempt)   ½
Interest from government stocks   1
Dividends   ½
Personal allowance   ½
Income tax liability   1
Income tax suffered at source   1

      6

(ii) *Income tax payments*
Balancing payment   1½
Payments on account   1½

      3

(d) Interest   1
Calculation   1
Surcharge   1

      3
      25

(a) **Na Style trading profits 2009/10, 2010/11 and 2011/12**

Year	Basis period	Working	Taxable Profits £
2009/10	1.01.10 – 5.4.10	£25,200 × 3/6	12,600
2010/11	1.01.10 – 31.12.10 (N)	£25,200 + £21,600 × 6/12	36,000
2011/12	1.7.10 – 30.6.11		21,600

Note. Because the accounting period ending in the second tax year is less than twelve months, the basis period for that year is the first twelve months of trading.

Overlap profits

Overlap period	Working	Overlap profits £
1.01.10 – 5.4.10	£25,200 × 3/6	12,600
1.07.10 – 31.12.10	£21,600 × 6/12	10,800

(b) **Na Style tax adjusted trading profit for year ended 30 June 2012**

		£	£
Net profit			23,000
Add:	depreciation	1,300	
	motor expenses – private use		
	7,000/8,000 × £2,200	1,925	
	professional fees – accountancy	0	
	professional fees – lease (N)	1,260	
	property expenses – private use		
	1/3 × £12,900	4,300	
	purchases – goods taken for own use (selling price)	450	
	other expenses – fine	400	
	other expenses – political party donation	80	
	other expenses – trade subscription	0	
			9,715
			32,715
Less:	telephone – business use 20% × £1,200	240	
	capital allowances	810	(1,050)
Tax adjusted trading profit			31,665

Note. Legal expenses relating to the *grant* of a short lease are not allowable.

(c) (i) **Na Style tax payable for 2012/13**

	Non-savings income £	Savings income £	Dividend income £	Total £
Trading income (part (b))	31,665			
BSI £560 × 100/80		700		
ISA interest (exempt)		0		
NS&I interest (exempt)		0		
Interest from stocks (gross)		1,440		
UK dividends £1,080 × 100/90			1,200	
Net income	31,665	2,140	1,200	35,005
Less: personal allowance	(8,105)			
Taxable income	23,560	2,140	1,200	26,900

	£	£
Income tax		
Non-savings income		
£23,560 × 20%		4,712
Savings income		
£2,140 × 20%		428
Dividend income		
£1,200 × 10%		120
Tax liability		5,260

	£	£
Less: tax suffered		
Tax credit on dividend income £1,200 × 10%	120	
Tax on building society interest £700 × 20%	140	
		(260)
Tax payable		5,000

(ii) **Na Style balancing payment for 2012/13**

	£
Tax payable (part (i))	5,000
Less: payments on account	(3,200)
Balancing payment due 31 January 2014	1,800
First payment on account 2013/14	
½ × £5,000 due 31 January 2014	2,500
Second payment on account 2013/14	
½ × £5,000 due 31 July 2014	2,500

(d) **Consequences of not making balancing payment until 31 May 2014**

Interest is charged where a balancing payment is paid late. This will run from 1 February 2014 to 31 May 2014.

The interest charge will be £1,800 × 3% × 4/12 = **£18**.

In addition, a penalty of £1,800 @ 5% = **£90** will be imposed as the balancing payment is made after the penalty date (30 days after the due date) but not more than five months after the penalty date.

12 Simon House

Text references. The badges of trade are discussed in Chapter 7 which also deals with the computation of trading profit. Chapter 2 deals with income tax computation. Chapter 13 covers computation of chargeable gains for individuals.

Top tips. Think carefully about what costs are allowable as part of trading expenses in part (b) and, alternatively, as part of the cost of the asset in part (c). Not all the expenses are allowable in both cases.

Easy marks. The examiner gave you the badges of trade in part (a) so it should have been easy marks to comment on them.

Examiner's comments. This question was very well answered, and often helped marginal candidates to achieve a pass mark. In part (a) a number of candidates failed to score any marks because they did not state what did or did not indicate trading. For example, stating that the 'length of ownership' means how long an item has owned did not score any marks. It was necessary to explain that the sale of property within a short time of its acquisition is an indication of trading. Part (b) presented no problems for most candidates. In this type of question it is always best to produce full computations for each option. This will maximise marks if any mistakes are made. It was pleasing to see that many candidates correctly restricted the Class 2 NIC to 19 weeks' contributions.

			Marks
(a)	Subject matter	½	
	Length of ownership	½	
	Frequency of transactions	½	
	Work done	½	
	Circumstances of realisation	½	
	Profit motive	½	
			3
(b)	Income	½	
	Acquisition of house	½	
	Legal fees on acquisition	½	
	Renovation costs	½	
	Legal fees on sale	½	
	Loan interest	1	
	Personal allowance	½	
	Income tax liability	1	
	Class 4 NICs	1½	
	Class 2 NICs	1½	
			8
(c)	Sale proceeds	½	
	Legal fees on sale	½	
	Cost of house	½	
	Legal fees on acquisition	½	
	Enhancement expenditure	½	
	Loan interest – not allowable	½	
	Annual exempt amount	½	
	Capital gains tax liability	½	
			4
			15

(a) **Badges of trade**

Subject matter

Some assets are commonly held as investments for their intrinsic value, for example an individual may buy shares for dividend income produced by them or may buy a painting to enjoy it as a work of art. A subsequent disposal of an investment asset usually produces a capital gain. Where the subject matter of a transaction is not an investment asset, any profit on resale is usually a trading profit.

Length of ownership

If items purchased are sold soon afterwards, this indicates trading transactions.

Frequency of transactions

Transactions which may, in isolation, be of a capital nature will be interpreted as trading transactions where their frequency indicates the carrying on of a trade.

Work done

When work is done to make an asset more marketable, or steps are taken to find purchasers, this is likely to be indicative of trading.

Length of ownership

If items purchased are sold soon afterwards, this indicates trading.

Circumstances of realisation

A forced sale, for example to realise funds for an emergency, is not likely to be treated as trading.

Motive

The absence of a profit motive will not necessarily preclude a tax charge as trading income, but its presence is a strong indication that a person is trading.

(b) **Simon House income tax and NICs for 2012/13 if trading**

	£	£
Income		260,000
Less: *costs incurred*		
house	127,000	
legal fees on acquisition	1,800	
renovation	50,600	
legal fees on sale	2,600	
loan interest		
£150,000 × 6% × 4/12	3,000	
		(185,000)
Trading income/Net income		75,000
Less: personal allowance		(8,105)
Taxable income		66,895
Income tax		
£34,370 @ 20%		6,874
£32,525 @ 40%		13,010
Income tax liability		19,884
Class 4 NICs		
£(42,475 – 7,605) = £34,870 @ 9%		3,138
£(75,000 – 42,475) = £32,525 @ 2%		650
Total Class 4 NICs		3,788
Class 2 NICs		
£2.65 × 19 weeks (N)		50

Note. Marks were awarded for any reasonable attempt at calculating the number of weeks. ½ mark was deducted if 52 weeks were used.

(c) **Simon House capital gains tax 2012/13 if not trading**

	£	£
Sale proceeds		260,000
Less: legal fees on sale		(2,600)
Net proceeds of sale		257,400
Less: cost of house	127,000	
legal fees on acquisition	1,800	
Renovation	50,600	
loan interest (N)	0	
		(179,400)
Chargeable gain		78,000
Less: annual exempt amount		(10,600)
Taxable gain		67,400

	£	£
Capital gains tax		
£34,370 @ 18%		6,187
£(67,400 – 34,370) = 33,030 @ 28%		9,248
Capital gains tax liability		15,435

Note. The loan interest is a revenue expense and so is not allowable in computing the chargeable gain.

13 Bayle Defender

Text references. Adjustment of profit is dealt with in Chapter 7. Employment income is covered in Chapter 3. The income tax computation is the subject of Chapter 2. Self-assessment is dealt with in Chapter 17. NICs for both employees and the self-employed are covered in Chapter 12. The basis of assessment will be found in Chapter 9 and partnerships are dealt with in Chapter 11.

Top tips. You must start your adjustment of profit computation with the net profit. Don't forget to include any items which do not require adjustment (such as the impairment loss) with a zero.

Easy marks. There were plenty of easy marks for the adjustment of profit computation with standard items such as gifts to customers which should have been well-known. The balancing payment and payments on account should also have yielded easy marks.

Examiner's comments. Parts (a) (i), (a) (ii) and (b)(i) were generally well answered, but candidates had more difficultly with the other sections. In part (a)(i) the only consistent problem was the revenue received in respect of a previously written off impairment loss. Most candidates did not appreciate that no adjustment was necessary. In part (a)(ii) it was often not appreciated that one of the bonuses was treated as being received in the previous tax year, and often bonuses were included or excluded without any explanation as to why. It should have been obvious that with income of over £250,000 no personal allowance was available, yet many candidates wasted time by showing a calculation for this. Many candidates simply ignored part (a)(iii), and very few appreciated that both the balancing payment for 2012/13 and the first payment on account for 2013/14 were due on 31 January 2014. In part (b)(i) it was pleasing to see several candidates correctly restricted NIC contributions to the four months of employment. Although there were also many good answers to part (b)(ii), there were also a lot of candidates who wasted time by doing NIC calculations for both the taxpayer and the new person, or NIC calculations for both years, instead of just the one required.

Marking scheme

				Marks
(a)	(i)	Impairment loss	½	
		Gifts to customers	1	
		Donations to political parties	½	
		Lease of motor car	1	
		Personal tax advice	½	
		Property expenses	1	
		Parking fines	½	
		Professional subscription	½	
		Golf membership fee	½	
				6

				Marks
	(ii)	Trading profits	½	
		Director's remuneration	½	
		Bonus payments	1	
		Interest from savings certificates	½	
		Interest from government stocks	½	
		Dividends	½	
		Personal allowance	1	
		Income tax	2	
		Tax suffered at source	1½	
				8
	(iii)	**Tax payments**		
		Balancing payment	1	
		Payments on account	1	
		Interest and penalties		
		Interest	1½	
		Penalties	1½	
				5
(b)	(i)	Monthly earnings period thresholds	1	
		Employee Class 1 NIC	1½	
		Employer Class 1 NIC	1½	
				4
	(ii)	**Trading income assessments**		
		2012/13	1½	
		2013/14	2½	
				4
		NIC		
		Class 2 NIC	1½	
		Class 4 NIC	1	
		Bayle	½	
				3
				30

(a)   (i)   **Bayle Defender – Trading profit for the year ended 30 September 2012**

		£
Net profit		172,400
Add: Impairment loss		0
Gifts to customers - Clocks		3,300
- Bottles of champagne		2,480
Donations to political parties		2,900
Lease of motor car £10,360 × 15%		1,554
Personal tax advice		600
Property expenses £46,240 × 2/5		18,496
Parking fines		520
Professional subscriptions		0
Golf club membership fee		960
Taxable trading profit		203,210

Tutorial notes

(1)   The recovered impairments loss will have been allowed as a deduction when originally written off, so the recovery is now taxable. Therefore no adjustment is required.

(2)   Gifts to customers are only an allowable deduction if they cost less than £50 per recipient per tax year, are not of food, drink, tobacco or vouchers for exchangeable goods and carry a conspicuous advertisement for the trader making the gift.

(3)   The motor car has a CO_2 emission rate in excess of 160 grams per kilometre, so 15% of the leasing costs are not allowed.

(ii)   **Bayle Defender – Income tax computation 2012/13**

	Non-savings income £	Savings income £	Dividend income £	Total £
Trading profit (from a(i) above)	203,210			
Employment income £(42,000 + 6,000)	48,000			
Interest from savings certificates (exempt)		0		
Interest from gilts (gross)		3,600		
Dividends (£9,900 × 100/90)			11,000	
Net income	251,210	3,600	11,000	265,810
Less: PA	(0)	(0)	(0)	(0)
Taxable income	251,210	3,600	11,000	265,810

Tax	£	£
£34,370 @ 20%		6,874
£(150,000 – 34,370) = 115,630 @ 40%		46,252
£(251,210 – 150,000 + 3,600) = 104,810 @ 50%		52,405
£11,000 @ 42.5%		4,675
Income tax liability		110,206
Tax suffered at source		
PAYE £48,000 @ 50%	24,000	
Dividends £11,000 @ 10%	1,100	(25,100)
Income tax payable		85,106

Tutorial notes

(1)   The bonus payment of £6,000 that Bayle became entitled to on 10 March 2012 will have been treated as being received during 2011/12.

(2)   Interest received on maturity of savings certificates issued by National Savings and Investments is exempt.

(3)   No personal allowance is available as Bayle's net income of £265,810 exceeds £116,210.

(iii)   **Tax payments**

Bayle's balancing payment for 2012/13 will be £31,580 (85,106 – 53,526).

In addition, she will have to make the first payment on account for 2013/14 of £42,553 (85,106 x 50%), so the total amount payable on 31 January 2014 will be £74,133 (31,580 + 42,553).

Interest and penalties

Interest is charged where payments are made late. This will run from the end of the due date of 31 January 2014 to 31 August 2014.

The interest charge will be £1,297 (74,133 × 3% × 7/12).

Two penalties each of £1,579 (31,580 at 5%) will be imposed on the balancing payment, one when it is thirty days late and the other when it is a further five months late.

(b)　(i)　The monthly primary earnings threshold is £634 (7,605/12) and the monthly secondary earnings threshold is £624 (7,488/12).

Fyle will pay employee Class 1 NIC for 2012/13 of £1,280 (£(3,300 – 634) = 2,666 @ 12% × 4).

Bayle will pay employer's Class 1 NIC for 2012/13 of £1,477 (£(3,300 – 624) = 2,676 @ 13.8% × 4).

Tutorial note:

The alternative approach using the annual earnings threshold and then taking 4/12ths of an annual NIC figure is acceptable.

　　(ii)　(1)　**Trading income assessments**

Fyle's trading income assessment for 2012/13 is £14,400 calculated as follows:

	£
Basis period: 1 December 2012 to 5 April 2013	
£216,000 × 4/12	72,000
Profit share £72,000 × 20%	14,400

The assessment for 2013/14 is £44,000 calculated as follows:

	£
Basis period: 1 December 2012 to 30 November 2013	
£216,000 × 10/12	180,000
£240,000 × 2/12	40,000
	220,000
Profit share £220,000 × 20%	44,000

Tutorial notes

(1)　The commencement rules apply to Fyle for 2012/13 since he will join as a partner on 1 December 2012.

(2)　The assessment for 2013/14 is for the 12 months from when Fyle joins the partnership.

　(2)　**NIC**

Fyle will pay Class 2 NIC for 2012/13 of £(2.65 × 18) = £48.

He will pay Class 4 NIC for 2012/13 of £(14,400 – 7,605) = 6,795 @ 9% = £612.

There are no NIC implications for Bayle.

14 Samantha Fabrique

Text references. Chapter 10 deals with trading losses.

Top tips. You should use the standard layout for losses: set up the columns and lines required and then slot in the numbers. A loss memorandum is also useful as a double check that you have used the losses correctly.

Easy marks. There were easy marks for setting out the trading income and gains stated in the question and using the personal allowance and annual exempt amount.

Examiner's comments. In part (a) many candidates explained the loss reliefs that were available rather than the factors that must be taken into account when deciding which loss reliefs to actually claim. In part (b) many candidates claimed loss relief against the total income for the year of the loss despite this income clearly being covered by the personal allowance. Very few candidates, even if they showed the capital gains separately, claimed loss relief against capital gains.

			Marks
(a)	Rate of tax	1	
	Timing of relief	1	
	Waste of personal allowance/annual exempt amount	1	
			3
(b)	Trading income	½	
	Trading loss relief carried forward	1	
	Building society interest	½	
	Trading loss relief against general income	1	
	Personal allowance	½	
	Gains	½	
	Capital loss relief carried forward	1	
	Trading loss relief against gains	1	
	Annual exempt amount	1	7
			10

(a) Factors that will influence an individual's choice of loss relief claim are:

(i) The rate of income tax or capital gains tax at which relief will be obtained, with preference being given to income charged at the additional rate of 50%, then the higher rate of 40%.

(ii) The timing of the relief obtained, with a claim against general income/capital gains of the current year or preceding year resulting in earlier relief than a carry forward claim against future trading profits.

(iii) The extent to which the income tax personal allowance and the capital gains tax annual exempt amount will be wasted by using a claim against general income/capital gains.

(b) **Samantha Fabrique – taxable income**

	2010/11 £	2011/12 £	2012/13 £	2013/14 £
Trading income	7,290	52,600	0	13,390
Less: trading loss relief carried forward	(0)	(0)	(0)	(7,000)
	7,290	52,600	0	6,390
Building society interest	0	2,100	3,800	2,130
	7,290	54,700	3,800	8,520
Less: trading loss relief against general income (N)	(0)	(54,700)	(0)	(0)
Net income	7,290	0	3,800	8,520
Less: personal allowance	(7,290)	(0)	(3,800)	(8,105)
Taxable income	0	0	0	415

Samantha Fabrique – taxable gains

	2010/11 £	2011/12 £	2012/13 £	2013/14 £
Gains	20,600	23,300	0	14,000
Less: trading loss relief against gains (note)	(0)	(23,300)	(0)	(0)
	20,600	0	0	14,000
Less: capital loss carried forward	(0)	(0)	(0)	(3,400)
	20,600	0	0	10,600
Less: annual exempt amount	(10,600)	(0)	(0)	(10,600)
Taxable gains	10,000	0	0	0

Note. Loss relief has been claimed against general income and gains for 2011/12 since this gives relief at the earliest date and at the highest rates of tax. No claim should be made to set the loss against general income in 2012/13 since this is already covered by the personal allowance for that year.

Trading loss memorandum

	£
Loss 2012/13	85,000
Less: used 2011/12 (income)	(54,700)
used 2011/12 (gains)	(23,300)
Available for c/f	7,000
Less: used 2013/14	(7,000)
Loss unused	0

15 Michael and Sean

Text references. Chapter 1 covers the overall function and purpose of taxation in a modern economy. Chapter 10 deals with trading losses.

Top tips. Remember that if a taxpayer claims loss relief against general income, the benefit of the personal allowance may be lost.

Easy marks. A few minutes thought should have enabled you to identify the points required for part (a). One mark usually indicates one point needs to be made so don't write more than one or two sentences for each part.

Examiner's comments. Part (a) was generally well answered, although candidates should note that where just one or two marks are available for a requirement then just a short sentence is required – not a detailed explanation. Not surprisingly, it was part (b) that caused the most problems in the exam paper. For Michael, the claims should have been fairly straightforward given that he only had one source of income for each year. However, some candidates were not even aware that a claim could be made against total income. For Sean, a few candidates suggested that the loss be carried forward despite the trade ceasing. In both cases, it was generally not appreciated that the most advantageous choice of loss relief claims would generally preserve the benefit of personal allowances.

Marking scheme

				Marks
(a)	(i)	Saving		1
	(ii)	Charitable support		1
	(iii)	Capital gains reliefs	1	
		Plant and machinery	1	
				2
(b)	**Michael**			
	Relief against total income		1	
	Claims		1	
	Rate of tax saved	– 2008/09	1	
		– 2009/10	1	
	Carry forward		1	
	Sean			
	Available loss		1	
	Terminal loss relief		1	
	Claims		1	
	Rates of tax saved		1½	
	Relief against total income		1½	
				11
				15

(a) (i) Saving is encouraged by offering individuals tax incentives such as income tax and capital gains tax exemptions on individual savings accounts and income tax relief on pension contributions.

(ii) Charitable support is encouraged by giving individuals income tax relief on donations made through the gift aid scheme or by payroll deduction.

(iii) Entrepreneurs are encouraged to build their own businesses through various capital gains tax reliefs such as entrepreneurs' relief.

Investment in plant and machinery is encouraged through capital allowances.

(b) **Michael**

The loss of £25,230 for 2011/12 can be claimed against general income for the three preceding years, under early years loss relief, earliest year first, since it is incurred in the first four years of trading.

The loss relief claim will therefore be £17,430 in 2008/09 and £(25,230 – 17,430) = £7,800 in 2009/10.

For 2008/09 this will waste Michael's personal allowance, with the balance of the claim of £(17,430 – 8,105) = £9,325 saving income tax at the basic rate of 20%.

For 2009/10 Michael has income of £(50,600 – 8,105 – 34,370) = £8,125 subject to income tax at the higher rate of 40%, so the claim of £7,800 will save tax at the higher rate.

Alternatively, Michael could have carried the trading loss forward against future trading profits, but the trading profit of £7,730 for 2012/13 is covered by the personal allowance, and there is no information regarding future trading profits.

Tutorial note

A claim for loss relief against general income for 2011/12 and/or 2010/11 is not possible since Michael does not have any income for either of these years.

Sean

The unused overlap profits brought forward are added to the loss for the year ended 31 December 2012, so the total loss for 2012/13 is £(23,100 + 3,600) = £26,700.

The whole of the loss can be claimed as a terminal since it is for the final 12 months of trading. The claim is against trading income for the year of the loss (2012/13 – nil) and the three preceding years, latest first.

The terminal loss claim will therefore be £3,700 in 2011/12, £18,900 in 2010/11 and £(26,700 – 3,700 – 18,900) = £4,100 in 2009/10.

The property business profits are sufficient to utilise Sean's personal allowance for each year, so the loss relief claims will save income tax at the basic rate of 20%.

Alternatively, Sean could have initially claimed loss relief against his general income for 2012/13 and/or 2011/12, but this would have wasted his personal allowance for either or both of those years.

16 Ae, Bee, Cae, Dee and Eu

Text references. Partnerships are covered in Chapter 11. Assessable trading income is dealt with in Chapter 9 and capital allowances are covered in Chapter 8.

Top tips. You must attempt each part of a multi-part question like this one to ensure you have a good chance of passing the exam.

Easy marks. Obtaining relief for overlap profits in part (c) was an easy mark.

Examiner's comments. This question was extremely well answered by the majority of candidates, many of whom scored maximum marks. One of the main problems in the answers of poorer candidates was not showing the appropriate tax years, thus losing a lot of marks throughout. The only common mistake was that in part (b) for the year of change, candidates often used an actual basis rather than the 12 months to the new accounting date.

			Marks
(a)	2010/11		1½
	2011/12		1
	2012/13	– Ae and Bee	1
		– Cae	1½
			5
(b)	(i) 2010/11		1
	2011/12		2
	2012/13		1
			4
	(ii) Overlap profits		1
(c)	2013/14	– Assessment	1
		– Capital allowances	½
	2014/15	– Assessment	1
		– Capital allowances	1½
		– Relief for overlap profits	1
			5
			15

(a) **Division of partnership profits for A, B and C**

	Total £	A £	B £	C £
y/e 30.6.11	54,000	27,000	27,000	–
y/e 30.6.12	66,000	33,000	33,000	–
y/e 30.6.13	87,000	29,000	29,000	29,000

Then allocate to tax years:
2010/11
A and B – First year
Actual basis 1.7.10 – 5.4.11

		A	B	C
9/12 x £27,000		20,250	20,250	–

2011/12
A and B – Second year

	A	B	C
First 12 months y/e 30.6.11	27,000	27,000	–

2012/13
A and B – Third year

	A	B
CYB y/e 30.6.12	33,000	33,000

C – First year
Actual basis 1.7.12 – 5.4.13

	C
9/12 x £29,000	21,750

(b)　(i)　**Change of accounting date for D**

	£	£
2010/11		
CYB y/e 5.4.11		32,880
2011/12 (year of change)		
Basis period is 12 months to new a/cting date – 31.7.11		
1.8.10 – 5.4.11		
8/12 × £32,880	21,920	
6.4.11 - 31.07.11	16,240	38,160
2012/13		
CYB y/e 31.7.12		54,120

　　(ii)　Overlap profits
　　　　　1.8.10 – 5.4.11
　　　　　8/12 × £32,880　　　　　　　　　　　　　　　　　　　21,920

(c)　**Cessation for E**

	£	£
2013/14		
CYB y/e 30.6.13 Trading income	62,775	
Less: CAs (W)	(1,575)	61,200
2014/15		
Cessation y/e 30.6.14 and p/e 30.09.14	72,000	
Trading income £(57,600 + 14,400)		
Less: CAs £(1,292 + 3,108)(W)	(4,400)	
Overlap profits	(19,800)	47,800

Working

	Main pool	Allowances
	£	£
y/e 30.6.13		
TWDV b/f	8,750	
WDA @ 18%	(1,575)	1,575
TWDV c/f	7,175	
y/e 30.6.14		
WDA @ 18%	(1,292)	1,292
TWDV c/f	5,883	
p/e 30.9.14		
Addition	2,400	
Disposal	(5,175)	
BA	3,108	3,108

17 Auy Man and Bim Men

> **Text references.** Residence is dealt with in Chapter 2. Adjustment of profit is covered in Chapter 7 and capital allowances in Chapter 8. Assessable trading income is dealt with in Chapter 9 and partnerships in Chapter 11. National insurance contributions are the subject of Chapter 12. VAT is covered in Chapters 26 and 27.
>
> **Top tips.** You need to look carefully at the CO_2 emissions of the motor cars to determine the capital allowances treatment. Remember that the detail on this is in the tax tables available in the exam.
>
> **Easy marks.** There were easy marks for the adjustment of profit in part (b) if you followed the instructions to start with the profit before taxation figure and indicated with a zero any items which did not require adjustment.
>
> **Examiner's comments.** This question was well answered, especially parts (b) and (c). In part (a) several candidates simply repeated the information contained within the question rather than explaining the 183 day rule and the substantial visits rule. There were generally no problems with part (b) although a number of candidates did not appreciate that they had to deduct the salary and interest on capital before allocating the balance of profits. Most candidates scored maximum marks for part (c). In part (d) the tax point was explained reasonably well, although some candidates wasted time by also giving details for the supply of goods. Some students struggled with the VAT calculation, assuming this to be much more complicated than it actually was. For 2 marks, all that was required was to select the output VAT of £25,600 and input VAT of £140 and £180 from the text, and then calculate the amount payable of £25,280. It was not necessary to calculate any VAT. The main problem as regards the VAT calculation using the flat rate scheme was that candidates incorrectly deducted input VAT.

Marking scheme

				Marks
(a)	Auy Man		1	
	Bim Men		1	
				2
(b)	**Trading profit**			
	Depreciation		½	
	Input VAT		½	
	Motor expenses		1	
	Entertaining employees		½	
	Appropriation of profit		½	
	Excessive salary		½	
	Deduction of capital allowances		½	
	Capital allowances	- Main pool	2	
		- Motor car [1]	1½	
		- Motor car [2]	2	
		- Special rate pool	1½	
		- First year allowance	1½	
	Trading income assessments			
	Salary		½	
	Interest on capital		1	
	Balance of profits		1	
				15
(c)	Auy Man		2	
	Bim Men		1	
				3
(d)	(i)	**Tax point**		
		Basic tax point	1	
		Payment received or invoice issued	1	
		Issue of invoice within 14 days	1	
				3

(ii) **VAT paid**
Output VAT and input VAT — 1
Calculation — 1
— 2

(iii) **Flat rate scheme**
Joining the scheme — 1
Continuing to use the scheme — 1½
VAT payable — 2
VAT saving — ½
— 5
— 30

(a) **Residence status**

Auy will be treated as resident in the United Kingdom for 2012/13 as she was present in the United Kingdom for 183 days or more. Bim will be treated as resident in the United Kingdom for 2012/13 as she has made substantial visits to the United Kingdom. Her visits have averaged 91 days or more over four consecutive tax years.

(b) **Adjusted trading profit for y/e 5 April 2013**

	£	£
Profit before taxation		80,562
Add: depreciation	3,400	
input VAT	0	
motor expenses £2,600 × 30%	780	
entertaining employees	0	
appropriation of profit: salary for Bim	4,000	
appropriation of profit: excessive salary for Auy's husband £(15,000 – 10,000)	5,000	
		13,180
		93,742
Less: capital allowances (W)		(13,742)
Tax adjusted trading profit		80,000

Working

Capital allowances y/e 5 April 2013

	£	Main pool £	Motor car [1] £	Motor car [2] £	Special rate pool £	Allow-ances £
TWDV b/f		3,100	18,000	14,000		
Additions						
Motor car [4]		14,200				
Motor car [5]					10,875	
		17,300				
Disposal						
Motor car [2]				(13,100)		
BA				(900) × 70%		630
WDA @ 18%		(3,114)				3,114
WDA @ 8%			(1,440) × 70%		(870)	1,878
Addition						
Motor car [3]	11,600					
FYA @ 100%	(11,600) × 70%					8,120
	0					
TWDV c/f		14,186	16,560		10,005	
Allowances						13,742

Motor car [1] and Motor car [5] have CO_2 emissions over 160 grams per kilometre and therefore qualify for writing down allowances at the rate of 8%. Motor car [1] is in a single asset pool because of private use by a partner. Motor car [5] is in the special pool because it is used wholly for business purposes.

Motor car [3] has CO_2 emissions of less than 110 grams per kilometre and therefore qualifies for the 100% first year allowance.

Motor car [4] has CO_2 emissions between 111 and 160 grams per kilometre, and therefore qualifies for writing down allowances at the rate of 18% as part of the main pool.

Trading income assessments 2012/13

	Total £	Auy Man £	Bim Men £
Salary	4,000	0	4,000
Interest £56,000/34,000 @ 5%	4,500	2,800	1,700
Balance (80:20)	71,500	57,200	14,300
	80,000	60,000	20,000

(c)   **Auy Man and Bim Men – national insurance contributions 2012/13**

Auy Man

	£
Main rate: £(42,475 – 7,605) = 34,870 @ 9%	3,138
Additional rate: £(60,000 – 42,475) = 17,525 @ 2%	351
	3,489

Bim Men

	£
Main rate only: £ (20,000 – 7,605) = 12,395 @ 9%	£1,116

(d)   (i)   **Tax point**

The basic tax point is the date when services are completed.

If an invoice is issued or payment received before the basic tax point, then this becomes the actual tax point.

If an invoice is issued within 14 days of the basic tax point, the invoice date will usually be the actual tax point.

(ii)   **VAT paid for the year ended 5 April 2013**

The partnership's output VAT is £25,600 and its total input VAT is £(180 + 140) = £320.

Therefore VAT of £25,280 (25,600 – 320) will have been paid to HM Revenue & Customs during the year ended 5 April 2013.

(iii)   **Flat rate scheme**

The partnership can join the flat rate scheme if its expected taxable turnover (excluding VAT) for the next 12 months does not exceed £150,000.

The partnership can continue to use the scheme until its total turnover (including VAT, but excluding sales of capital assets) for the previous year exceeds £230,000.

If the partnership had used the flat rate scheme throughout the year ended 5 April 2013 then it would have paid VAT of £(140,762 + 25,600) = £166,362 @ 14% = £23,291.

This is a saving of £(25,280 – 23,291) = £1,989 for the year.

18 Flick Pick

Text references. Employment income is covered in Chapter 3 and taxable benefits in Chapter 4. Taxable income is covered in Chapter 2. Partnerships are the subject of Chapter 11. Property income is dealt with in Chapter 6. National insurance contributions are in Chapter 12. Choice of accounting date is covered in Chapter 9, which also contains the rules on basis periods. VAT will be found in Chapters 26 and 27.

Top tips. In a multiple part question such as this, it is really important to attempt all the parts in order to gain a pass mark.

Easy marks. There were plenty of easy marks to be obtained in this question. The living accommodation benefit should have been familiar and the property income computation was straightforward. A quick look at the tax tables would have given the classes of national insurance contributions required for part (b). Part (d)(iii) might have looked a little unusual but was really a basic question on the tax point.

Examiner's comments. There were many very good answers to part (a). The aspects that caused problems were not appreciating that:

- When calculating Flick's share of the partnership profits, the capital allowances had to be deducted before allocating the profit.

- When calculating the property business profit, no deduction is given for the cost of replacement furniture when the wear and tear allowance is claimed.

There were many very good answers to part (b), but some candidates missed some very easy marks by explaining NIC in detail, but not actually answering the requirements of the question. In part (c), quite a few candidates appreciated that an accounting date of 30 April would result in overlap profits and that the basis period rules would be more complicated. Very few knew that the interval between earning profits and paying the related tax liability would be longer or that it would be easier to implement tax planning. In part (d), although it was disappointing to see a number of candidates deduct inputs when calculating VAT using the flat rate basis, the first requirement was otherwise generally answered very well. The second requirement caused a lot of confusion, with quite a few candidates discussing VAT registration – the correct answer was simply that voluntary VAT registration reduced the partnership's profits by the amount of VAT payable calculated in the first requirement. For the final requirement, quite a few candidates just explained the time of supply rules, without relating them to the information given in the question. It was clearly stated that an invoice was issued on the date of a film being screened – so the 14-day rule for issuing an invoice was irrelevant.

Marking scheme

			Marks
(a)	Salary		½
	Living accommodation	– Annual value	½
		– Additional benefit	2
		– Furniture	1
	Trading profit	– Profit share	2
		– Assessment	1
		– Capital allowances	2
	Property business profit	– Rent receivable	½
		– Council tax	½
		– Wear and tear allowance	1
		– Furniture	½
	Personal allowance		½
			12

				Marks
(b)	Class 1 NIC		1	
	Class 1A NIC		1	
	Class 2 NIC		1	
	Class 4 NIC		1	
				4
(c)	Interval		1	
	Tax planning		1	
	Basis period rules more complicated		1	
	Profit assessed in the year of cessation		1	
				4
(d)	(i)	Flat rate scheme	1	
		Normal basis	1	
		Conclusion	1	
				3
	(ii)	No recovery of VAT by customers	1	
		Possible need to absorb VAT	1	
		Conclusion	1	
				3
	(iii)	VAT period	1	
		Basic tax point	1	
		Deposit	1	
		Balance	1	
				4
				30

(a) **Flick Pick – Taxable income 2012/13**

			Non-savings income £
Employment income			
Salary			24,330
Living accommodation	– Annual value		4,600
	– Additional benefit (W1)		2,760
	– Furniture £9,400 × 20%		1,880
			33,570
Trading profit (W2)			8,220
Property income (W3)			5,940
Net income			47,730
Less personal allowance			(8,105)
Taxable income			39,625

Workings

1   *Living accommodation additional benefit*

	£
Market value	144,000
Less limit	(75,000)
	69,000
Additional benefit £69,000 × 4%	2,760

Tutorial note

Since the property was acquired more than 6 years before being provided to Flick, the market value at the date it was provided to her is used as the cost of providing the benefit, instead of the original cost.

2   *Trading profit*

First work out the capital allowances for the partnership.

	Motor car	Allowances @ 60%
	£	£
Purchase	18,750	
WDA @ 8% × 4/12	(500)	300
TWDV c/f	18,250	

Tutorial note

The partnership's motor car has CO_2 emissions over 160 g/km and therefore qualifies for writing allowance at the rate of 8%.

Flick's share of the partnership's trading profit for the period ended 30 April 2013 is then calculated as follows.

	£
Trading profit	29,700
Less capital allowances	(300)
	29,400
Less salary paid to Art £6,000 × 4/12	(2,000)
Profits available for profit sharing	27,400
Profit share for Flick £27,400 × 40%	10,960
Flick's trading income for 2012/13 £10,960 × 3/4	8,220

Tutorial note

Flick's basis period for 2012/13 is 1 January 2013 to 5 April 2013 since this is her first year of trading.

3   *Property business profit*

	£	£
Rent receivable £660 × 12		7,920
Less council tax	1,320	
wear and tear allowance £(7,920 – 1,320) × 10%	660	
Furniture	0	
		(1,980)
		5,940

Tutorial note

No deduction is available for replacement furniture where the wear and tear allowance is claimed.

(b)   3D Ltd will be responsible for paying class 1 NIC (both primary and secondary contributions) in respect of Flick's salary.

3D Ltd will be responsible for paying class 1A NIC in respect of Flick's taxable benefits.

Flick will be responsible for paying class 2 NIC in respect of her trading income.

Flick will be responsible for paying class 4 NIC in respect of her trading income.

(c)   **Advantages**

The interval between earning profits and paying the related tax liability will be 11 months longer. This can be particularly beneficial where profits are rising.

It will be possible to calculate taxable profits well in advance of the end of the tax year, making it much easier to implement tax planning and make pension contributions.

Disadvantages

The application of the basis period rules is more complicated.

The amount of profit assessed in the year of cessation could potentially be quite high as the basis period will be up to 23 months in length. Although overlap profits are deductible, these might be insignificant if the opening years' profits are low.

(d)   (i)   Using the flat rate scheme to calculate its VAT liability the partnership will have paid VAT of £(59,700 x 12%) = £7,164 for the quarter ended 31 March 2013.

If the partnership had used the normal basis it would have paid VAT of £(59,700 – 27,300 = 32,400 x 20/120) = £5,400.

It was therefore not beneficial to use the flat rate scheme as the additional cost of £(7,164 – 5,400) = £1,764 for the quarter would appear to outweigh the advantage of simplified VAT administration.

(ii)   The partnership's sales are all to members of the general public, who cannot recover the input VAT.

It may not therefore be possible to pass the output VAT on to customers in the prices charged. To the extent this is not possible the partnership would have had to absorb all or some of this amount itself as a cost.

It was therefore not beneficial for the partnership to have voluntarily registered for VAT from 1 January 2013. For the quarter ended 31 March 2013 voluntary registration reduced the partnership's profits by a maximum of £7,164 (£5,400 if the normal basis had been used).

(iii)   Output VAT must be accounted for according to the VAT period in which the supply is treated as being made. This is determined by the tax point.

The basic tax point is the date when the service is completed, which will be the date that a film is screened.

Where payment is received before the basic tax point, then this date becomes the actual tax point. The tax point for each 25% deposit is therefore the date that it is received.

Invoices are issued on the same day as the basic tax point, so this is the tax point for the balance of 75%.

19 Pi Casso

Text references. Chapter 17 covers self assessment and payment by individuals.

Top tips. Take care to start with the correct tax year. You need to realise that if you are paying tax for 2012/13 that the payments on account will be based on the previous year 2011/12. Take care when stating payment dates. Take the time to start correctly and then be methodical.

Easy marks. Parts (c) and (d) required you to write out the rules for filing returns and compliance check enquiries. These should be easy marks.

Examiner's comments. Part (a) caused the most problems, with the vast majority of candidates not being able to demonstrate how payments are calculated and paid under the self-assessment system. Class 2 national insurance contributions were often incorrectly included, whilst few candidates appreciated that a claim to reduce payments on account was possible. In part (b) most candidates appreciated that interest would be due, but very few mentioned the potential penalty that could be charged. It was disappointing that the self-assessment tax return submission dates were often not know in part (c). The same comment applies to part (d). Candidates often gave a long list of reasons why HMRC could make a compliance check enquiry on a return, but failed to mention that an enquiry might be on a completely random basis.

			Marks
(a)	Second payment on account for 2011/12	2	
	Balancing payment for 2011/12	2	
	Claim to reduce payments on account	1	
	Payments on account for 2012/13	1	
	Balancing payment for 2012/13	1	
	First payment on account for 2013/14	1	
			8
(b)	Interest	1	
	Penalty	1	
			2
(c)	Paper based return	1	
	Return filed online	1	
			2
(d)	Notification date	1	
	Random bases	1	
	Income/Deductions	1	
			3
			15

(a)

Due date	Tax year	Payment	£
31 July 2012	2011/12	Second payment on account (N1)	2,240
31 January 2013	2011/12	Balancing payment (N2)	5,490
31 January 2013	2012/13	First payment on account (N3)	1,860
31 July 2013	2012/13	Second payment on account	1,860
31 January 2014	2012/13	Balancing payment (N4)	Nil
31 January 2014	2013/14	First payment on account (N5)	1,860

Notes

(1) The second payment on account for 2011/12 is based on Pi's income tax and Class 4 NIC liability for 2010/11. It is therefore £2,240 ((3,240 + 1,240 = 4,480) × 50%).

(2) The balancing payment for 2011/12 is £5,490 (4,100 + 990 + 4,880) = £9,970 less the payments on account of £4,480 (£2,240 × 2)).

(3) Pi will make a claim to reduce her total payments on account for 2012/13 to £3,720 (2,730 + 990), so each payment will be £1,860 (3,720 × 50%).

(4) The balancing payment for 2012/13 is £Nil (3,720 less the payments on account of 3,720 (1,860 × 2)).

(5) The first payment on account for 2013/14 is based on Pi's income tax and Class 4 NIC liability for 2012/13. It is therefore £1,860 ((2,730 + 990 = 3,720) × 50%).

(b) (1) If Pi's payments on account for 2012/13 were reduced to nil, then she would be charged interest on the payments due of £1,860 from the relevant due date to the date of payment.

(2) A penalty of the difference between the reduced payment on account and the correct payment on account may be charged if the claim to reduce the payments on account to nil was made fraudulently or negligently.

(c) (1) Unless the return is issued after 31 July 2013, the latest date that Pi can submit a paper based self-assessment tax return for 2012/13 is 31 October 2013.

(2) Alternatively, Pi has until 31 January 2014 to file her self-assessment tax return for 2012/13 online.

(d) (1) If HMRC intend to make a compliance check enquiry on Pi's 2012/13 tax return they will have to notify her within twelve months of the actual filing date if the return was delivered on or before the due date.

(2) HMRC have the right to make a compliance check enquiry into the completeness and accuracy of any return and such an enquiry may be made on a completely random basis.

(3) However, compliance check enquiries are generally made because of a suspicion that income has been undeclared or because deductions have been incorrectly claimed.

20 Ernest Vader

Text references. Self assessment for individuals is covered in Chapter 17. Ethics are covered in Chapter 1.

Top tips. The number of marks for each part gives an indication of the scope of the answer required. Part (c) was only awarded 1 mark so should have been answered by a single sentence.

Easy marks. The calculation of interest in part (e) required very little technical knowledge – 2 easy marks.

Examiner's comments. This question was not well answered, with many candidates attempting it as their final question or omitting it altogether. In part (a) most candidates knew the difference between tax evasion and tax avoidance, but many failed to score an easy mark by not stating that the taxpayer's actions would be viewed as tax evasion. Part (b) caused problems for most candidates but a common sense approach would have gained most of the available marks. Unfortunately, far too many candidates instead just incorrectly explained that it would be necessary to inform HMRC themselves. In part (c) far too many candidates wrote at length about a compliance check enquiry rather than just stating that HMRC would issue a written information notice. The time limits in part (d) were often not known and most candidates were unaware of the use of a discovery assessment despite being given help in the wording of the requirement. There was little excuse for getting the interest calculation wrong in part (e) as candidates were given the tax liability, the due date, the payment date and the rate of interest.

Marking scheme

				Marks
(a)	Tax evasion		1	
	Tax avoidance		1	
	Non-disclosure of disposal		1	
				3
(b)	Professional judgement: standard of conduct		1	
	Advise disclosure		1	
	Obligation to report for money laundering		½	
	Cease to act and inform HMRC		½	
				3
(c)	Written information notice			1
(d)	Lack of sufficient information		1	
	Time limits		1	
				2
(e)	(i)	Interest period	1	
		Calculation	1	
				2
	(ii)	Maximum penalty	1	
		Link to behaviour	1	
		Actual penalty	1	
		Disclosure	1	
				4
				15

(a) **Tax evasion and tax avoidance**

Tax evasion is illegal and involves the reduction of tax liabilities by not providing information to which HMRC is entitled or providing HMRC with deliberately false information.

In contrast, tax avoidance involves the minimisation of tax liabilities by the use of any lawful means, although certain tax avoidance schemes must be disclosed to HMRC.

If Ernest makes no disclosure of the capital gain then this will be viewed as tax evasion as his tax liability for 2012/13 will be understated by £18,000.

(b) **Ethics**

The matter is one of professional judgement. A trainee Chartered Certified Accountant would be expected to act honestly and with integrity.

Ernest should therefore be advised to disclose details of the capital gain to HMRC.

If such disclosure is not made you would be obliged to report under the money laundering regulations and you should also consider ceasing to act for Ernest. In these circumstances you would be advised to notify HMRC that you no longer act for him although you would not need to provide any reason for this.

(c) **Obtaining information from taxpayer**

HMRC can request information from Ernest by issuing a written information notice.

(d) **Discovery assessment**

A discovery assessment can be raised because Ernest's self-assessment tax return did not contain sufficient information to make HMRC aware of the capital gain.

The normal time limit for making a discovery assessment is 4 years after the end of the tax year, but this is extended to 6 years if there has been careless understatement and 20 years if there has been deliberate understatement.

(e) (i) **Interest**

Interest will run from the end of the due date of 31 January 2014 to the payment date of 31 July 2014.

The interest charge will therefore be £18,000 × 3.0% × 6/12 = £270.

(ii) **Penalties**

The amount of penalty is based on the tax due but unpaid as a result of the failure to notify and the maximum penalty is 100% of that tax due.

However, the actual penalty will be linked to Ernest's behaviour.

Since Ernest would appear to have deliberately failed to notify HMRC of his capital gain, the actual penalty is likely to be 70% of the tax unpaid which is £18,000 × 70% = £12,600. This assumes that there is no attempt at concealment.

The penalty would have been substantially reduced if Ernest had disclosed the capital gain, especially if the disclosure had been unprompted by HMRC prior to discovery. The maximum reduction would be to 20% of the tax unpaid.

21 Aloi, Bon, Cherry and Dinah

Text references. Entrepreneurs' relief is dealt with in Chapter 15. Shares are covered in Chapter 16. Computing chargeable gains and the calculation of capital gains tax is the subject of Chapter 13.

Top tips. Par value means the face value of the shares. Aloi therefore had a cost of £50,000 for her first 50,000 £1 shares in Alphabet Ltd.

Easy marks. Make sure that you remember to deduct the annual exempt amount before computing the capital gains tax liability.

Examiner's comments. Answers to this question either tended to be very good or quite poor, with many candidates making the calculations far more complicated than they actually were. In part (a) many candidates simply reproduced the qualifying conditions for entrepreneurs' relief, without relating them to the information given for each of the three shareholders. In part (b) a number of candidates included taxable income as part of their calculations, and the annual exempt amount was often omitted. For the fourth shareholder, it should have been obvious that with sales proceeds of just £6,600 there would be no capital gains tax liability, yet the vast majority of candidates wasted time attempting to calculate a liability. Similarly, there was little awareness that the transfer on death was an exempt disposal.

Marking scheme

			Marks
(a)	Bon	1	
	Cherry	1	
	Dinah	1	
			3
(b)	**Aloi**		
	Alphabet Ltd – Disposal proceeds	½	
	– Cost	1	
	Investment property	½	
	Annual exempt amount	1	
	Capital gains tax	1	
	Bon		
	Deemed proceeds	1	
	Cost	1	
	Annual exempt amount	½	
	Capital gains tax	½	
	Cherry		
	Disposal proceeds	½	
	Cost	½	
	Annual exempt amount	½	
	Capital gains tax	2	
	Dinah		
	Sale of shares	1	
	Exempt disposal on death	½	
			12
			15

(a) Bon only acquired her shareholding and became a director on 1 February 2012, so the qualifying conditions were not met for one year prior to the date of disposal.

Cherry was not an officer or an employee of Alphabet Ltd.

Dinah's shareholding of 3% (3,000/100,000 × 100) is less than the minimum required holding of 5%.

(b) **Aloi – Capital gains tax (CGT) liability 2012/13**

Summary

	Gains £	CGT £
Gain qualifying for entrepreneurs' relief		
Ordinary shares in Alphabet Ltd		
Proceeds of sale (60,000 × £6)	360,000	
Less costs (50,000 + 18,600)	(68,600)	
Gain	291,400	
CGT @ 10% on £291,400		29,140
Gain not qualifying for entrepreneurs' relief		
Investment property	22,600	
Less: annual exempt amount (best use as saves tax @ 28%)	(10,600)	
Taxable gain	12,000	
CGT @ 28% on £12,000		3,360
Total CGT due		32,500

Bon – Capital gains tax (CGT) liability 2012/13

	£
Ordinary shares in XYZ plc	
Deemed proceeds of sale (10,000 × £7.12 (W1))	71,200
Less cost (W2)	(36,880)
Gain	34,320
Less: annual exempt amount	(10,600)
Taxable gain	23,720
CGT @ 28% on £23,720	6,642

Workings

1 The shares in XYZ plc are valued at 710 + ¼ × (718 – 710) = 712p. There are no recorded bargains on the date of the gift so the average bargain basis does not apply.

2 Following the takeover, Bon received 25,000 shares in XYZ plc. The cost of the original shareholding is passed on to the new shareholding so the cost attributable to the 10,000 shares sold is £36,880 (92,200 × 10,000/25,000).

Cherry – Capital gains tax (CGT) liability 2012/13

	£
Ordinary shares in Alphabet Ltd	
Disposal proceeds	72,000
Less cost	(23,900)
Gain	48,100
Less: annual exempt amount	(10,600)
Taxable gain	37,500
CGT @ 18% on £7,400 (W)	1,332
CGT @ 28% on £30,100	8,428
Total CGT liability	9,760

Working

Cherry's basic rate band limit is increased to £(34,370 + 3,400) = £37,770, of which £(37,770 – 30,370) = £7,400 is unused.

Dinah

There is no CGT liability on the sale of the XYZ plc shares as the gain of £5,000 (6,600 – (4,800 × 1,000/3,000)) is less than the annual exempt amount.

The transfer of the XYZ plc shares on Dinah's death is an exempt disposal.

22 Winston King

Marking scheme

				Marks
(a)	(i)	Resident in the UK	½	
		Ordinarily resident in the UK	½	
				1
	(ii)	Resident in the UK		1
(b)	(i)	Annual exempt amount	1	
		Unused basic rate band	½	
		Capital gains tax	1½	
				3
	(ii)	Freehold shop	½	
		Painting	½	
		Capital loss	1	
		Annual exempt amount	½	
		Capital gains tax	1½	
				4
(c)	(i)	Proceeds	½	
		Costs of disposal	½	
		Cost	½	
		Costs of acquisition	½	
		Indexation allowance	1	
				3
	(ii)	Freehold factory	1½	
		Freehold office building	1½	
				3
				15

(a) (i)   Individuals are subject to capital gains tax (CGT) on the disposal of chargeable assets during any tax year in which they are either resident or ordinarily resident in the UK.

     (ii) Companies are subject to corporation tax on gains from the disposal of chargeable assets if they are resident in the UK.

(b) (i) **Winston King – CGT liability 2012/13**

	£
Chargeable gain on painting	45,860
Less annual exempt amount	(10,600)
Taxable gain	35,260
CGT liability: £(34,370 – 21,770) = 12,600 @ 18%	2,268
£(35,260 – 12,600) = 22,660 @ 28%	6,345
	8,613

(ii) **Winston King – Revised CGT liability 2012/13**

	£
Gain qualifying for entrepreneurs' relief	
Gain on freehold shop £(140,000 – 80,000)	60,000
Gain not qualifying for entrepreneurs' relief	
Painting	45,860
Less allowable loss on warehouse £(102,000 – 88,000)	(14,000)
Net gain	31,860
Less annual exempt amount	(10,600)
Taxable gain	21,260
CGT liability: £60,000 @ 10%	6,000
£21,260 @ 28%	5,953
	11,953

Tutorial notes

(1) The capital loss on the sale of the freehold warehouse and the annual exempt amount are set against the chargeable gain from the sale of the painting as this saves CGT at the higher rate of 28%. Although the warehouse is being sold with the business, it was never actually used in the business, and so this aspect of the sale does not qualify for entrepreneurs' relief. If it had been used in the business, the loss of £14,000 would have been deducted from the gain on the shop to give a net gain on sale of the business of £46,000. CGT would then be charged on £46,000 at 10%.

(2) The unused basic rate tax band of £12,600 is set against the gain qualifying for entrepreneurs' relief of £60,000 even though this has no effect on the 10% tax rate.

(c) (i) **Wiki Ltd – Chargeable gain on disposal of warehouse**

	£	£
Disposal proceeds		312,000
Less incidental costs of disposal		(3,400)
		308,600
Less cost	171,000	
incidental costs of acquisition	2,200	
		(173,200)
		135,400
Less indexation allowance		
$\dfrac{247.1 - 178.2}{178.2}$ (= 0.387) × £173,200		(67,028)
Chargeable gain		68,372

(ii) **Freehold factory**

No rollover relief is available as the amount not reinvested of £(308,600 – 166,000) = £142,600 exceeds the chargeable gain.

The base cost of the factory will be £166,000.

Freehold office building

The net sale proceeds are not fully reinvested, and so £(308,600 – 296,000) = £12,600 of the chargeable gain cannot be rolled over.

The base cost of the office building will be £296,000 – £(68,372 – 12,600) = £240,228.

Tutorial note

Equivalent marks were awarded if the gross proceeds of £312,000 were used instead of the net proceeds of £308,600.

23 Jorge Jung

Text references. Chapter 13 deals with the basic computation of chargeable gains, including the annual exempt amount. Chapter 14 covers wasting assets, chattels, and the principal private residence exemption. Chapter 15 deals with business reliefs including gift relief.

Top tips. Remember that deemed periods of occupation for principal private residence relief must usually be preceded by a period of actual occupation and followed by a period of actual occupation.

Easy marks. The painting and the motor car were easy half marks. Don't forget to deduct the annual exempt amount for another easy half mark.

Examiner's comments This question was well answered, with only the principal private residence consistently causing problems. However, quite a few candidates wasted time by calculating the taxpayer's tax liability when the requirement was to just calculate the taxable gains. The easiest approach to the principal private residence exemption was to start with the total period of ownership and then to deduct the exempt periods. Most of these were straightforward, being the periods of actual occupation, any period up to 36 months, working elsewhere in the UK up to 48 months, and the final 36 months of ownership. The only difficult aspect was a period working overseas which was not exempt as it was not followed by a period of actual occupation. The easy half-mark for deducting the annual exempt amount was often missed.

	Marks
House	
Proceeds	½
Cost	½
Period of exemption	3
Principal private residence exemption	1
Letting exemption	1
Copyright	
Proceeds	½
Cost	1½
Painting	½
Motor car	½
Land	
Proceeds	½
Cost – probate value taken over on transfer from spouse	1
Apportionment of cost	1
	Marks
Shares	
Deemed proceeds	1
Cost	½
Gift relief	1½
Annual exempt amount	½
	15

Jorge Jung – Taxable gains computation 2012/13

	£
House (W1)	0
Copyright (W4)	2,600
Painting (W5) – exempt as proceeds and cost £6,000 or less	0
Motor car (W6) – exempt asset so loss not allowable	0
Land (W7)	71,760
Ordinary shares in Futuristic Ltd (W8)	13,700
Chargeable gains	88,060
Less: annual exempt amount	(10,600)
Taxable gains	77,460

Workings

1   *House*

	£
Proceeds	308,000
Less: cost	(98,000)
Gain	210,000
Less: principal private residence exemption (W2)	(188,000)
letting exemption (W3)	(22,000)
Gain after exemptions	0

2   *Principal private residence exemption*

	Exempt months	Chargeable months	Total Months
Actual occupation	16		16
Deemed occupation – up to 3 years any reason	18		18
Deemed occupation – any time employed overseas	24		24
Actual occupation	11		11
Deemed occupation – up to 4 years working elsewhere in UK	30		30
Deemed occupation – up to 3 years any reason balance (36 – 18) = 18, (22 – 18) = 4 chargeable	18	4	22
Deemed occupation – up to 4 years working elsewhere in UK balance (48 – 30) = 18, (26 – 18) = 8 chargeable	18	8	26
Actual occupation	17		17
Working overseas (12 - [36 – 21 – 13] = 10 chargeable		10	10
Last 36 months – always treated as period of occupation	36	—	36
Totals	188	22	210

Principal private residence exemption £210,000 × 188/210	£188,000

Tutorial note

In calculating the principal private residence exemption, any periods of absence while working overseas, a maximum of four years absence while working elsewhere in the UK, and a maximum of three years absence for any reason are treated as deemed occupation, usually provided that they are preceded and followed by a period of actual occupation. The second period working overseas is therefore not a period of deemed occupation as it was not followed by a period of actual occupation.

Alternative approach

An alternative approach, suggested as the easiest by the examiner, is to calculate the chargeable months as follows:

Total period of ownership		210
Less: Actual occupation (16 + 11 + 17)		(44)
Deemed occupation	- any reason up to 3 years	(36)
	- employed overseas without limit	(24)
	- working in UK up to 4 years	(48)
Last 36 months - always treated as period of occupation		(36)
Chargeable months		22

3   *Letting exemption*

Lowest of:

(i)	Gain in letting period £210,000 × 22/210		£22,000
(ii)	Gain exempt under PPR (W2)		£188,000
(iii)	Maximum exemption		£40,000

Therefore letting exemption is   £22,000

4   *Copyright*

	£
Proceeds	8,200
Less cost: £7,000 × 8/10 (N)	(5,600)
Gain	2,600

Tutorial note

The copyright is a wasting asset. The cost of £7,000 must therefore be depreciated based on an unexpired life of ten years at the date of acquisition and an unexpired life of eight years at the date of disposal.

5   *Painting*

Non-wasting chattel. Gain is exempt as gross sale proceeds are £6,000 or less.

6   *Motor car*

Exempt asset for capital gains tax so loss of £(14,600 − 10,700) = £3,900 is not allowable.

7   *Land*

	£
Proceeds	92,000
Less: cost £28,600 (N) × $\dfrac{92,000}{92,000 + 38,000}$	(20,240)
Gain	71,760

Tutorial note

The cost of the land is £28,600 which is the value when Jorge's father-in-law died. Jorge would have taken over this cost when his wife transferred the land to him.

8   *Ordinary shares in Futuristic Ltd*

	£
Deemed proceeds – market value (N)	64,800
Less: cost	(26,300)
Gain	38,500
Less: gift relief – balancing figure £(38,500 – 13,700)	(24,800)
Gain chargeable – excess of actual proceeds over cost £(40,000 – 26,300)	13,700

Jorge and his sister are connected persons and therefore the market value of the ordinary shares in Futuristic Ltd is used.

24 Nim and Mae

Text references. Chapters 13 to 16 deal with the computation of chargeable gains.

Top tips. Questions may be set about spouses or civil partners. Transfers between these are on a no gain/ no loss basis.

Easy marks. Remembering to deduct the annual exempt amount for each taxpayer and applying the rate of tax should have been 2 easy marks.

Examiner's comments. For the husband, quite a few candidates surprisingly had problems with the valuation rules for quoted shares. It was also not always appreciated that the transfer between spouses and the sale of the UK Government securities were respectively at no gain, no loss, and exempt. Candidates thus wasted time performing unnecessary calculations. Many candidates had difficulty with the cost of the quoted shares disposed of, and they incorrectly included the purchase within the following 30 days as part of the share pool. The restriction of the brought forward capital losses so that chargeable gains were reduced to the amount of the annual exempt amount was often missed. For the wife, many candidates treated the private portion of the principal private residence as taxable rather than the business portion. The investment property included within the disposal of the business was sometimes treated as exempt from CGT and sometimes entrepreneurs' relief was claimed in respect of it. Only a minority of candidates correctly calculate the cost of the wasting asset.

Marking scheme

		Marks
Nim Lom		
Kapook plc	Deemed proceeds	2
	Cost	1
	Share pool	2
Jooba Ltd		1
Antique table		1½
UK Government securities		½
Capital losses brought forward		1
Annual exempt amount		½
Capital losses carried forward		½
Mae Lom		
Jooba Ltd	Proceeds	½
	Cost	1
House	Proceeds	½
	Cost	½
	Exemption	1
Business	Goodwill	½
	Office building	½
	Investment property	½
		Marks
Copyright	Proceeds	½
	Cost	1½
Capital losses brought forward		½
Annual exempt amount		½
Capital gains tax		2
		20

Nim Lom – CGT liability 2012/13

	£	£
Ordinary shares in Kapook plc		
Deemed proceeds (10,000 × £3.70) (W1)	37,000	
Less: cost (W2)	(23,400)	
		13,600
Ordinary shares in Jooba Ltd (no gain, no loss transfer between spouses)		–
Antique table (W3)		3,500
UK Government securities (exempt)		–
Chargeable gains		17,100
Less: losses b/f (W4)		(6,500)
Net chargeable gains		10,600
Less: annual exempt amount		(10,600)
Taxable gains		Nil

Nim therefore has a <u>nil</u> liability to capital gains tax in 2012/13 and capital losses carried forward of £(16,200 – 6,500) = <u>£9,700</u>.

Workings

1   The shares in Kapook plc are valued at the lower of:

   (a)   370 + ¼ × (390 – 370) = 375;

   (b) $\dfrac{360 + 380}{2}$ = 370

   ie 370.

2   The disposal is first matched against the purchase on 24 July 2012 (this is within the following 30 days) and then against the shares in the share pool. The cost of the shares disposed of is, therefore, £23,400 (5,800 + 17,600).

Share pool	*No. of shares*	*Cost*
	£	£
Purchase 19 February 2002	8,000	16,200
Purchase 6 June 2007	6,000	14,600
	14,000	30,800
Disposal 20 July 2012 £30,800 × 8,000/14,000	(8,000)	(17,600)
Balance c/f	6,000	13,200

3   The antique table is a non-wasting chattel.

	£
Proceeds	8,700
Less cost	(5,200)
Gain	3,500

The maximum gain is 5/3 × £(8,700 – 6,000) = £4,500. The chargeable gain is the lower of £3,500 and £4,500, so it is £3,500.

4   The set off of the brought forward capital losses is restricted to £6,500 (17,100 – 10,600) so that chargeable gains are reduced to the amount of the annual exempt amount.

Mae Lom – CGT liability 2012/13

	£	Gains qualifying for entrepreneurs' relief £	Gains not qualifying for entrepreneurs' relief £
Ordinary shares in Jooba Ltd			
Disposal proceeds	30,400		
Less: cost £16,000 × 2,000/5,000 (N1)	(6,400)		
			24,000
House			
Disposal proceeds	186,000		
Less: cost	(122,000)		
	64,000		
Less: principal private residence exemption (W)	(56,000)		
			8,000
Business			
Goodwill	80,000		
Freehold office building	136,000		
		216,000	
Investment property (N2)		_____	34,000
Copyright			
Disposal proceeds	9,600		
Less: cost £10,000 × 15/20 (N3)	(7,500)		
			2,100
Chargeable gains			68,100
Less: losses b/f (best use)			(8,500)
Net chargeable gains			59,600
Less: annual exempt amount (best use)		_____	(10,600)
Taxable gains		216,000	49,000
Capital gains tax @ 10%/28% (N4)		21,600	13,720
Capital gains tax liability 2012/13 £(21,600 + 13,720)			35,320

Working

One of the eight rooms in Mae's house was always used exclusively for business purposes, so the principal private residence exemption is restricted to £(64,000 × 7/8) = £56,000.

Notes

1   Nim's original cost is used in calculating the capital gain on the disposal of the shares in Jooba Ltd because the transfer between the spouses was on a no gain/no loss basis.

2   The investment property does not qualify for entrepreneurs' relief because it was never used for business purposes.

3   The copyright is a wasting asset. The cost of £10,000 must therefore be depreciated based on an unexpired life of 20 years at the date of acquisition and an unexpired life of 15 years at the date of disposal.

4   Mae's taxable income plus the gains qualifying for entrepreneurs' relief use up her basic rate band, so the gains not qualifying for entrepreneurs' relief are taxable at 28%.

25 Amanda, Bo and Charles

> **Text references.** The calculation of chargeable gains for individuals is covered in Chapter 13. Business reliefs are in Chapter 15 and principal private residence relief is in Chapter 14.
>
> **Top tips.** You were asked to state the chargeable gain for each taxpayer – this is the gain before the annual exempt amount and so you should not have wasted time by deducting the exempt amount. Also note that in the first two parts of the question, entrepreneurs' relief was to be ignored.
>
> **Easy marks.** There were easy marks to be gained by calculating the gains before reliefs were applied.
>
> **Examiner's comments.** This question was not as well answered as would have been expected given that it was effectively three short separate questions on reasonably straightforward areas of capital gains tax. Base costs were often not shown despite these being required in parts (a) and (b). In part (a) far too many candidates treated this as one disposal rather than dealing with each asset separately. In the second section only a few candidates appreciated that incorporation relief was restricted according to the proportion of cash consideration to total consideration. Part (b) was reasonably well answered, although few candidates could correctly calculate the revised base cost following the restriction of holdover relief in the second section. Although there were some very good answers to part (c), far too many candidates had problems calculating the principal private residence exemption, and often lost marks by not showing detailed workings. Even when the correct exemption was calculated this was often shown as the amount chargeable rather than the exempt amount. In the second section it was not always appreciated that letting relief was available.

Marking scheme

				Marks
(a)	(i)	Goodwill gain	1	
		Freehold shop gain	1	
		Incorporation relief	1	
		Base cost of shares	1	
				4
	(ii)	Gain chargeable – explanation	1	
		– calculation	1	
		Base cost of shares	1	
				3
(b)	(i)	Gain	1	
		Gift relief	1	
		Base cost of shares	1	
				3
	(ii)	Gain chargeable	1	
		Base cost of shares	1	
				2
(c)	(i)	Gain	1	
		Period of exemption	3	
		PPR relief	1	
				5
	(ii)	Letting relief exemption	2	
		Revised gain	1	
				3
				20

(a) (i) **Amanda Moon: full incorporation relief**

	£	£
Proceeds of goodwill	90,000	
Less: cost	(nil)	90,000
Proceeds of shop	165,000	
Less: cost	(120,000)	45,000
Gains		135,000

Note. The net current assets are not chargeable assets and therefore are not part of the computation.

Incorporation relief will apply to the whole of the gains because:

- the business is transferred as a going concern
- all its assets (other than cash) are transferred
- the consideration is wholly in shares.

Therefore Amanda will not have any chargeable gains in 2012/13.

The base cost of her 300,000 £1 shares will be £(300,000 – 135,000) = £165,000.

(ii) **Amanda Moon: partial incorporation relief**

If Amanda takes 200,000 £1 shares and £100,000 in cash, the following partial incorporation relief will apply:

$$\text{Gain} \times \frac{\text{Value of shares received from the company}}{\text{Total value of consideration from the company}}$$

$$£135,000 \times \frac{£200,000}{£300,000} = £90,000$$

Amanda's chargeable gains in 2012/13 will therefore be £(135,000 – 90,000) = £45,000.

The base cost of her 200,000 £1 shares will be £(200,000 – 90,000) = £110,000.

(b) (i) **Bo Neptune: full gift relief**

	£
MV of shares	210,000
Less: cost	(94,000)
Gain	116,000

Gift relief will apply to the whole of the gain because the shares are qualifying business assets (unquoted trading company shares) and there is no consideration paid for the disposal.

Therefore Bo will not have a chargeable gain in 2012/13.

The base cost of the shares for Bo's son will be £(210,000 – 116,000) = £94,000.

(ii) **Bo Neptune: partial gift relief**

If Bo's son paid £160,000 for the shares, this is a sale at an undervalue and partial gift relief will be available. The part of the gain equal to the excess of actual consideration over actual cost is chargeable immediately and only the balance of the gain is deferred.

Bo's chargeable gain in 2012/13 will therefore be £(160,000 – 94,000) = £66,000. The remainder of the gain of £(116,000 – 66,000) = £50,000 will be deferred by gift relief.

The base cost of the shares for Bo's son will be £(210,000 – 50,000) = £160,000.

(c) (i) **Charles Orion: principal private residence relief**

		£
Sale proceeds		282,000
Less: cost		(110,000)
Gain		172,000
Less: PPR relief (W)		
$\dfrac{90}{144} \times £172,000$		(107,500)
Chargeable gain		64,500

Working

Period	Total months	Exempt months	Chargeable months
1.10.00 – 31.3.02 (occupied)	18	18	0
1.4.02 – 31.3.05 (see below)	36	36	0
1.4.05 – 30.9.09 (absent)	54	0	54
1.10.09 – 30.9.12 (last 36 months)	36	36	0
	144	90	54

During the period 1.4.02 and 31.3.05 (three years' absence for any reason), Charles is deemed to be resident in the property because he actually occupies the property both before and after the period of absence.

(ii) **Charles Orion: principal private residence relief and letting relief**

If Charles had rented out the house between 1 April 2002 and 31 December 2010, he would be entitled to letting relief in respect of the period of letting not covered by the main principal private resident relief (ie 54 months). This is the lowest of:

Gain exempt under PPR rules: $\dfrac{90}{144} \times £172,000$	£107,500
Gain attributable to letting: $\dfrac{54}{144} \times £172,000$	£64,500
£40,000 (maximum)	£40,000

The letting relief is therefore £40,000 and the chargeable gain is:

	£
Gain	172,000
Less: PPR relief	(107,500)
Less: letting relief	(40,000)
Chargeable gain	24,500

26 Naomi

Text references. Chapter 18 covers the inheritance tax examinable in F6.

Top tips. Deal with each transfer of value in date order. The question helpfully sets out how you should examine the transfers ie looking at the IHT implications during the donor's lifetime and then re-examining the effect of the donor's death.

Easy marks. There were easy marks for explaining the annual exemption and the spouse exemption.

Marking scheme

		Marks
(a)	*6 May each year*	
	Annual exemptions	1
	15 August 2004	
	Transfer of value	½
	Chargeable lifetime transfer	½
	Nil rate band available	½
	IHT on balance @ 20%	½
	12 September 2008	
	Transfer of value	1
	Potentially exempt transfer	½
	14 February 2011	
	Transfer of value	½
	Chargeable lifetime transfer	½
	Nil rate band available	½
	IHT on balance @ 20/80	½
	Gross transfer	½
		7
(b)	*6 May each year*	
	Remains exempt	½
	15 August 2004	
	Death more than 7 years of transfer - no additional tax chargeable	½
	No repayment of lifetime IHT	½
	12 September 2008	
	Transfer of value at date of gift	½
	Potentially exempt transfer becomes chargeable	½
	Nil rate band available	½
	IHT on balance @ 40%	½
	Taper relief	½
	14 February 2011	
	Transfer of value at date of gift	½
	Nil rate band available	½
	IHT on balance @ 40%	½
	Deduct lifetime tax	½
		6
(c)	Spouse exemption	½
	Residue chargeable	½
	Nil rate band available	½
	IHT @ 40%	½
		2
		15

(a) **IHT implications of lifetime gifts by Naomi**

6 May each year

The gift of quoted shares worth £3,000 on 6 May each year will use the annual exemption for the tax year starting on 6 April in that year.

15 August 2004

There is a transfer of value for inheritance tax of £313,000 as a gift is a gratuitous disposition which results in a diminution in the value of the donor's estate of this amount

This is a chargeable lifetime transfer because it is not an exempt transfer and not a transfer to another individual.

The nil rate band available is £263,000 because the donor did not make any chargeable transfers in the seven years before 15 August 2004 (transfers after 15 August 1997).

The inheritance tax payable on this transfer is calculated as follows:

			£
Gross transfer of value			313,000
			£
IHT	£263,000	× 0% =	Nil
	£ 50,000	× 20% =	10,000
	£313,000		10,000

12 September 2008

There is a transfer of value for inheritance tax as a gift is a gratuitous disposition which results in a diminution in the value of the donor's estate. This diminution is:

	£
Value of shares held before gift	50,000
Value of shares held after gift	(4,000)
Transfer of value	46,000

This is potentially exempt transfer because it is not an exempt transfer but it is a transfer to another individual. A potentially exempt transfer is exempt during the lifetime of the donor so there is no lifetime tax payable.

14 February 2011

There is a transfer of value for inheritance tax as a gift is a gratuitous disposition which results in a diminution in the value of the donor's estate. The diminution in value is the value of the house plus the lifetime inheritance tax that Naomi agrees to pay.

This is a chargeable lifetime transfer because it is not an exempt transfer and not a transfer to another individual.

There was a lifetime transfer of value of £313,000 in seven years before 14 February 2011 (transfers after 14 February 2004) so the nil rate band available was £(325,000 – 313,000) = £12,000.

The inheritance tax payable on this transfer is calculated as follows:

			£
Net transfer of value			82,000
			£
IHT	£12,000	× 0% =	Nil
	£ 70,000	× 20/80 =	17,500
	£82,000		17,500

The gross transfer is £(82,000 + 17,500) = £99,500.

Check

IHT	£12,000	× 0% =	Nil
	£ 87,500	× 20% =	17,500
	£99,500		17,500

(b) **IHT implications of Naomi's death on lifetime gifts**

6 May each year

These transfers remain exempt and there are no implications of Naomi's death on them.

15 August 2004

There is no additional tax charge on this transfer because the donor died more than seven years from making it.

There is no repayment of lifetime inheritance tax.

12 September 2008

This potentially exempt transfer becomes chargeable because of the donor's death within seven years of making it.

The transfer of value is £46,000 which was the diminution in value of the donor's estate at the date of the transfer. The subsequent sale does not affect this value.

There was a lifetime transfer of value of £313,000 in seven years before 12 September 2008 (transfers after 12 September 2001) so the nil rate band available is £(325,000 – 313,000) = £12,000.

The inheritance tax payable on this transfer is calculated as follows:

				£
Gross transfer of value				46,000
				£
IHT	£12,000	× 0% =		Nil
	£ 34,000	× 40% =		13,600
	£46,000			13,600
	Less taper relief @ 40% (death between 4 and 5 years after transfer)			(5,440)
IHT payable				8,160

14 February 2011

Additional tax is payable on this chargeable lifetime transfer because the donor died within seven years of making it.

The gross transfer of value is £99,500. The increase in value of the house at the date of the donor's death is not subject to inheritance tax.

There were lifetime transfers of value of £313,000 and £46,000 in seven years before 14 February 2011 (transfers after 14 February 2004) so the nil rate band of £325,000 is completely used up.

The inheritance tax payable on this transfer is calculated as follows:

		£
Gross transfer of value		99,500
IHT	£99,500 × 40% =	39,800
	Less: lifetime tax paid	(17,500)
Additional death tax		22,300

There is no taper relief because the donor died within three years of making the transfer.

(c) **Inheritance tax implications of the terms of Naomi's Will**

There is no inheritance tax on legacy of £250,000 given to Robert under Naomi's Will because of the spouse exemption.

The residue of the estate is chargeable to IHT as it a transfer of value to another individual.

There were lifetime transfers of value of £46,000 and £99,500 in seven years before 12 October 2012 (transfers after 12 October 2005) so the nil rate band available is £(325,000 – 46,000 – 99,500) = £179,500.

The inheritance tax payable on this transfer is calculated as follows:

		£
Gross transfer of value £(550,000 – 250,000)		300,000
IHT	£179,500 × 0% =	Nil
	£120,500 × 40% =	48,200
	£300,000	48,200

27 Ning Gao

Text references. Inheritance tax is covered in Chapter 18.

Top tips. In part (b) (ii) it was important to deal with the situation if Ning Gao lived for another six years and also if she lived for another seven years. You should have spotted that the gift to her son was a potentially exempt transfer which would become fully exempt once she survived seven years.

Easy marks. The death estate was quite straightforward as long as you did not confuse the exemptions for income tax and capital gains tax on certain investments with the inheritance tax position.

Examiner's comments. Part (a) was well answered, with candidates being given credit for their treatment of the PETs even if this was included in part (b). Part (b) was also well answered, although a number of candidates deducted the endowment mortgage (it would have been repaid upon death by the life assurance element of the mortgage) and the promise to pay a nephew's legal fee (not deductible being purely gratuitous). Somewhat surprisingly, there was often little knowledge of who was responsible for paying the tax – many candidates stated that it was the beneficiaries (or even the deceased!), rather than the personal representatives. The effect of living for another six years or another seven years was often not understood – the difference being that after seven years all the PETs would become exempt, thus increasing the available nil rate band. Too many candidates discussed taper relief despite this having no impact on the tax payable in respect of the estate.

Marking scheme

				Marks
(a)		Husband's nil rate band	1	
		Total nil rate band	1	
		PET on 7 November 2012	1	
		PET on 14 August 2002	1	
				4
(b)	(i)	Property one	½	
		Repayment mortgage	½	
		Property two	½	
		Endowment mortgage	½	
		Motor cars	½	
		Investments	1	
		Bank loan	½	
		Legal fees	1	
		IHT liability	1	
		Payment responsibility	1	
				7
	(ii)	Live for more than six years	1	
		Live for more than seven years	1	
				2
(c)		Exemption	1	
		Normal expenditure	½	
		Standard of living unaffected	½	
				2
				15

(a) Ning's personal representatives could claim her deceased husband's unused nil rate band of £325,000 x 70% = £227,500.

The total amount of nil rate band is therefore £(325,000 + 227,500) = £552,500.

The potentially exempt transfer on 7 November 2012 will utilise £220,000 of the nil rate band, so only £(552,500 – 220,000) = £332,500 is available against the death estate.

The potentially exempt transfer on 14 August 2002 is exempt from inheritance tax as it was made more than seven years before 20 March 2013.

(b) (i) **Ning Gao – Inheritance tax (IHT) on death estate 20 March 2013**

	£	£
Property one	674,000	
Less repayment mortgage	(160,000)	
		514,000
Property two		442,000
Motor cars		172,000
Investments £(47,000 + 36,000 + 69,000)		152,000
Gross estate		1,280,000
Less bank loan	22,400	
nephew's legal fees	0	
		(22,400)
Net estate		1,257,600
£332,500 @ 0%		0
£925,100 @ 40%		370,040
Inheritance tax liability		370,040

The personal representatives of Ning Gao's estate will be responsible for paying the inheritance tax.

Tutorial notes

1   There is no deduction in respect of the endowment mortgage as this will be repaid upon death by the life assurance element of the mortgage.

2   The promise to pay the nephew's legal fee is not deductible as it is purely gratuitous (not made for valuable consideration).

(ii) If Ning were to live for another six years until 20 March 2019 then the inheritance tax payable in respect of her estate would not alter, as the potentially exempt transfer on 7 November 2012 will still be made within the previous seven years.

If Ning were to live for another seven years until 20 March 2020 then the potentially exempt transfer will become exempt, and the inheritance tax payable in respect of her estate would therefore decrease by £220,000 @ 40% = £88,000.

(c) A lifetime transfer of value made out of income may be exempt under the normal expenditure out of income exemption.

The transfer of value must be part of the normal expenditure of the donor (regular payments, rather than a single gift).

The transfer must leave the donor with sufficient income to maintain her usual standard of living.

28 Artem

Text references. Chapter 18 covers the inheritance tax examinable in F6.

Top tips. Remember that potentially exempt transfers are treated as exempt during the donor's lifetime and will be exempt if the donor survives 7 years from making the gift.

Easy marks. There were easy marks for spotting various exemptions

Marks

(a) *10 December 2004*

Annual exemptions x 2	½
Potentially exempt transfer	½

17 January 2009

Annual exemptions x 2	½
Chargeable lifetime transfer	½
Nil rate band available	½
IHT on balance @ 20/80	½
Gross transfer	½

15 February 2009

Small gift exemption	½

18 August 2009

Annual exemption	½
Potentially exempt transfer	½

17 June 2010

Annual exemption	½
Chargeable lifetime transfer	½
Nil rate band available	½
IHT on balance @ 20%	½

1 August 2011

Marriage exemption	½
Annual exemption	½
Potentially exempt transfer	½

5 September 2011

Spouse exemption	½

9

(b) *10 December 2004*

Exempt as more than 7 years before death	½

17 January 2009

Within nil rate band at death	½

18 August 2009

Potentially exempt transfer now chargeable	½
Nil rate band available	½
IHT on balance @ 40%	½
Taper relief	½

17 June 2010

Nil rate band exceeded	½
IHT @ 40%	½
Lifetime tax deducted	½

1 August 2011

Potentially exempt transfer now chargeable	½
Nil rate band exceeded	½
IHT @ 40%	½

6

15

(a) **Lifetime inheritance tax implications**

10 December 2004

The first £6,000 of this transfer is an exempt transfer because of the annual exemptions for 2004/05 and 2003/04.

The remaining £(65,000 – 6,000) = £59,000 is a potentially exempt transfer as it is a gift to an individual. This is treated as an exempt transfer during Artem's life.

17 January 2009

The first £6,000 of this transfer is an exempt transfer because of the annual exemptions for 2008/09 and 2007/08.

The remaining £(323,000 – 6,000) = £317,000 is a chargeable lifetime transfer because it is not a transfer to another individual.

This is the first chargeable transfer that Artem makes and so the nil rate band is available in full.

The inheritance tax on this transfer is:

				£
Net transfer of value (Artem pays IHT)				317,000
				£
IHT	£312,000	× 0% =		Nil
	£ 5,000	× 20/80 =		1,250
	£317,000			1,250

The gross transfer of value for accumulation is £(317,000 + 1,250) = £318,250.

Check

IHT	£312,000	× 0% =		Nil
	£ 6,250	× 20% =		1,250
	£ 318,250			1,250

15 February 2009

The gift to the nephew is exempt as a small gift.

18 August 2009

The first £3,000 of this transfer is an exempt transfer because of the annual exemption for 2009/10.

The remaining £(46,000 – 3,000) = £43,000 is a potentially exempt transfer as it is a gift to an individual. This is treated as an exempt transfer during Artem's life.

17 June 2010

The first £3,000 of this transfer is an exempt transfer because of the annual exemption for 2010/11.

The remaining £(103,000 – 3,000) = £100,000 is a chargeable lifetime transfer because it is not a transfer to another individual.

There was a lifetime transfer of value of £318,250 in seven years before 17 June 2010 (transfers after 17 June 2003) so the nil rate band available was £(325,000 – 318,250) = £6,750.

The inheritance tax on this transfer is:

				£
Gross transfer of value (Trustees pay tax)				100,000
				£
IHT	£6,750	× 0% =		Nil
	£ 93,250	× 20% =		18,650
	£100,000			18,650

1 August 2011

The first £2,500 of this gift is exempt under the marriage exemption as a transfer from a remoter ancestor. The next £3,000 of this transfer is an exempt transfer because of the annual exemption for 2011/12.

The remaining £(66,000 – 2,500 – 3,000) = £60,500 is a potentially exempt transfer as it is a gift to an individual. This is treated as an exempt transfer during Artem's life.

5 September 2011

The gift to Artem's wife is an exempt transfer under the spouse exemption.

(b) **Death inheritance tax implications**

10 December 2004

The potentially exempt transfer of £59,000 is exempt because Artem died more than 7 years after making it.

17 January 2009

The gross chargeable lifetime transfer of £318,250 was made within 7 years before Artem's death and so additional inheritance tax might be payable.

However, the transfer is now covered by the nil rate band at the date of Artem's death of £325,000.

18 August 2009

The potentially exempt transfer of £43,000 is chargeable transfer because it was made within the 7 years before Artem's death.

There was a lifetime transfer of value of £318,250 in seven years before 18 August 2009 (transfers after 18 August 2002) so the nil rate band available is £(325,000 − 318,250) = £6,750.

The inheritance tax on this transfer is:

	£
Gross transfer of value	43,000

IHT	£6,750	× 0% =	Nil
	£36,250	× 40% =	14,500
	£43,000		14,500
Less: taper relief (3 to 4 years) @ 20%			(2,900)
Death tax payable			11,600

17 June 2010

The chargeable transfer of £100,000 was made within 7 years before Artem's death and so additional inheritance tax might be payable.

Lifetime transfers of value of £318,250 and £43,000 were made in seven years before 17 June 2010 (transfers after 17 June 2003) which exceed the nil rate band on death of £325,000.

The inheritance tax on this transfer is:

	£
Gross transfer of value	100,000

IHT	£100,000	× 40% =	40,000
Less: lifetime IHT paid			(18,650)
Death tax payable			21,350

There is no taper relief as Artem died within 3 years of making this transfer.

1 August 2011

The potentially exempt transfer of £60,500 is chargeable transfer because it was made within the 7 years before Artem's death.

Lifetime transfers of value of £318,250, £43,000 and £100,000 were made in seven years before 1 August 2011 (transfers after 1 August 2004). These exceed the nil rate band on death of £325,000.

The inheritance tax on this transfer is:

	£
Gross transfer of value	60,500

IHT	£60,500	× 40% =	24,200

There is no taper relief as Artem died within 3 years of making this transfer.

29 Jimmy

Marking scheme

				Marks
(a)	PET		1	
	CLT		1	
				2
(b)	**Lifetime transfers**			
	PET	– recognition as PET	½	
		– Marriage exemption	1	
		– Annual exemption	1	
	CLT	– recognition as CLT	½	
		– IHT liability	2	
	Additional liability arising on death			
	PET		1	
	CLT	– IHT liability	1	
		– IHT already paid	½	
	Death estate			
	Property		½	
	Building society deposits		½	
	Life assurance policy		1	
	Funeral expenses		1	
	Spouse exemption		1	
	IHT liability		½	
				12
(c)	Due date			1
				15

(a)   A potentially exempt transfer only becomes chargeable to inheritance tax (IHT) if the donor dies within seven years of making the gift.

In contrast, a chargeable lifetime transfer is immediately charged to IHT. An additional IHT liability may then arise if the donor dies within seven years of making the gift.

(b) **Jimmy – inheritance tax computation**

Lifetime transfers

2 August 2011

	£
Transfer of value	50,000
Less: marriage exemption	(2,500)
annual exemption 2011/12	(3,000)
annual exemption 2010/11 b/f	(3,000)
Potentially exempt transfer (no lifetime tax)	41,500

14 November 2011

	£
Net transfer of value (Jimmy pays IHT)	800,000

			£
IHT	£325,000	× 0% =	Nil
	£475,000	× 20/80 =	118,750
	£800,000		118,750

The gross transfer of value for accumulation is £(800,000 + 118,750) = £918,750.

Tutorial note

Check IHT using 20% rate on gross transfers

			£
IHT	£325,000	× 0% =	Nil
	£593,750	× 20% =	118,750
	£918,750		118,750

Additional liabilities arising on death

2 August 2011

	£
Potentially exempt transfer (within nil band at death, no tax to pay)	41,500

14 November 2011

There was a lifetime transfer of value of £41,500 in seven years before 14 November 2011 (transfers after 14 November 2004) so the nil rate band available is £(325,000 – 41,500) = £283,500. There is no taper relief as death occurred within three years of the transfer.

			£
Gross transfer of value			918,750
IHT	£283,500	× 0% =	Nil
	£635,250	× 40% =	254,100
	£918,750		254,100
Less: lifetime tax paid			(118,750)
Death tax payable			135,350

Death estate

14 February 2013

There were transfers of £(41,500 + 918,750) = £960,250 in seven years before 14 February 2013 (transfers after 14 February 2006) so there is no nil rate band available to be set against the death estate.

	£
Property	260,000
Building society deposits	515,600
Proceeds of life assurance policy	210,000
	985,600
Less: funeral expenses	(5,600)
Value of estate	980,000
Less: spouse exemption	(300,000)
Chargeable death estate	680,000
£680,000 × 40% =	272,000

(c) The due date on which the IHT liability of £272,000 will be payable by the personal representatives of Jimmy's estate is the earlier of 31 August 2013 or the date when they deliver their account to HMRC.

30 IHT transfers

Text references. Chapter 18 covers the inheritance tax examinable in F6.

Top tips. Where a question is divided into discrete parts such as this one, it is important to attempt ALL of the parts of the question to achieve a reasonable mark.

Easy marks. There were easy marks for explaining common exemptions such as the annual exemption, the marriage exemption and the small gifts exemption.

Marking scheme

			Marks
(a)	Gift is transfer of value	½	
	Annual exemptions	1	
	Marriage exemption	½	
	Potentially exempt transfer	1	
			3
(b)	Small gifts exemption		1
(c)	Sale at undervalue so diminution in estate	1	
	Transfer of value definition	1	
	No gratuitous intent so not transfer of value	1	
			3
(d)	Diminution in estate	1	
	Chargeable lifetime transfer	½	
	Nil rate band	½	
	Cumulation for seven years	1	
			3
(e)	Transfer of value but exempt	½	
	Out of income	½	
	Habitual	½	
	Maintains usual standard of living	½	
			2
(f)	Potentially exempt transfer	1	
	Chargeable on death within 7 years	½	
	Value of transfer	½	
	Better to give shares than cash	½	
	Taper relief	½	
			3
			15

(a) **Bilal**

The gift of £20,000 is a transfer of value for inheritance tax.

Bilal can use his £3,000 annual exemptions for 2012/13 and 2011/12 and also the marriage exemption which is £5,000 for a gift to the donor's child.

The remaining transfer of value is £(20,000 – 3,000 – 3,000 – 5,000) = £9,000. This is a potentially exempt transfer as it is a transfer to another individual. It will become a chargeable transfer if Bilal dies within seven years of making it but will be covered by his nil rate band.

(b)   **Sammy**

Gifts up to £250 per person in any one tax year are exempt under the small gifts exemption.

(c)   **Terry**

There has been a sale at an undervalue and Terry's estate has been reduced in value by £(20,000 – 1,000) = £19,000.

However, a transfer of value for IHT requires the diminution to be as a result of a gratuitous disposition. Since Terry thought that he was obtaining a market value for the value, his bad business deal is not a transfer of value as he had no gratuitous intent.

(d)   **Lucas**

There is a transfer of value as the gift is a gratuitous disposition which results in a diminution in the value of the donor's estate. This diminution is:

	£
Value of shares held before gift (8,000 × £37.50)	300,000
Value of shares held after gift (6,000 × £18.75)	(112,500)
Transfer of value	187,500

This is chargeable lifetime transfer as it is a transfer to trustees. However there is no lifetime tax payable because the transfer is within the available nil rate band of £325,000.

The transfer will be cumulated with any further transfers in the next seven years, including the death estate, if Lucas dies within this time.

(e)   **Donald**

There is a transfer of value of £1,000 each month. The transfers will be exempt under the normal expenditure out of income exemption because the transfer is:

- made out of income; and
- part of the normal expenditure of the donor (habitual); and
- leaves the donor with sufficient income to maintain his usual standard of living.

(f)   **Jas**

If either cash or shares are given, the transfer of value will be a potentially exempt transfer so the transfer will be treated as exempt while Jas is alive.

If Jas dies within seven years of making the transfer it will become a chargeable transfer and will be subject to death rates at the date of death. However, in either case, the transfer of value will be £100,000 as any increase in value of the shares is not be subject to inheritance tax. On purely IHT terms, Jas should therefore make a gift of the shares rather than cash.

If Jas dies between three and seven years of making the transfer, taper relief will reduce the death tax.

31 Molten-Metal plc

Marking scheme

		Marks
(a)	Trading profit	½
	Loan stock interest payable	1½
	Repairs to office building	1
	P&M - Office building	½
	- Ventilation system and lift	1
	- AIA	1
	- Machinery	½
	- Building alterations	½
	- Wall	½
	- Partition walls	1
	- AIA	1
	- Main pool	2
	- Special rate pool	1½
	- Short life asset	1
	Property business profit - Premium received	1½
	- Rent	1
	Interest income	2
	Chargeable gain - Disposal proceeds	½
	- Costs of disposal	½
	- Cost	½
	- Enhancement expenditure	1½
	- Indexation allowance	1½
	Corporation tax	½
		23
(b)	Instalment payment	1
	Due date	1
		2
		25

(a) **Molten-Metal plc – Corporation tax computation for the year ended 31 March 2013**

	£	£
Trading profit		2,138,415
Less: Loan stock interest payable £(22,500 + 3,700 – 4,200)	22,000	
Repairs to office building	0	
Capital allowances P&M (W1)	65,638	
		(87,638)
		2,050,777
Property business profit (W2)		68,400
Interest income (W3)		8,700
Chargeable gain (W4)		163,790
Taxable total profits		2,291,667
Corporation tax £2,291,667 @ 24%		550,000

Tutorial notes

(1)   Interest paid in respect of a loan used for trading purposes is deductible in calculating the trading profit.

(2)   The repairs to the office building are not deductible, being capital in nature, as the building was not in a useable state when purchased and this fact was reflected in the reduced purchased price.

Workings

1   *Capital allowances*

	AIA	Main pool	Special rate pool	Short life asset	Allowances
	£	£	£	£	£
TWDVs c/f		87,800			
Additions on which AIA claimed					
Office building	0				
Ventilation system	11,000				
Lift	12,000				
	23,000				
AIA – 100%	(23,000)				23,000
Transfer balance to special rate pool	0			0	
Machinery	61,600				
Building alterations	7,700				
Wall	0				
Partition walls	22,900				
	92,200				
AIA	(2,000)				2,000
Transfer balance to main pool	90,200	90,200			
Addition on which AIA not claimed					
Computer				2,500	
Additions not qualifying for AIA					
Motor car			24,000		
Motor cars £17,300 × 2		34,600			
		212,600			
WDA @ 18%		(38,268)		(450)	38,718
WDA @ 8%			(1,920)		1,920
TWDVs c/f		174,332	22,080	2,050	
Allowances					65,638

Tutorial notes

(1) The ventilation system and lift are both integral to a building and so are special rate pool expenditure. It is beneficial to claim the annual investment allowance of £25,000 initially against this expenditure, as it would otherwise only qualify for writing down allowance at the rate of 8%.

(2) The building alterations were necessary for the installation of the machinery, and therefore qualify for capital allowances. Walls are specifically excluded, with the exception of partition walls which are movable and intended to be so moved.

(3) The computer will be depooled by making the election and treated as a short life asset. The annual investment allowance should not be claimed against this asset as this will effectively disapply the depooling election.

(4) The motor car acquired in November 2012 has CO_2 emissions over 160 grams per kilometre, and therefore qualifies for writing down allowances at the rate of 8% as part of the special rate pool.

(5) The motor cars acquired in March 2013 have CO_2 emissions between 111 and 160 grams per kilometre, and therefore qualify for writing down allowances at the rate of 18% as part of the main pool. The private use of a motor car is irrelevant, since such usage will be assessed on the employee as a benefit.

2 *Property Business Profit*

	£
Premium received	68,000
Less: £68,000 × 2% × (6 – 1)	(6,800)
	61,200
Rent receivable £((78,800 – 68,000) = 10,800) × 2/3	7,200
Property business profit	68,400

3 *Interest income*

	£
Loan interest receivable £(9,800 + 3,100)	12,900
Bank interest receivable	2,600
	15,500
Less: interest payable	(6,800)
Net interest income	8,700

4 *Chargeable gain*

	£	£
Disposal proceeds		872,000
Less: costs of disposal		(28,400)
Net proceeds of disposal		843,600
Cost	396,200	
Enhancement expenditure - Extension	146,000	
- Roof	0	
		(542,200)
		301,400
Indexation allowance		
Cost £396,200 × 0.302	119,652	
Enhancement expenditure £146,000 × 0.123	17,958	
		(137,610)
Chargeable gain		163,790

Tutorial note

The cost of replacing part of the roof is not enhancement expenditure as the office building is simply being restored to its original state prior to the fire.

(b) The fourth and final quarterly instalment payment will be for £(550,000 – 398,200) = <u>£151,800</u>.

This is due on 14 July 2013.

32 Crash-Bash Ltd

Text references. Capital allowances are covered in Chapter 8. Computing taxable total profits is in Chapter 19 and the computation of corporation tax in Chapter 20. Overseas matters for companies is covered in Chapter 24. VAT is dealt with in Chapters 26 and 27.

Top tips. You could start with part (b) if you are confident about VAT since you were told that it was independent of part (a).

Easy marks. Registration for VAT is often examined so you should have been able to gain easy marks in part (b)(i).

Examiner's comments. In the first section of part (a) most candidates were not aware that the essential point regarding residence is where a company's central management and control is exercised. Most candidates had little difficulty with the corporation tax computation, and there were many perfect answers to this part of the question. However, the overseas income was often treated as franked investment income or simply ignored. The double taxation relief was sometimes used to reduce the overseas income rather than the corporation tax liability. As regards transfer pricing, very few candidates gave detailed enough answers to score more than one or two marks. It was surprising that very few candidates even appreciated that the pricing policy would result in the company's UK corporation tax liability being reduced.

In part (b) the VAT aspects of the question were not so well answered. Many candidates incorrectly stated that VAT registration was necessary because the company had exceeded the registration limit over the previous 12 months. They even gave the wrong date of registration despite this being given in the question. A number of candidates prepared the company's VAT return showing output VAT and input VAT, rather than calculating the amount of pre-registration input VAT. Very few candidates were aware of when default interest is charged.

Marking scheme

				Marks
(a)	(i)	Central control and management in the UK	1	
		Board meetings held in the UK	1	
				2
	(ii)	UK trading profit	½	
		Advertising expenditure	1	
		Plant and machinery – AIA	1	
		– FYA @ 100%	1	
		– disposal	½	
		– WDA	1	
		Capital gain on factory	1	
		Rollover relief	1	
		Overseas income	1	
		Overseas dividend	1	
		FII	1	
		Corporation tax	2	
		Double taxation relief	2	
				14
	(iii)	Reduction in UK corporation tax	1	
		Use of market value	1	
		Definition of market value	1	
		Adjustment under self assessment	1	
				4

(b)	(i)	Registration limit	1
		Taxable supplies for September 2012	1
		Notification	<u>1</u>
			3
	(ii)	Inventory – explanation	1
		– calculation	½
		Services – explanation	1
		– calculation	1
		Total VAT recovery	<u>½</u>
			4
	(iii)	Net errors less than limit	1
		Net errors exceeding limit	1
		Default interest	<u>1</u>
			<u>3</u>
			<u><u>30</u></u>

(a) (i) **Residence of Crash-Bash Ltd in the United Kingdom**

Companies that are incorporated overseas are only treated as being resident in the UK if their central management and control is exercised in the UK.

Since the directors are UK based and hold their board meetings in the UK, this would indicate that Crash-Bash Ltd is managed and controlled from the UK and therefore it is resident in the UK.

(ii) **Crash-Bash Ltd corporation tax liability for nine months ended 31 March 2013**

	£
UK trading profit (W1)	320,000
Overseas branch trading profit	20,000
Capital gain (W3)	<u>20,000</u>
Taxable total profits	360,000
FII £36,000 × 100/90 (N)	<u>40,000</u>
Augmented profits	<u>400,000</u>

Corporation tax (W4)	£
FY 2012	
£360,000 × 24%	86,400
Less: 1/100 × (562,500 − 400,000) × (360,000/400,000)	<u>(1,463)</u>
	84,937
Less: DTR (W5)	<u>(4,719)</u>
CT liability	<u>80,218</u>

Note. The dividend from Safety Inc is not FII because it is received from a 51% group company. It is exempt from UK corporation tax.

Workings

1	*UK trading profit*	£
	Tax adjusted trading profit	365,148
	Less: pre-trading advertising expenditure (N)	(12,840)
	capital allowances (W2)	<u>(32,308)</u>
		<u>320,000</u>

Note. The advertising expenditure incurred in June 2012 is pre-trading expenditure within seven years prior to the commencement of trading and is treated as incurred on the first day of trading (1 July 2012).

2   Plant and machinery

	AIA £	FYA @ 100% £	Main pool £	Allowances £
Additions qualifying for AIA				
2.10.12	25,000			
AIA £25,000 × 9/12	(18,750)			18,750
	6,250			
Transfer balance to pool	(6,250)		6,250	
Additions qualifying for FYA @ 100%				
28.11.12 Car		13,200		
FYA @ 100%		(13,200)		13,200
Disposal				
12.2.13			(3,600)	
			2,650	
WDA @ 18% × 9/12			(358)	358
TWDV c/f			2,292	
Allowances				32,308

Note. The annual investment allowance is reduced to £18,750 (25,000 × 9/12) because Crash–Bash Ltd's accounting period is nine months long. The writing down allowance is similarly restricted to 9/12.

3   *Capital gain*

	£
Disposal proceeds	500,000
Less: indexed cost	(375,000)
Gain	125,000
Less: gain rolled over into new warehouse (balance)	(105,000)
Gain left in charge - amount not reinvested £(500,000 – 480,000)	20,000

4   *Corporation tax limits*

	FY 2012 9 months to 31 March 2013 £
Augmented profits	400,000
Lower limit	
£300,000 × 9/12 × ½	112,500
Upper limit	
£1,500,000 × 9/12 × ½	562,500

There is one associated company (Safety Inc) so the limits are one-half of the usual limits. Marginal relief applies because augmented profits fall between the lower and upper limits.

5   *Double taxation relief*

Lower of:

(i)   UK corporation tax on overseas trading income:

$$\frac{20,000}{360,000} \times £84,937 = \quad £4,719$$

(ii) Overseas tax £20,000 @ 25% =   £5,000

ie £4,719

(iii)   **Crash-Bash Ltd and Safety Inc transfer pricing**

Invoicing for the exported crash helmets at less than the market price will reduce the UK trading profits of Crash-Bash Ltd and therefore its UK corporation tax.

A true market price will therefore have to be substituted for the transfer price. This will be the 'arms length' price that would be charged if the parties to the transaction were independent of each other.

Crash-Bash Ltd will be required to make the adjustment in its corporation tax self-assessment tax return.

(b)   (i)   **Crash-Bash Ltd compulsory VAT registration**

Traders must register for VAT if at any time they expect their taxable supplies for the following 30-day period to exceed £77,000.

Crash–Bash Ltd realised that its taxable supplies for September 2012 were going to be at least £100,000. The company was therefore liable to register from 1 September 2012 (the start of the 30-day period).

Crash–Bash Ltd had to notify HMRC by 30 September 2012 (the end of the 30-day period).

(ii)   **Crash-Bash Ltd pre-registration VAT**

VAT incurred before registration can be treated as input tax and recovered from HMRC subject to certain conditions.

If the claim is for input tax suffered on goods purchased prior to registration then the following conditions must be satisfied.

- The goods were acquired for the purpose of the business which either was carried on or was to be carried on by the trader at the time of supply.

- The goods have not been supplied onwards or consumed before the date of registration.

- The VAT must have been incurred in the four years prior to the effective date of registration.

Crash-Bash Ltd can therefore recover the input VAT paid on the inventory held at 1 September 2012. The input VAT recoverable is £108,600 × 20% = £21,720.

If the claim is for input tax suffered on the supply of services prior to registration then the following conditions must be satisfied.

- The services were supplied for the purposes of a business which either was carried on or was to be carried on by the trader at the time of supply.

- The services were supplied within the six months prior to the date of registration.

Crash-Bash Ltd can therefore recover the input VAT paid on the services incurred in July and August 2012. The input VAT on the services recoverable is £(22,300 + 32,700 = £55,000) × 20% = £11,000.

The total input VAT recovery is therefore £(21,720 + 11,000) = £32,720.

(iii)   **Crash-Bash Ltd VAT errors**

If the errors on a VAT return for the period ending 30 November 2012 did not exceed the greater of:

- £10,000 (net under-declaration minus over-declaration); or
- 1% x net VAT turnover for return period ended 30 November 2012 (maximum £50,000);

then the errors can be corrected on the return for the quarter ended 28 February 2013.

Errors in excess of the limit should be notified to HMRC in writing eg by letter.

Default interest will only be charged where the limit for notifying errors in the next return is exceeded.

33 Mice Ltd

Text references. Property business income is dealt with in Chapters 6 and 19. Losses for companies are in Chapter 22 and group relief in Chapter 23. Capital allowances are covered in Chapter 8. Calculation of income tax is in Chapter 2 and national insurance contributions in Chapter 12.

Top tips. You should use the loss relief pro-forma in part (a)(ii).

Easy marks. The calculation of property business profit in part (a) was straightforward and should have been easy marks.

Examiner's comments. This question was generally very well answered, especially the calculation of the property business profit in part (a) where most candidates scored virtually maximum marks. In part (b) several candidates explained whether or not group relief would be available rather than calculating the amount of relief. In part (c) most candidates were aware of what capital allowances were available. Many candidates complicated part (d) by performing long calculations, making this much more time consuming than necessary for 3 marks. However, they should have appreciated that this was additional remuneration so the calculations were simply £40,000 × 40%, £40,000 × 2% and £40,000 × 13.8% for the 3 marks.

Marking scheme

				Marks
(a)	(i)	Lease premium received	1½	
		Rent receivable - Property 1	1	
		- Property 2	½	
		- Property 3	½	
		Business rates	½	
		Repairs	1	
		Advertising	½	
		Insurance	1½	
		Loan interest	1	
				8
	(ii)	**Year ended 31 March 2013**		
		Property business profit	½	
		Loan interest	1½	
		Overseas income	1	
		Chargeable gain	½	
		Loss relief	1	
		Other periods		
		Trading profit	½	
		Property business profit	½	
		Loss relief	1	
		Qualifying charitable donations	½	
				7
(b)		Period ending 30 June 2012	1½	
		Year ended 30 June 2013	1½	
				3
(c)		Equipment	2	
		Ventilation system	2	
				4
(d)		Income tax	1	
		Employee's NIC	1	
		Employer's NIC	1	
				3
				25

(a) (i) **Mice Ltd – property business profit y/e 31 March 2013**

	£	£
Premium received for lease	18,000	
Less: £18,000 × 2% × (8 – 1)	(2,520)	
Amount taxable as property business income		15,480
Property 1 rent accrued £3,200 × 4		12,800
Property 2 rent accrued		6,000
Property 3 rent accrued		0
Gross income accrued		34,280
Less: expenses accrued		
business rates	2,200	
repairs (N1)	1,060	
Advertising	680	
insurance £(460 + 310 + (480 × 3/12))	890	
loan interest (N2)	0	
		(4,830)
Property business profit		29,450

Notes

1   The enlargement of the car park is capital expenditure which cannot be deducted when calculating the property business profit.

2   Interest paid in respect of a loan to purchase property is set off under the loan relationship rules.

(ii) **Mice Ltd – taxable total profits y/e 31 March 2013**

	£	£
Property business profit		29,450
Loan interest		
Received 31 December 2012	6,400	
Accrued 31 March 2013	3,200	
Paid on property 3 loan – 1 January 2013 to 31 March 2013	(1,800)	
		7,800
Overseas income (N)		0
Chargeable gain		2,750
Total profits		40,000
Less: current period loss relief		(40,000)
Taxable total profits		0

Note. The overseas dividend income is exempt. However, it is franked investment income and would be relevant when calculating the rate of corporation tax (not relevant here because there are no taxable total profits).

Mice Ltd – total taxable profits for periods ending 31 March 2010, 2011 and 2012

	p/e 31.3.10	y/e 31.3.11	y/e 31.3.12
	£	£	£
Trading profit	83,200	24,700	51,200
Property business profit	2,800	7,100	12,200
Total profits	86,000	31,800	63,400
Less: carry back loss relief	(0)	(0)	(63,400)
	86,000	31,800	0
Less: qualifying charitable donation	(1,000)	(1,500)	(0)
Taxable total profits	85,000	30,300	0

There is no loss relief in the period to 31 March 2010 or the year ended 31 March 2011 because loss relief for a continuing business is restricted to 12 months before the loss making period.

(b)   **Mice Ltd and Web-Cam Ltd – group relief**

For the three-month period ended 30 June 2012 group relief is restricted to the profit of £28,000, as this is lower than the loss of £180,000 x 3/12 = £45,000 for the corresponding period.

For the year ended 30 June 2013, group relief is restricted to the loss of £180,000 × 9/12 = £135,000 for the corresponding period, as this is lower than the corresponding profit of £224,000 × 9/12 = £168,000.

(c)   **Mice Ltd – capital allowance**

Equipment

The first £25,000 of expenditure will qualify for the annual investment allowance at the rate of 100%. The remainder of the expenditure will be added to the main pool and therefore will be eligible for writing down allowance at the rate of 18%.

Capital allowances for the year ended 31 March 2013 will therefore be £25,000 + (£100,000 × 18%) = £43,000.

Ventilation system

The annual investment allowance will be available as above. The ventilation system will be integral to the factory, and so the balance of expenditure will only qualify for writing down allowances at the rate of 8%.

Capital allowances for the year ended 31 March 2013 will therefore be £25,000 + (£100,000 × 8%) = £33,000.

(d)   **Director's income tax and national insurance contributions**

The managing director's additional income tax liability for 2012/13 will be £40,000 @ 40% = £16,000.

The additional employee's Class 1 NIC will be £40,000 @ 2% = £800.

The additional employer's Class 1 NIC will be £40,000 @ 13.8% = £5,520.

34 Do-Not-Panic Ltd

Text references. Chapters 19 and 20 cover computing taxable total profits and the corporation tax liability.

Top tips. Split out the long period correctly into the two accounting periods. Remember it is always the first twelve months and then the balance (in this case three months).

Easy marks. Allocating the figures between the two accounting periods should be straightforward.

Examiner's comments. Depending on whether candidates appreciated that the period of account needed to be split into a twelve-month period and a three-month period, this question was either answered very well or quite badly. Invariably many of the less well prepared candidates calculated corporation tax based on a fifteen-month period. The due dates were often omitted or incorrect.

Marking scheme

		Marks
Trading profit		1
Capital allowances	– period ended 31 March 2013	1
Interest income	– period ended 31 March 2013	1
Capital gains		1
Franked investment income		1
Corporation tax	– year ended 31 December 2012	2
	– period ended 31 March 2013	2
Due dates		1
		10

Do-Not-Panic Ltd – Corporation tax liabilities for the fifteen-month period ended 31 March 2013

	Year ended 31 December 2012 £	Period ended 31 March 2013 £
Trading profit (12:3)	228,000	57,000
Capital allowances (W)	–	(5,000)
	228,000	52,000
Interest income (accruals basis)	–	7,500
Capital gains (39,000 – 4,250)	–	34,750
Taxable total profits	228,000	94,250
Franked investment income	–	25,000
Augmented profits	228,000	119,250

y/e 31.12.12	*FY 2011/FY 2012* £	*FY 2012*
Limits for FY 2011 and FY 2012 are same so can be dealt with together		
Taxable total profits/augmented profits	228,000	
Lower limit £300,000		
Small profits rate applies in both financial years at 20% so can be dealt with together		
FY 2011/FY 2012		
£228,000 × 20%/CT for y/e 31.12.12	45,600	

p/e 31.3.13
FY 2012
Lower limit
$\qquad$ £300,000 × 3/12 = £75,000
Upper limit
$\qquad$ £1,500,000 × 3/12 = £375,000

			£
Marginal relief applies			
$\qquad$ £94,250 × 24%			22,620
Less: $\dfrac{1}{100} \times$ £(375,000 – 119,250) $\times \dfrac{94,250}{119,250}$			(2,021)
CT for p/e 31.3.13			20,599
Due dates		1 October 2013	1 January 2014

Working

Period ended 31 March 2013

	AIA £	Main pool £	Allowances £
Equipment	5,000		
AIA £25,000 × 3/12 = £6,250 maximum	(5,000)		5,000
TWDV carried forward		–	

35 Quagmire plc

Marking scheme

			Marks
(a)	Large company	1	
	Associated company	1	
	No exception	1	
			3
(b)	Corporation tax liability	1	
	Instalments	1	
	Due dates	1	
			3
(c)	Augmented profit	1	
	No longer a large company	½	
	Due date	½	
	Corporation tax	2	
			4
			10

(a) **Quagmire plc – payment of corporation tax**

Large companies have to make quarterly instalment payments in respect of their corporation tax liability. A large company is one paying corporation tax at the main rate.

Quagmire plc has one associated company, so the upper limit is reduced to £750,000 (1,500,000/2). Corporation tax will therefore be at the main rate for the year ended 31 March 2013.

There is an exception for the first year that a company is large, provided augmented profits do not exceed £10 million. No exception applies because Quagmire plc was also a large company for the year ended 31 March 2012.

(b) **Quagmire plc – corporation tax liability**

Quagmire plc's corporation tax liability for the year ended 31 March 2013 is £(1,200,000 × 24%) = £288,000

The company will have paid this in four quarterly instalments of £288,000/4 = £72,000.

The instalments will have been due on 14 October 2012, 14 January 2013, 14 April 2013 and 14 July 2013.

(c) **Effect of no associated company**

Quagmire plc's augmented profits for the year ended 31 March 2013 are £1,200,000 plus franked investment income of £200,000 = £1,400,000.

Quagmire plc is no longer a large company since its augmented profits are below the upper limit of £1,500,000. The corporation tax liability will therefore be due in one amount on 1 January 2014.

The corporation tax liability will be calculated as follows:

	£
£1,200,000 × 24%	288,000
Less marginal relief	
£(1,500,000 – 1,400,000) × (1,200,000/1,400,000) × $\frac{1}{100}$	(857)
Corporation tax liability	287,143

36 Heavy Ltd and Soft Ltd

Text references. Chapter 19 covers the computation of taxable total profits and Chapter 20 deals with the computation of the corporation tax liability. Details of capital allowances are to be found in Chapter 8.

Top tips. A chargeable period of account for corporation tax cannot exceed 12 months in length. A long period of account must therefore be divided into two chargeable accounting periods – the first period is always 12 months and the second period is the balance.

Easy marks. There was an easy mark in this question for adding back depreciation and amortisation. The main capital allowances should also have yielded easy marks, even if you missed the more unusual small pool write-off and the restriction for the short accounting period.

Examiner's comments. There were many very good answers to part (a). The aspects that caused problems were not appreciating that:

- There was no chargeable gain on a disposal of an office building to Soft Ltd because of the 75% group relationship.

- As the accounting period spanned 31 March 2012 it was necessary to apportion the taxable total profits between the financial years 2011 and 2012. (*BPP note:* this comment only now applies to Heavy Ltd).

- The balance on main capital allowances pool could be fully written off as it was less than £1,000.

- There was no balancing allowance on the special rate pool despite all the items included therein having been sold.

Part (b) was often not well answered, with the main problem being that candidates simply did not know the long period of account rules. This lack of a basic piece of knowledge cost many candidates several very easy marks. Even those candidates who knew the rules often deducted the capital loss in the second period, when it should have simply been carried forward.

BPP note. This question has been slightly changed from that originally set in June 2012 and reviewed by the examiner.

			Marks
(a)	Operating profit		½
	Depreciation		½
	Amortisation		½
	Lease premium	– Assessable amount	1½
		– Deduction	1
	Capital allowances	– AIA	1
		– Main pool	1
		– Short life asset	1½
		– Special rate pool	1½
	Interest income		2
	Chargeable gain		1
	Franked investment income		2
	Corporation tax	– Upper limit	½
		– Apportionment to tax years	½
		– Main rates	1
		– Marginal reliefs	2
			18
(b)	Trading profits		1
	Capital allowances	– Year ended 31 August 2013	1
		– Period ended 31 December 2013	1½
	Chargeable gain/allowable loss		1½
	Corporation tax	– Year ended 31 August 2013	1
		– Period ended 31 December 2013	1
			7
			25

(a) **Heavy Ltd – Corporation tax computation for the year ended 31 December 2012**

	£
Operating profit	417,340
Depreciation	12,880
Amortisation	9,000
Deduction for lease premium (W1)	(7,380)
Capital allowances (W2)	(22,840)
Trading profit	409,000
Interest income (W3)	11,000
Chargeable gain	0
Taxable total profits	420,000
Add: franked investment income (W4)	30,000
Augmented profits	450,000

Y/e 31.12.12 FY 2011 and FY 2012
Upper limit £1,500,000/2 = £750,000
Lower limit £300,000/2 = £150,000
Marginal relief applies in both financial years

	£
FY 2011 (1 January 2012 – 31 March 2012)	
£420,000 × 3/12 × 26%	27,300
Less marginal relief £(750,000 – 450,000) $\times \dfrac{420,000}{450,000} \times 3/12 \times 3/200$	(1,050)
FY 2012 (1 April 2012 – 31 December 2012)	
£420,000 × 9/12 × 24%	75,600
Less marginal relief £(750,000 – 450,000) $\times \dfrac{420,000}{450,000} \times 9/12 \times 1/100$	(2,100)
Corporation tax liability for the year ended 31 December 2012	99,750

Tutorial notes

1　The sale of the office building does not give rise to a chargeable gain as this is a no gain, no loss disposal since Heavy Ltd and Soft Ltd are members of a 75% capital gains group.

2　As far as Paper F6 (UK) is concerned, all overseas dividends are exempt from UK corporation tax. They are included as franked investment income when calculating a company's augmented profits in exactly the same way as UK dividends.

3　Heavy Ltd has one associated company (Soft Ltd) and so the upper limit and the lower limit are divided by two. A company which has only been associated for part of an accounting period is deemed to have been associated for the whole period for the purpose of determining the profit limits.

4　The taxable total profits must be apportioned between the Financial Years 2011 and 2012 because of the change in the main rate of corporation tax.

Workings

1　*Deduction for lease premium*

	£
Premium received	90,000
Less £90,000 × 2% × (10 -1)	(16,200)
Amount assessable on landlord as property business income	73,800
Deductible for year ended 31 December 2012 £73,800/10	7,380

Tutorial note

The office building has been used for business purposes and so the proportion of the lease premium assessed as property business income on the landlord can be deducted, spread over the life of the lease.

2　*Capital allowances*

	AIA £	Main pool £	Special rate pool £	Short life asset £	Allowances £
TWDVs b/f		900	21,700	3,200	
Addition qualifying for AIA					
Office equipment	22,400				
AIA	(22,400)				22,400
Disposal					
Special rate pool			(9,950)		
			11,750		
Short life asset				(4,600)	
Balancing charge				1,400	(1,400)
WDA – small pool		(900)			900
WDA @ 8%			(940)		940
TWDV c/f		0	10,810		
Allowances					22,840

Tutorial notes

1 The balance on the main pool is less than £1,000 so a writing down allowance equal to the unrelieved expenditure can be claimed.

2 Although all the items included in the special rate pool have been sold, there is no balancing allowance as the business has not ceased. Compare this to the short life asset which is held in a single asset pool and does have a balancing adjustment when the business is continuing.

3 *Interest income*

	£
Loan interest receivable £(8,800 + 1,500)	10,300
Bank interest receivable	1,600
	11,900
Less loan interest payable	(900)
Net interest income	11,000

4 *Franked investment income*

	£
Unconnected UK company	18,000
Soft Limited (group dividend)	0
Unconnected overseas company	9,000
Total dividends	27,000
Franked investment income £27,000 × 100/90	30,000

(b) **Soft Ltd – Corporation tax liabilities for the 16-month period ended 31 December 2013**

	Y/e 31.8.13 £	P/e 31.12.13 £
Trading profit 12:4	90,150	30,050
Less capital allowances (W)	(4,320)	(947)
	85,830	29,103
Chargeable gain	16,170	0
Taxable total profits	102,000	29,103

Y/e 31.8.13 FY 2012 and FY 2013
Lower limit £300,000/2 = £150,000
P/e 31.12.13 FY 2013
Lower limit £300,000/2 × 4/12 = £50,000
Small profits rate applies in both financial years
FY 2012 and FY 2013

£102,000 × 20%	20,400	
£29,103 × 20%		5,821

Tutorial notes

1 Trading profits are allocated on a time basis between the two chargeable accounting periods. However, capital allowances are calculated separately for each chargeable accounting period.

2 The capital loss for £2,900 for the period ended 31 December 2013 is carried forward. It cannot be carried back against the gain in the year ended 31 August 2013.

3 Soft Ltd has one associated company (Heavy Ltd) and so the lower limit is divided by two. For the short period of 4 months ended 31 December 2013, the limit must also be reduced proportionately.

Working

	Main pool £	Allowances £
Year ended 31 August 2013		
TWDV b/f	24,000	
WDA @ 18%	(4,320)	4,320
	19,680	
Period ended 31 December 2013		
Disposal	(3,900)	
	15,780	
WDA @ 18% × 4/12	(947)	947
TWDV c/f	14,833	

37 Thai Curry Ltd

Text references. Chapters 19 and 20 for calculation of augmented profits and taxable total profits. Chapter 8 covers capital allowances. Chapter 25 for corporation tax administration.

Top tips. It is essential to set out your capital allowances proforma in the correct layout to achieve maximum marks. Ensure that you state all of your assumptions so that you do not miss out on any method marks.

You cannot avoid administration questions in the exam so make sure you know due dates for returns and tax payments.

				Marks
(a)	Capital allowances			
		TWDV b/f	½	
		AIA	2	
		Disposals	2	
		WDA @ 18%	1	
		WDA @ 8%	1	
		FYA @ 100%	1	
	Trading loss		½	
	Deduct allowances		1	
				9
(b)	Trading profit nil		½	
	Property income			
	Property 1	– rent	1	
		– expense	½	
		– bad debt	1	
	Property 2	– rent	½	
		– lease premium	1½	
	Interest		1	
	Chargeable gain		½	
	Deduct CY loss		1	
	FII		½	
	CT limits		1	
	CT @ 24%		½	
	Marginal relief		1½	
				11
(c)	(i)	Return deadline	1	
		Fixed penalty	1	
		Tax geared penalty	1	
				3

(ii)	9 months 1 day		1
	Late payment interest		1
	Interest calculation		1
			$\underline{3}$
			$\underline{26}$

(a) **Thai Curry Ltd's adjusted trading loss y/e 31 March 2013**

	£
Trading loss	(55,036)
Less: Capital allowances (W)	(34,894)
Allowable trading loss	(89,930)

Working

Capital allowances

	AIA	FYA @ 100%	Main pool	Special rate pool	Allowances
	£	£	£	£	£
TWDV b/f			10,600	16,400	
Additions qualifying for AIA					
8.7.12 Equipment	9,460				
20.3.13 Office (N1)	12,750				
	22,210				
AIA	(22,210)				22,210
Additions not qualifying for AIA					
26.8.12 Car			15,800		
Disposals					
1.5.12 Equipment			(12,800)		
			13,600		
WDA @ 18%			(2,448)		2,448
14.7.12 Car				(9,700)	
				6,700	
WDA @ 8%				(536)	536
Addition qualifying for FYA					
19.11.12 Car		9,700			
100% FYA		(9,700)			9,700
TWDV c/f			11,152	6,164	
Allowances					34,894

Notes

The items included within the cost of the office building purchased on 20 March 2013 will qualify for plant and machinery capital allowances. All of the expenditure is covered by the AIA so it is not necessary to distinguish between main pool and special rate pool expenditure. The disposal of the car from the special rate pool does not result in a balancing allowance as the business is continuing. The balance of the expenditure will continue to be written down at 8%.

(b) **Corporation tax liability y/e 31 March 2013**

	£
Trading profit	Nil
Property income (W1)	72,800
Interest (W3)	11,500
Chargeable gain	152,300
Total profits	236,600
Less: current year loss relief	(89,930)
Taxable total profits	146,670
Add: gross dividends: £36,000 × 100/90	40,000
Augmented profits	186,670

CT liability (W4)	£
FY 2012: £146,670 × 24%	35,201
Less 1/100 (375,000 − 186,670) × (146,670/186,670)	(1,480)
CT liability	33,721

Workings

1   *Property income*

Property 1

	£	£
8m × £2,200	17,600	
Less: redecoration costs	(8,800)	
Less: rent not recoverable: 2m × £2,200	(4,400)	
Property income		4,400

Property 2

	£	£
8/12 × £18,000	12,000	
Premium taxable as income (W2)	56,400	
Property income		68,400
Total property income		72,800

2   *Lease premium*

	£
Premium (P)	60,000
Less: 2% × (n-1) × P	
2% × (4-1) × 60,000	(3,600)
Taxable as income	56,400

3   *Loan interest*

	£
Received at 30.9.12	8,000
Accrued at 31.3.13	3,500
Total amount (accruals basis)	11,500

4

	FY 2012 *12 months to 31.3.13*
Taxable total profits	146,670
Augmented profits	186,670
Lower limit	
£300,000/4	75,000
Upper limit	
£1,500,000/4	375,000

Therefore marginal relief applies.

(c) (i) **Date for return submission and penalties**

The CT return must be submitted one year after the end of the period of account ie by 31 March 2014.

If the return is not submitted until 30 November 2014 it will be 8 months late. If the return is up to 3 months late there is a fixed penalty of £100. If it more than 3 months late, as it is here, the fixed penalty increases to £200.

As the return is more than 6 months late there is also a tax geared penalty if the tax is unpaid six months after the return is due. The penalty is 10% × unpaid tax, ie 10% × £33,721 = £3,372.

(ii) **Date for CT payment & interest**

As the company is not large it must pay its corporation tax by 9 months and 1 day after the accounting period, ie by 1 January 2014.

If the tax is not paid until 30 November 2014 it will be 11 months late and interest will be charged from the due date. (In practice, interest is calculated on a daily basis.)

The rate of interest on unpaid tax is 3% and therefore the amount that will be charged is:

3% × 11/12 × £33,721 = £927.

38 Hawk Ltd

Text reference. Chargeable gains for companies are covered in Chapter 21.

Top tips. Work out each of the gains separately and then bring them together in a summary. Even if you are unsure about how to deal with one of the gains, make sure that you attempt the calculation of tax.

Easy marks. The calculation of corporation tax was an easy mark.

Marking scheme

		Marks
(a)	**Office building**	
	Disposal proceeds	½
	Costs of disposal	½
	Cost	½
	Costs of acquisition	½
	Enhancement expenditure	½
	Indexation – Cost	1
	– Enhancement	1
	Albatross plc	
	Proceeds	½
	Cost	2
	Cuckoo plc	
	Proceeds	½
	Value of shares – Ordinary shares	1
	– Preference shares	1
	Cost	1½
	Land	
	Proceeds	½
	Costs	2
	Corporation tax liability	
	Net chargeable gains	1
	Calculation	1½
		16

(b)	(i)	Qualifying disposal	1	
		Amount of reinvestment	1	2
	(ii)	Period of reinvestment		1
	(iii)	Corporation tax savings		1
				20

(a) **Corporation tax liability y/e 31 March 2013**

	£
Trading income	125,000
Net chargeable gains (W5)	132,137
Taxable total profits	257,137

Hawk Ltd is a small profit company

£257,137 × 20%	51,427

Workings

1 *Office building*

	£
Proceeds	270,000
Less: disposal costs	(5,726)
Net proceeds of sale	264,274
Less: original costs £(81,000 + 3,200)	(84,200)
enhancement expenditure	(43,000)
Unindexed gain	137,074
Less: indexation allowance	
on original cost	
$\dfrac{(242.6 - 186.8)}{186.8}(0.299) \times £84,200$	(25,176)
on enhancement	
$\dfrac{(242.6 - 197.7)}{197.7}(0.227) \times £43,000$	(9,761)
Indexed gain	102,137

2 *Albatross plc shares*

FA 1985 pool

	No. of shares	Cost
		£
1.8.12 Acquisition	6,000	18,600
17.8.12 Acquisition	2,000	9,400
	8,000	28,000
29.8.12 Disposal	(5,000)	(17,500)
c/f	3,000	10,500

	£
Proceeds	42,500
Less: cost	(17,500)
Gain (no indexation allowance)	25,000

3 *Cuckoo plc preference shares*
Reorganisation

	MV	Cost
	£	£
15,000 Ordinary shares (5,000 × 3) × £4.50	67,500	45,000
10,000 Preference shares (5,000 × 2) × £2.25	22,500	15,000
	90,000	60,000

		£
Proceeds		32,000
Less: cost		(15,000)
Gain (no indexation allowance)		17,000

4   *Land*

		£
Proceeds		120,000
Less: costs £203,500 × $\dfrac{120,000}{120,000 + 65,000}$		(132,000)
Loss		(12,000)

5   *Net chargeable gains*

	£
Office building (W1)	102,137
Albatross plc Shares (W2)	25,000
Cuckoo plc preference shares (W3)	17,000
Land (W4)	(12,000)
Net chargeable gains	132,137

(b)   (i)   The only disposal that qualifies for rollover relief is the sale of the freehold office building. Shares do not qualify and the land has not been used for business purposes.

The office building was sold for £270,000, and this is therefore the amount that Hawk Ltd will have to reinvest in order to claim the maximum possible amount of rollover relief.

Tutorial note. It would also have been acceptable to state that the net disposal proceeds (£264,274) had to be reinvested to claim the maximum possible of rollover relief.

(ii)   The reinvestment will have to take place between 1 May 2011 and 30 April 2015, which is the period starting one year before and ending three years after the date of disposal.

(iii)   Corporation tax of £20,427 (£102,137 × 20%) will be saved if the maximum possible amount of rollover relief is claimed.

39 Problematic Ltd

Text references. Chargeable gains for companies are covered in Chapter 21. Taxable total profits are defined in Chapter 20.

Top tips. Make sure you use the three column pro-forma for the FA 1985 pool.

Easy marks. The calculations of taxable total profits simply required the gains calculated to be added together with the figure for trading profit.

Examiner's comments. It was pleasing to see that this question was well answered. On an overall note, it does not create a very good impression when candidates deduct the annual exempt amount when dealing with a company. The only aspect that consistently caused problems in part (a) was the restoration of the asset. Despite the question telling candidates that a claim to defer the gain had been made, many insisted that such a claim was not possible and instead calculated a capital loss. Many candidates did not even attempt part (b) despite the fact that this section generally just required them to provide figures already calculated in part (a).

			Marks
(a)	**Easy plc**		
	FA 1985 pool - Purchase	½	
	- Rights issue	1½	
	- Indexation	2	
	- Disposal	1	
	Chargeable gain	1½	
	Office building		
	Proceeds fully reinvested	1	
	No disposal on receipt of proceeds	1	
	Freehold factory		
	Disposal proceeds	½	
	Indexed cost	½	
	Rollover relief	2	
	Land		
	Proceeds	½	
	Incidental costs of disposal	1	
	Cost	2	
	Taxable total profits		
	Chargeable gains	½	
	Calculation	½	
			16
(b)	Ordinary shares in Easy plc	½	
	Office building	1½	
	Leasehold factory	1	
	Land	1	
			4
			20

(a) **Problematic plc – taxable total profits for y/e 31 March 2013**

	£
Easy plc shares (W1)	31,929
Office building (W2)	0
Freehold factory (W3)	16,200
Land (W4)	45,550
Trading profit	106,321
Taxable total profits	200,000

Workings

(1) *Easy plc shares*

FA85 pool

	No. of shares	Cost	Indexed cost
		£	£
Purchase 26.6.05	15,000	12,600	12,600
Index to September 2008			
$\frac{(218.4 - 192.2)}{192.2} \times £12,600$			1,718
Rights issue 1 for 3 @ £2.20	5,000	11,000	11,000
c/f	20,000	23,600	25,318

	No. of shares	Cost	Indexed cost
		£	£
b/f	20,000	23,600	25,318
Index to June 2012			
$\dfrac{(242.3 - 218.4)}{218.4} \times £25,318$			2,771
			28,089
Sale	(16,000)	(18,880)	(22,471)
C/f	4,000	4,720	5,618

Gain	
	£
Proceeds	54,400
Less: cost	(18,880)
	35,520
Less: indexation £ (22,471 – 18,880)	(3,591)
Chargeable gain	31,929

(2)   *Office building*

The insurance proceeds of £36,000 received by Problematic Ltd have been fully applied in restoring the office building.

There is therefore no disposal on the receipt of the insurance proceeds.

(3)   *Freehold factory*

	£
Proceeds	171,000
Less: indexed cost	(127,000)
	44,000
Less: gain deferred on purchase of leasehold factory £(44,000 – 16,200)	(27,800)
Chargeable gain (amount not reinvested £(171,000 – 154,800))	16,200

(4)   *Land*

	£
Proceeds	130,000
Less: disposal costs	(3,200)
Net disposal proceeds	126,800
Less: indexed cost	
$\dfrac{130,000}{130,000 + 350,000} \times £300,000$	(81,250)
Chargeable gain	45,550

(b)   **Carried forward indexed base costs**

The 4,000 £1 ordinary shares in Easy plc have an indexed base cost of £5,618

The indexed base cost of the office building is £(169,000 – 36,000 + 41,000) = £174,000.

The leasehold factory is a depreciating asset, so there is no adjustment to the base cost of £154,800.

The indexed base cost of the remaining three acres of land is £(300,000 – 81,250) = £218,750.

Tutorial note. When a replacement asset is a depreciating asset then the gain is not rolled over by reducing the cost of the replacement asset. Instead, the gain is deferred until it crystallises on the earliest of:

−   The disposal of the replacement asset.

−   The date the replacement asset is no longer used in the business.

−   Ten years after the acquisition of the replacement asset which in this case is 10 December 2022.

40 Lim Lam

Marking scheme

				Marks
(a)	Land	– Proceeds	½	
		– Cost	½	
	Oily plc	– Deemed proceeds	2	
		– Cost	1	
	Mal-Mil Ltd	– Proceeds	½	
		– Cost	1	
	Annual exempt amount	– Use first against gains not qualifying for ER	1	
	Capital gains tax @ 28%		½	
	Capital gains tax @ 10%		½	
	Due date		½	
				8
(b)	**Chargeable gain**			
	Proceeds		½	
	Incidental costs of disposal		½	
	Cost		1½	
	Enhancement expenditure		1	
	Indexation		1½	
	Corporation tax liability			
	Calculation		1½	
	Due date		½	
				7
				15

(a) **Lim Lam – Capital gains tax liability 2012/13**

Summary

	£	Gains not qualifying for entrepreneurs' relief £	Gains qualifying for entrepreneurs' relief £
Land			
Disposal proceeds	260,000		
Less: cost	(182,000)		
		78,000	
Ordinary shares in Oily plc			
Deemed proceeds	37,200		
(5,000 × £7.44) (W1)			
Less: cost	(15,925)		
		21,275	
Ordinary shares in Mal-Mil Ltd			
Disposal proceeds	280,000		
Less: cost (W2)	(56,000)		
			224,000
Chargeable gains		99,275	224,000
Less: annual exempt amount (N1)		(10,600)	
Taxable gains		88,675	224,000
Capital gains tax on 88,675 @ 28% (N2)		24,829	
Capital gains tax on 224,000 @ 10%			22,400
Capital gains tax liability 2012/13		£47,229	

Lim's capital gains tax liability should be paid by 31 January 2014.

Workings

1   The shares in Oily plc are valued at £7.44 (£7.40 + ¼(£7.56 − £7.40)) as this is lower than £7.48 ((£7.36 + £7.60)/2).

2   Share pool

	Number	Cost £
Purchase 8 June 2005	125,000	142,000
Purchase 23 May 2007	60,000	117,000
	185,000	259,000
Disposal 22 March 2013 (259,000 × 40,000/185,000)	(40,000)	(56,000)
Balance carried forward	145,000	203,000

Tutorial notes

1   The annual exempt amount is set against the gains not qualifying for entrepreneurs' relief as this gives the best use of the annual exempt amount as it reduces tax at 28%.

2   The gains qualifying for entrepreneurs' relief are the lowest part of the gains and therefore use up the remaining basic rate band of £6,370 (34,370 − 28,000). This means that the gains not qualifying for entrepreneurs' relief are all taxed at 28%.

(b) **Mal-Mil Ltd – Chargeable gain on the disposal of the land**

	£	£
Disposal proceeds		162,000
Incidental costs of disposal		(3,800)
		158,200
Less: cost (W1)	101,250	
Enhancement expenditure (W2)	12,150	
		(113,400)
Less: indexation allowance £113,400 × 0.020 (W3)		(2,268)
Chargeable gain		42,532

Workings

1 *Cost of land*

The cost relating to the two acres of land sold is £101,250 (260,000 × 162,000/416,000 (162,000 + 254,000)).

2 *Enhancement expenditure*

The levelling of the land is enhancement expenditure. The cost relating to the two acres of land sold is £12,150 (31,200 × 162,000/416,000).

3 *Indexation factor*

Both the cost and the enhancement expenditure were incurred during July 2012. The relevant indexation factor is therefore $\frac{(246.6 - 241.7)}{241.7} = 0.020$.

Corporation tax liability

Mal-Mil Ltd's taxable total profits for the year ended 31 December 2012 are £(163,000 + 42,532) = £205,532.

Mal-Mil Ltd's corporation tax liability for the year ended 31 December 2012 is £41,106 (£205,532 × 20% – FYs 2011 & 2012 same rate for small profits). This is due on 1 October 2013.

41 Starfish Ltd

Text references. Computing taxable total profits is covered in Chapter 19. Corporation tax losses are dealt with in Chapter 22. Chapters 26 and 27 cover value added tax.

Top tips. Make sure that you set out the computation of taxable total profits in part (c) using the standard layout, leaving space for losses carried forward against trading profits and losses carried back against total profits.

Easy marks. The adjustment of profit computation was reasonably straightforward.

Examiner's comments. Part (a) surprisingly caused quite a few problems, with a number of candidates discussing long periods of account or, even worse, the basis period rules for unincorporated businesses. Some candidates just stated that an accounting period starts when trading commences, and ends when trading ceases – which would imply that all companies have just one long accounting period. Part (b) was very well answered, with many very good answers. The only aspect consistently answered incorrectly was the treatment of a purchased asset. In the final capital allowances computation no allowances are given, so the addition should simply have been added to the main pool. In part (c) many candidates overlooked the trading loss for the final period of trading. The VAT calculation in part (d) was generally well answered, although few candidates appreciated that output VAT would not be due on the sale of inventory and non-current assets if the business was sold as a going concern. Many candidates simply stated that no VAT would be due, which was too vague to score marks.

				Marks
(a)	Start of accounting period		2	
	Finish of accounting period		2	
				4
(b)	Depreciation		½	
	Donations		1½	
	Impairment loss		1	
	Legal fees		1½	
	Entertaining customers		½	
	Entertaining employees		½	
	Counselling services		½	
	Plant and machinery	– WDV brought forward	1	
		– Addition	1½	
		– Main pool proceeds	2	
		– Motor car proceeds	1	
		– Balancing adjustments	½	
				12
(c)	Trading profit		½	
	Relief for 2009 loss	– Period ended 31 March 2009	½	
		– Carry forward	½	
	Bank interest		½	
	Relief for 2013 loss	– Year ended 31 March 2010	1	
		– Other periods	1	
	Qualifying charitable donations		1	
				5
(d)	(i)	Output VAT	– Cash sales revenue	1½	
			– Credit sales revenue	1½	
			– Inventory	1	
			– Sale of non-current assets	½	
		Input VAT	– Expenses	1	
			– Impairment loss	1	
			– Purchase of non-current asset	½	
					7
	(ii)	Output VAT not due on TOGC		1	
		VAT refund		1	
					2
					30

(a)   **Start and finish of accounting periods**

An accounting period will normally start immediately after the end of the preceding accounting period.

An accounting period will also start when a company starts to trade, or otherwise becomes liable to corporation tax.

An accounting period will normally finish 12 months after the beginning of the accounting period or at the end of a company's period of account (if less than 12 months).

An accounting period will also finish when a company ceases to trade, when it ceases to otherwise be liable to corporation tax, when it ceases to be resident in the UK, or on the commencement of winding up procedures.

(b) **Starfish Ltd – Trading loss for the period ended 31 March 2013**

	£	£
Loss before taxation		(190,000)
Add: Depreciation	25,030	
Donation to political party	300	
Donation (not qualifying charitable donation)	600	
Donation paid (qualifying charitable donation)	750	
Impairment loss	0	
Legal fees – Internet domain name	0	
– Misleading advertisement	2,020	
– Issue of loan notes (N1)	0	
Entertaining customers (N2)	3,600	
Entertaining employees (N2)	0	
Counselling services (N3)	0	
		32,300
		(157,700)
Less: Capital allowances (W1)		(2,300)
Adjusted trading loss		(160,000)

Workings

1 *Capital allowances*

	Main pool	Special rate pool	Allowances
	£	£	£
TWDVs b/f	23,600	13,200	
Addition – computer (W2) (N4)	2,600		
	26,200		
Disposals (W3)	(27,500)	(9,600)	
Balancing charge	(1,300)		(1,300)
Balancing allowance		3,600	3,600
Total allowances			2,300

2 *Computer*

The input VAT on the computer is recoverable and so only the cost net of VAT is eligible expenditure which is £3,120 × 100/120 = £2,600.

3 *Disposal proceeds*

The output VAT charged on the disposals is not part of the proceeds for capital allowance purposes. The main pool proceeds are therefore £([31,200 + 1,800] × 100/120) = £27,500. There is no VAT charged on the sale of the car, as none was recovered on purchase (owing to private usage).

Tutorial notes

1 The cost of obtaining loan finance, even if abortive, is allowable as a trading loan relationship debit.

2 The only exception to the non-deductibility of entertainment expenditure is when it is in respect of employees.

3 The costs of counselling services for redundant employees are deductible if they qualify for exemption from the employment income charge on employees.

4 The annual investment allowance and writing down allowances are not given for the period in which a trade ceases. Therefore the addition is simply added into the main pool.

(c) **Starfish Ltd – Taxable total profits**

	P/e 31.3.09	Y/e 31.3.10	Y/e 31.3.11	Y/e 31.3.12	P/e 31.12.12
	£	£	£	£	£
Trading profit	0	64,200	53,900	14,700	49,900
Less: c/f loss relief (N1)	0	(12,600)	0	0	0
	0	51,600	53,900	14,700	49,900
Bank interest	600	1,400	1,700	0	0
	600	53,000	55,600	14,700	49,900
Less: c/b loss relief (N2)	(0)	(13,250)	(55,600)	(14,700)	(49,900)
	600	39,750	0	0	0
Less: qualifying charitable donations (N3)	(600)	(1,000)	(0)	(0)	(0)
Taxable total profits	0	38,750	0	0	0

Tutorial notes

1   Starfish Ltd would not have made a loss relief claim against total profits for the period ended 31 March 2009 as this would have wasted the £600 of relieved qualifying charitable donations for that period.

2   The trading loss for the period ended 31 March 2013 can be relieved against total profits for the 3 years immediately preceding the start of the loss making period since it is a terminal loss. The 3 year period is between 1 January 2010 and 31 December 2012. Relief is as follows:

	£
Loss of 3 month p/e 31.3.13	160,000
Less: used in p/e 31.12.12	(49,900)
	110,100
Less: used in y/e 31.3.12	(14,700)
	95,400
Less: used in y/e 31.3.11	(55,600)
	39,800
Less: used in y/e 31.3.10 (restricted to 3/12 × £53,000)	(13,250)
Balance unrelieved	26,550

3   The qualifying charitable donations in the period ending 31 March 2013, and earlier years, are also unrelieved.

(d) (i)   **Starfish Ltd – VAT return for the quarter ended 31 March 2013**

	£	£
Output VAT		
Cash sales revenue £38,520 × 20/120		6,420
Credit sales revenue £2,000 × (100 – 4)% × 20%		384
Sale of inventory on cessation £28,800 × 20/120		4,800
Sale of non-current assets £([31,200 + 1,800] × 20/120)		5,500
Input VAT		
Expenses £([69,960 – 4,320] = £65,640) × 20/120	10,940	
Impairment loss	384	
Purchase of non-current asset (computer)	520	
		(11,844)
VAT payable		5,260

Tutorial notes

1   The calculation of output VAT on the credit sales revenue takes into account the discount for prompt payment, even for the 40% of customers that did not take it.

2   Input VAT on business entertainment for UK customers is not recoverable.

3   Relief for the impairment loss is available because the claim is made more than six months from the time that payment was due, and the debt has been written off in the company's books.

(ii)   A sale of a business as a going concern is outside the scope of VAT, and therefore output VAT would not have been due on the sale of the inventory or the sale of the non-current assets.

Instead of VAT being payable, Starfish Ltd would have been due a refund of £5,040 (5,260 – 4,800 – 5,500).

42 Volatile Ltd

Text references. Corporation tax losses are covered in Chapter 22.

Top tips. Don't forget to set up a loss memorandum for each loss so that you can see how the loss is utilised.

Easy marks. You should have been able to state at least 2 of the principles of claiming loss relief in part (a).

Examiner's comments. This question was not particularly well answered. In part (a) far too many candidates explained the loss reliefs available rather than the factors influencing the choice of claims. In part (b) many candidates approached this on a year by year basis, rather than one computation with a column for each of the four periods. This not only wasted time in having to write out four computations, but also made it very difficult to calculate the correct loss relief claims. Other common mistakes included treating the chargeable gains separately (rather than as part of the taxable total profits), and deducting qualifying charitable donations from trading profits rather than total profits after loss relief.

Marking scheme

			Marks
(a)	Rate of tax	1	
	Timing of relief	1	
	Qualifying charitable donations not relieved	1	
			3
(b)	Trading income	½	
	Property business income	½	
	Chargeable gains	½	
	Loss relief – y/e 31 December 2009	2	
	Loss relief – y/e 30 September 2012	2½	
	Qualifying charitable donations	½	
	Unrelieved losses	½	
			7
			10

(a)   **Choice of loss relief**

The three factors that will influence a company's choice of loss relief claims are:

- The rate at which relief will be obtained:

    - 25% if marginal relief applies (best use)
    - 24% at the main rate (second best use)
    - 20% at the small profits rate (third best use)

- How quickly relief will be obtained: loss relief against total profits is quicker than carry forward loss relief.

- The extent to which relief for qualifying charitable donations might be lost.

(b) **Volatile Ltd**

	P/e 31.12.08 £	Y/e 31.12.09 £	Y/e 31.12.10 £	P/e 30.09.11 £
Trading income	44,000	0	95,200	78,700
Less: carry forward loss relief	(0)	(0)	(8,700)	(0)
	44,000	0	86,500	78,700
Property business income	9,400	6,600	6,500	0
Chargeable gains	5,100	0	0	9,700
Total profits	58,500	6,600	93,000	88,400
Less: current period loss relief	(0)	(6,600)	(0)	(0)
Less: carry back loss relief	(58,500)		(23,250)	(88,400)
	0	0	69,750	0
Less: qualifying charitable donations	(0)	(0)	(1,200)	(0)
Taxable total profits	0	0	68,550	0

Loss memorandum

	£
Loss in y/e 31.12.09	73,800
Less: used y/e 31.12.09	(6,600)
Less: used p/e 31.12.08	(58,500)
Less: used y/e 31.12.10	(8,700)
Loss remaining unrelieved	0

	£
Loss in y/e 30.9.12	186,800
Less: used p/e 30.9.11	(88,400)
Less: used y/e 31.12.10	
3 months to 31.12.10	
£93,000 × 3/12	(23,250)
Loss remaining unrelieved	75,150

The loss of y/e 30.9.12 can be carried back against total profits of the previous 12 months ie against the 9 month period ending 30.9.11 and 3 months of the y/e 31.12.10.

43 Jogger Ltd

Marking scheme

			Marks	
(a)	(i)	Operating loss	½	
		Depreciation	½	
		P&M – AIA	1½	
		– Main pool	1½	
		– Special rate pool	1½	
		– Short life asset	1½	
				7
	(ii)	Property business profit	2	
		Bank interest	½	
		Loan interest	1	
		Chargeable gain	½	
		Loss relief	1	
		Franked investment income	1	
		Corporation tax	2	
				8
	(iii)	Due date	1	
		Fixed penalty	1½	
		Corporation tax related penalty	1½	
				4
(b)	(i)	Quarter ended 30 September 2011	2	
		Quarter ended 31 March 2012	2	
		Quarter ended 31 March 2013	2	
				6
	(ii)	One VAT return	1½	
		Payments on account	1½	
		Limit	1	
		VAT returns	1	
				5
				30

(a) (i) Trading loss y/e 31.3.13

	£
Operating loss	(81,518)
Add: depreciation	58,840
	(22,678)
Less: capital allowances (W)	(33,182)
Adjusted trading loss	(55,860)

Working

Plant and machinery

	AIA	Main pool	Special rate pool	SLA	Allowances
	£	£	£	£	£
TWDV b/f		26,600	18,800		
Additions qualifying for AIA					
30.9.12 Machinery	25,000				
AIA	(25,000)				25,000
Additions qualifying for AIA but not claimed					
15.12.12 Computer				12,500	
Additions not qualifying for AIA					
31.7.12 Car		11,800			
Disposals					
20.7.12 Car			(11,700)		
BC			7,100		
14.3.13 Lorry		(8,600)			
		29,800			
WDA @ 18%		(5,364)		(2,250)	7,614
WDA @ 8%			(568)		568
TWDV c/f		24,436	6,532	10,250	
Allowances					33,182

(ii) **Jogger Ltd – corporation tax computation y/e 31.3.13**

	£
Interest income (W1)	33,060
Property income (W2)	126,000
Chargeable gain	98,300
Total profits	257,360
Less: loss relief	(55,860)
Taxable total profits	201,500
Add: FII £45,000 × 100/90	50,000
Augmented profits	251,500

Corporation tax

Upper limit £1,500,000 / 3 associated companies	500,000
Lower limit £300,000 / 3 associated companies	100,000

Marginal relief applies

£201,500 × 24%	48,360
Less: 1/100 × £(500,000 – 251,500) × 201,500/251,500	(1,991)
Corporation tax payable	46,369

Workings

1   *Interest income*

	£
Bank interest receivable	8,460
Loan interest – received 31.12.12	16,400
– accrued 31.3.13	8,200
	33,060

2   *Property income*

	£
Premium received	100,000
Less: 2% × (10 − 1) × £100,000	(18,000)
Taxable as property income	82,000
Add: rental income accrued	44,000
	126,000

(iii)   Jogger Ltd's self-assessment tax return for the year ended 31 March 2013 must be submitted by 31 March 2014.

If the company submits its self-assessment tax return eight months late, then there will be an automatic fixed penalty of £200, since the return is more than three months late.

There will also be an additional corporation tax geared penalty of £4,637 (£46,369 × 10%) which is 10% of the tax unpaid six months after the return was due as the total delay is less than 12 months.

Tutorial note

The question states that the corporation tax liability is paid at the same time the self-assessment tax return is submitted which is eight months late.

(b)   (i)   The late submission of the VAT return for the quarter ended 30 September 2011 will have resulted in HM Revenue and Customs (HMRC) issuing a surcharge liability notice specifying a surcharge period running to 30 September 2012.

The late payment of VAT for the quarter ended 31 March 2012 will have resulted in a surcharge of £778 (£38,900 × 2%) because this is the first default in the surcharge period. The surcharge period will also have been extended to 31 March 2013.

The late payment of VAT for the quarter ended 31 March 2013 will therefore have resulted in a surcharge of £4,455 (£89,100 × 5%) because this is the second default in the surcharge period. The surcharge period will also have been extended to 31 March 2014.

(ii)   **Annual accounting scheme**

The reduced administration from only having to submit one VAT return each year should mean that default surcharges are avoided in respect of the late submission of VAT returns.

In addition, making payments on account based on the previous year's VAT liability will improve both budgeting and possibly cash flow if Jogger Ltd's business is expanding.

Jogger Ltd can apply to use the annual accounting scheme if its expected taxable turnover for the next 12 months does not exceed £1,350,000 exclusive of VAT.

However, the company must be up to date with its VAT returns before it is allowed to use the scheme.

44 Black Ltd, Brown Ltd and Blu Reddy

> **Text references.** Group relief is covered in Chapter 23. Double taxation relief is dealt with in Chapter 24. Inheritance tax is the subject of Chapter 18.
>
> **Top tips.** It is very important that you read the questions carefully and comply with any detailed instructions. For example, in each of the three parts of this question, you were given notes about your answer such as to set out your answer in a particular way or to ignore exemptions.
>
> **Easy marks.** The inheritance tax part of this question was probably the easiest on which to obtain marks. The loss to the donor principle is an important aspect of inheritance tax and quite straightforward to deal with.
>
> **Examiner's comments.** Part (a) was not as complicated as candidates tried to make it, and remembering basic principles would have eliminated the worst of the errors – only current year losses can be group relieved, with no relief available for capital losses. In part (b), a surprisingly common mistake was to deduct double taxation relief from taxable total profits rather than reducing the corporation tax liability. Candidates were helped in part (c) by being told to ignore annual exemptions, but many also ignored these instructions. They were not penalised for this, but it made the calculations a bit more complicated than was necessary. When calculating the additional liability arising on death many candidates had problems computing the amount of brought forward gross chargeable transfer, and taper relief was often calculated and deducted at the wrong point in the computation. Candidates should also appreciate that examinations are not quite the same as real life. With a six mark section it should be obvious that the value of the transfer was more than the nil rate band of £325,000 - many candidates calculating the transfer as 200,000 x £1 = £200,000. Using any of the other values would have enabled some marks to be obtained. However, there were many perfect answers to part (c), with the six marks obtained often being the difference between a pass and a fail.

Marking scheme

			Marks	
(a)	**Maximum potential claim by Black Ltd**			
	After losses brought forward used	1		
	Qualifying charitable donations	½		
	Maximum claim	½		
	Maximum surrender by White Ltd			
	Trading loss – current period only/maximum claim	1		
	Qualifying charitable donations	1		
	Capital losses	½		
	Maximum group relief claim that can be made	½		
			5	
(b)	(i)	UK trading profits	½	
		Branch one: profit	½	
		Branch two: loss	½	
		Corporation tax	½	
		Double tax relief	1	
			3	
	(ii)	Corporation tax on UK trading profits only	1	

(c) **Lifetime transfer**

Value transferred	2
IHT liability	1½
Additional tax on death	
Gross chargeable transfer	½
IHT liability	½
Taper relief	1
IHT already paid	½
	6
	15

(a) **Black Ltd – Group relief claim for year ended 31 March 2013**

Maximum potential claim by Black Ltd

Black Ltd uses its own losses brought forward in working out the taxable total profits against which it may claim group relief.

Furthermore, group relief is against taxable total profits after all other reliefs for the current period (for example qualifying charitable donations).

The maximum potential claim by Black Ltd is therefore £(396,800 – 57,900 + 21,100 – 4,400) = £355,600.

Maximum potential surrender by White Ltd

White Ltd may surrender its current period trading losses of £351,300. Only current period losses are available for group relief so White Ltd's loss of £21,800 brought forward cannot be group relieved.

White Ltd may also surrender excess qualifying charitable donations (ie to the extent that they exceed total profits before taking account of any losses). Since the qualifying charitable donations of £5,600 do not exceed the total profits of £26,700, there is no excess.

It is not possible to surrender capital losses as part of a group relief claim.

The maximum potential surrender by White Ltd is therefore £351,300.

Maximum group relief claim

The maximum group relief claim is the lower of the claim that can be made by Black Ltd and the surrender that can be made by White Ltd ie £351,300.

(b) (i) **Brown Ltd – Corporation tax liability for year ended 31 March 2013 if no election made**

	£
UK trading profit	30,000
Branch one trading profit	200,000
Branch two trading loss	(22,000)
Taxable total profits	208,000
Small profit rate applies (below lower limit)	
£208,000 × 20%	41,600
Less: DTR	
Branch one: lower of £(200,000 × 20%) =£40,000 and £32,000 (overseas tax)	(32,000)
Corporation tax liability	9,600

(ii) **Brown Ltd – Corporation tax liability for year ended 31 March 2013 if election made**

£30,000 × 20%	6,000

(c)   **Blu Reddy – Inheritance tax on transfer of Purple Ltd shares**

	£
Lifetime transfer 15 January 2013	
Value of shares held before the transfer	1,200,000
300,000 × £4	
Value of shares held after the transfer	
100,000 × £2	(200,000)
Net chargeable transfer	1,000,000
IHT liability	
£325,000 × 0%	0
£675,000 × 20/80	168,750
ifetime IHT payable	168,750
Gross chargeable transfer £(1,000,000 + 168,750)	1,168,750
Additional IHT arising death 31 May 2017	
Gross transfer of value	1,168,750
IHT liability	
£325,000 × 0%	0
£843,750 × 40%	337,500
	337,500
Less: taper relief (4 to 5 years @ 40%)	(135,000)
Death tax	202,500
Less: lifetime tax paid	(168,750)
Additional IHT payable	33,750

45 Neung Ltd

Text references. Taxable total profits are covered in Chapter 19 and the computation of corporation tax in Chapter 20. VAT is dealt with in Chapters 26 and 27.

Top tips. Set out your capital allowance computation in the standard columnar format – you might want to do this computation at the start of the question and then slot the total into the calculation of taxable total profits.

Easy marks. The rules on associated companies should be well known and so part (a)(i) should have given easy marks. Keep your points short and relevant to the question asked. For example, you did not need to deal with the position of non-UK companies in this part, although this was relevant in part (a)(iii).

Examiner's comments. This question was generally well answered, and there were many very good answers. In part (a)(i), candidates should realise that when given a list of four companies, it is good exam technique to explain for each company whether it is or is not treated as being associated. In part (a)(ii), several candidates treated the lease premium as income rather than as a deduction. Candidates should try to use a new page for large capital allowances computations. In part (a)(iii), most candidates correctly stated that the conversion of the overseas branches into subsidiaries would increase the number of associated companies, but only a few were aware that UK loss relief and UK capital allowances would not then be available. Part (b)(i) was well answered, although a number of candidates did not appreciate that the tax point for services supplied was when the invoice was issued, as this was before the basic tax point or the date of payment. Some candidates showed (an incorrect) input VAT figure for the cost of fuel despite the question only requiring a calculation of the output VAT. Part (b)(ii) was not as well answered as would have been expected, and too many candidates simply explained the default surcharge rules without applying them to the company's situation. Part (b)(iii) was also often not well answered, with far too many candidates stating that a VAT invoice would not have to be issued if the company was not registered for VAT, when quite clearly it was registered.

					Marks
(a)	(i)	Second Ltd and Fourth Ltd		1	
		Third Ltd and Fifth Ltd		1	
					2
	(ii)	Operating profit		½	
		Depreciation		½	
		Lease premium	– Assessable amount	1½	
			– Deduction	1	
		Capital allowances	– AIA	1	
			– Main pool	1½	
			– Special rate pool	1½	
		Overseas branches		1	
		Loan interest		1	
		Franked investment income		1	
		Group dividend		½	
		Corporation tax		2	
					13
	(iii)	Relief for trading losses		1	
		Availability of capital allowances		1	
		Associated company		1	
					3
	(iv)	Overseas branch loss not relievable		1	
		Election takes effect in next accounting period		1	
					2
(b)	(i)	Sales – VAT registered customers		1	
		– Additional contract		1	
		– Non-VAT registered customers		1	
		Fuel scale charge		1	
					4
	(ii)	Previous late submissions		1	
		Surcharge		1	
		Extension of surcharge period		1	
					3
	(iii)	Circumstances		2	
		Period		1	
					3
					30

(a)   (i)   **Associated companies**

Second Ltd and Fourth Ltd are not associated companies as Neung Ltd has a shareholding of less than 50% in Second Ltd, and Fourth Ltd is dormant.

Third Ltd and Fifth Ltd are associated companies as Neung Ltd has a shareholding of over 50% in each case, and both are trading companies.

(ii)   **Neung Ltd – Corporation tax computation for the year ended 31 March 2013**

	£
Operating profit	289,694
Depreciation	18,830
Deduction for lease premium (W1)	(4,340)
Capital allowances (W2)	(29,284)
UK trading profit	274,900
First overseas branch trading profit	41,000
Second overseas branch trading loss	(15,700)
Net trading profit	300,200
Loan interest (25,200 + 12,600)	37,800
Taxable total profits	338,000
Franked investment income (37,800 × 100/90)	42,000
Augmented profits	380,000
Corporation tax (338,000 @ 24%)	81,120
Marginal relief	
1/100 (500,000 – 380,000) × 338,000/380,000	(1,067)
	80,053

Neung Ltd has two associated companies, so the upper limit is reduced to £500,000 (1,500,000/3).

Tutorial note

The dividend of £16,200 from Third Ltd is not included as franked investment income as it is a group dividend.

Workings

1   *Deduction for lease premium*

The amount assessed on the landlord is £86,800 calculated as follows:

	£
Premium received	140,000
Less: 140,000 × 2% × (20 – 1)	(53,200)
	86,800

This is deductible over the life of the lease, so the deduction for the year ended 31 March 2013 is £4,340 (86,800/20).

Tutorial note

The office building has been used for business purposes, and so the proportion of the lease premium assessed on the landlord can be deducted, spread over the life of the lease.

2   *Capital allowances*

	AIA £	Main pool £	Special rate pool £	Allowances £
WDV brought forward		4,800	25,500	
Additions qualifying for AIA				
Ventilation system	20,000			
AIA	(20,000)			20,000
Other additions				
Motor car [1]			15,400	
Motor car [2]		28,600		
		33,400	40,900	
WDA – 18%		(6,012)		6,012
WDA – 8%			(3,272)	3,272
WDV carried forward		27,388	37,628	
Total allowances				29,284

Tutorial notes:

1   Motor car [1] has CO_2 emissions over 160 grams per kilometre and therefore only qualifies for writing down allowances at the rate of 8% as part of the special rate pool.

2   Motor car [2] has CO_2 emissions between 111 and 160 grams per kilometre and therefore qualifies for writing down allowances at the rate of 18% as part of the main pool.

(iii)   **Branch or subsidiary**

UK relief is not usually available for trading losses incurred by an overseas subsidiary company, whereas relief is usually available for trading losses incurred by an overseas branch, unless an exemption election has been made.

UK capital allowances will be available for capital expenditure incurred by an overseas branch, again unless an exemption election has been made. For expenditure incurred by an overseas subsidiary company, relief is not available in the UK, and may not be available overseas.

An overseas subsidiary company will be an associated company, and so the UK corporation tax limits will be reduced accordingly. An overseas branch is part of the UK company and so its existence does not affect the limits.

(iv)   **Branch exemption**

The taxation disadvantage of making the election is that losses of overseas branches will not be relievable against UK profits.

The election takes effect from the start of the accounting period after the one in which the election is made.

(b)   (i)   **Neung Ltd – Output VAT for the quarter ended 31 March 2013**

	£
Sales	
VAT registered customers (44,600 – 35,200 = 9,400) × 20%	1,880
Additional contract	1,600
Non-VAT registered customers (289,300 – 242,300 = 47,000) × 20/120	7,833
Fuel scale charge (467 × 20/120)	78
	11,391

Tutorial note

The basic tax point for a supply of services is the date that they are completed, but if a VAT invoice is issued or payment received before the basic tax point, then this becomes the actual tax point. Therefore the tax point for the contract is when the VAT invoice was issued on 1 March 2013.

(ii)   **Default surcharge**

Neung Ltd was late in submitting VAT returns and paying the related VAT liability for two previous quarters. The company has not managed to revert to a clean default surcharge record by submitting four consecutive VAT returns on time.

The late payment of VAT for the quarter ended 31 March 2013 will therefore result in a surcharge of 5% of the VAT liability for that period, although this will not be collected if it is less than £400.

In addition, the surcharge period will be extended to 31 March 2014.

(iii)   **VAT invoices**

Neung Ltd must issue a VAT invoice when it makes a standard rated supply to a VAT registered customer, but there is no requirement to do so if the supply is exempt or if the supply is to a non-VAT registered customer.

A VAT invoice should be issued within 30 days of the date that the supply is treated as being made.

46 A Ltd

> **Text references.** Chapters 19, 20, 23 and 25 are required reading for this question.
>
> **Top tips.** B Ltd's loss could be set only against the available profits of the corresponding accounting period.

		Marks
(a)	Trading income	½
	Property business income	½
	Interest income	½
	Qualifying charitable donation	1
	Group relief	3
	FII	½
	CT calculation	2
		8
(b)	Payment date	1
(c)	Filing date	1
		10

(a) **Corporation Tax computation 9 m/e 31 December 2012**

	£	£
Trading income		342,000
Property income		10,000
Interest income		16,000
Total profits		368,000
Less: qualifying charitable donation		(17,000)
		351,000
Less: group relief (W1)		(34,000)
Taxable total profits		317,000
Add: Franked Investment Income		1,000
Augmented profits		318,000

	£
Corporation tax	
FY 2012	
£317,000 × 24%	76,080
Less marginal relief	
$1/100 \ (£562,500 - 318,000) \times \dfrac{317,000}{318,000}$	(2,437)
Corporation tax payable	73,643

Note. It is assumed that the loan interest arose on a non-trading loan and is therefore taxable as interest income.

Workings

1 B Ltd joined the group with A Ltd on 1 July 2012 so for A Ltd's profit making accounting period to 31 December 2012 there are 6 months in common with B Ltd's loss making period.

A Ltd 6/9 × £351,000 = £234,000
B Ltd 6/12 × (£68,000) = £34,000

Maximum group relief available is lower of two, ie £34,000.

2   The 9 months to 31 December 2012 falls into FY 2012.

Augmented profits are between the upper and lower limits of £1,500,000 × 9/12 ÷ 2 = £562,500 and £300,000 × 9/12 ÷ 2 = £112,500, so marginal relief applies.

(b)   The corporation tax of £73,643 for the nine-month period ended 31 December 2012 must be paid by <u>1 October 2013</u>.

(c)   The corporation tax return for the nine-month period ended 31 December 2012 must be filed by <u>31 December 2013</u>.

47 Apple Ltd

Text references. Corporation tax computations are covered in Chapter 20. Chargeable gains for companies are dealt with in Chapters 21. Group relief is covered in Chapter 23.

Top tips. When using losses, consider the marginal rates of tax of each company.

Marking scheme

		Marks
(a)	*Taxable total profits*	
	Apple – Trading profits	1
	– Capital gains	1
	Bramley Ltd's Loss	1
	Cox Ltd's loss	1
	Delicious Ltd's loss	1
		5

		Marks
(b)	*Corporation tax saving*	
	Capital loss – use in Apple Ltd	2
	Rollover relief	1
	Proceeds not reinvested still chargeable	1
	Corporation tax saving	1
	Use of Bramley Ltd's loss	2
	Use of Cox Ltd's loss	2
	Delicious Ltd's loss – not advantageous to transfer	1
		10
		15

(a)   **Apple Ltd**

	Years ended 31 March		
	2011	2012	2013
	£	£	£
Trading profits	620,000	250,000	585,000
Capital gain	–	120,000	80,000
Taxable total profits	620,000	370,000	665,000

Bramley Ltd

	Years ended 31 March		
	2011	2012	2013
	£	£	£
Trading profits/total profits	–	52,000	70,000
Less: carry forward loss relief	–	(52,000)	(12,000)
Taxable total profits	–	–	58,000

Cox Ltd

	Years ended 31 March		
	2011	2012	2013
	£	£	£
Trading profits/total profits	83,000	–	40,000
Less: carry back loss relief	(58,000)	–	–
Taxable total profits	25,000	–	40,000

Delicious Ltd

	Years ended 31 March		
	2011	2012	2013
	£	£	£
Trading profits/total profits	–	90,000	–
Less: carry back loss relief	–	(15,000)	–
Taxable total profits	–	75,000	–

(b) **Apple Ltd**

	Years ended 31 March		
	2011	2012	2013
	£	£	£
Trading profits	620,000	250,000	585,000
Chargeable gain	–	20,000	36,000
Total profits	620,000	270,000	621,000
Less group relief	(64,000)	(58,000)	(0)
Taxable total profits	556,000	212,000	621,000

In the year to 31 March 2011 group relief has been claimed for Bramley Ltd's loss. This saves Apple Ltd corporation tax of £15,360 (£64,000 × 24%). If the loss had been carried forward as shown above it would have saved Bramley Ltd tax of £12,800 (20% × £64,000). The overall tax saving to the group arising as a result of the group relief claim is £2,560.

Rollover relief has been claimed to defer £100,000 of the chargeable gain arising in the year to 31 March 2012. The £20,000 gain remaining chargeable is equal to the amount of proceeds not reinvested by Cox Ltd in the freehold factory. The lower limit for the year to 31 March 2012 is £75,000 so the rollover relief saves Apple Ltd corporation tax of £25,000 (£100,000 × 25%).

It is assumed that Delicious Ltd and Apple Ltd will make an election to transfer the loss on the leasehold factory to Apple Ltd. If this occurs, Apple Ltd will be able to relieve the £44,000 loss by setting it against its chargeable gain for the year, saving tax of £10,560 (£44,000 × 24%).

In the year to 31 March 2012 group relief has been claimed for Cox Ltd's loss. This saves corporation tax of £14,500 (£58,000 × 25%). If the loss had been carried back as shown above, it would have saved Cox Ltd corporation tax of £11,600 (£58,000 × 20%). The overall tax saving to the group of a group relief claim is therefore £2,900 (£14,500 − £11,600).

Delicious Ltd could surrender its loss of £15,000 in the year to 31 March 2013 to Cox Ltd. This would not be beneficial as the tax saving would be at 20% whereas the tax saving will be at 25% if the carry back relief claim shown in (a) above is made.

48 Sofa Ltd

Text references. Chapter 19 deals with adjustment of profit for companies. Chapter 23 covers groups.

Top tips. Make sure you read the information given in the question very carefully. You were told the figure to start your adjustment of profit.

Easy marks. The capital allowances computation was straightforward if you used the standard format. The items to be disallowed should also have been well-known.

Marking scheme

			Marks
(a)	**Adjustment to profit**		
	Loss before taxation		½
	Depreciation		½
	Accountancy fees		½
	Legal fees – share capital		½
	Legal fees – renewal of short lease		½
	Legal fees – loan relationship		½
	New wall		½
	Repair to existing wall		½
	Business entertaining		½
	Staff entertaining		½
	Redundancy counselling		½
	Health and safety fine		½
	Profit on sale of shares		½
	Bank interest receivable		½
	Loan stock interest payable		1
	Capital allowances on P&M		
	TWDVs b/f		½
	Additions qualifying for AIA:	equipment	½
		Fixtures	½
	AIA		1
	Main pool		1
	Special rate pool		1
	Disposals		1
	WDAs		1
	Additions qualifying for FYA:	low emission car	½
	FYA @ 100%		½
	TWDVs c/f		½
	Allowances		1
			17
(b)	**Settee Ltd**		
	Availability of group relief		½
	Corresponding period 1		1
	Corresponding period 2		1
	Couch Ltd		
	No group relief – not in 75% group		1
	Futon Ltd		
	Availability of group relief		½
	Corresponding period		1
			5
			22

(a) Sofa Ltd – tax adjusted trading loss

	£	£
Loss before taxation		(255,002)
Add: depreciation	87,100	
professional fees: accountancy and audit	0	
professional fees (N1): share capital	7,800	
professional fees (N1): renewal of short lease	0	
professional fees (N1): issue of loan stock	0	
repairs and renewals (N2): new wall	9,700	
repairs and renewals (N2): repair to existing wall	0	
other expenses (N3): entertaining suppliers	1,360	
other expenses (N3): entertaining employees	0	
other expenses (N3): counselling on redundancy	0	
other expenses (N3): fine	420	
interest payable (N1)	0	106,380
		(148,622)
Less: profit on sale of shares	3,300	
bank interest – taxed as interest income	8,400	
CAs on plant and machinery (W)	32,078	(43,778)
Tax adjusted trading loss		(192,400)

Notes

1. The legal fees related to the renewal of a short lease (less than 50 years) are allowable. The cost of obtaining loan finance is allowable as a trading expense under the loan relationship rules as the loan was used for trading purposes. The loan stock interest payable is also allowable for the same reason. The cost of legal fees relating to the issue of share capital is not allowable as it is a capital expense.

2. The cost of the new wall is not allowable because it is a capital expense. The repair to the existing wall is allowable as a revenue expense.

3. Business entertaining is not allowable. Staff entertaining is allowable. Counselling on redundancy is specifically allowable. The health and safety fine is not allowable.

Working: Capital allowances on plant and machinery

	FYA £	AIA £	Main pool £	Special rate pool £	Allowances £
TWDV b/f			27,800	16,400	
Additions qualifying for AIA					
12.5.12 Equipment		1,400			
10.2.13 Fixtures (N)		11,200			
		12,600			
AIA		(12,600)			12,600
Additions not qualifying for AIA					
8.6.12 Car				22,200	
2.8.12 Car			10,900		
Disposals					
8.6.12 Car				(17,800)	
				20,800	
8.1.13 Lorry			(7,600)		
18.1.13 Car			(8,800)		
			22,300		
WDA @ 18%			(4,014)		4,014
WDA @ 8%				(1,664)	1,664
Addition qualifying for FYA					
19.10.12 Car	13,800				
FYA @ 100%	(13,800)				13,800
TWDV c/f			18,286	19,136	
Allowances					32,078

Note

The sale price put on the fixtures can be an amount up to their original cost. Since it has been agreed that Sofa Ltd is to obtain maximum capital allowances on the fixtures, the election must have been the maximum amount possible.

(b)   **Settee Ltd**

Group relief is available between Sofa Ltd and Settee Ltd because they are part of a 75% group.

Group relief applies to corresponding accounting periods.

Corresponding period 1 (1 April 2012 to 30 June 2012)
Loss of Sofa Ltd
3/12 × £192,400   £48,100

Profit of Settee Ltd
3/12 × £240,000   £60,000

Maximum group relief is lower of these two figures ie   £48,100

Corresponding period 2 (1 July 2012 to 31 March 2013)
Loss of Sofa Ltd
9/12 × £192,400   £144,300

Profit of Settee Ltd
9/12 × £90,000   £67,500

Maximum group relief is lower of these two figures ie   £67,500

Couch Ltd

There is no group relief available between Sofa Ltd and Couch Ltd because they are not members of a 75% group as Couch Ltd is only a 60% subsidiary.

Futon Ltd

Group relief is available between Sofa Ltd and Futon Ltd because they are part of a 75% group.

Corresponding period (1 January 2013 to 31 March 2013)
Loss of Sofa Ltd
3/12 × £192,400   £48,100

Profit of Futon Ltd   £60,000

Maximum group relief is lower of these two figures ie   £48,100

49 Gastron Ltd

Marking scheme

		Marks	
(a)	Profit before taxation	½	
	Depreciation	½	
	Amortisation of leasehold property	½	
	Gifts of pens to customers	½	
	Gifts of hampers to customers	½	
	Donation	½	
	Legal fees re renewal of lease	½	
	Legal fees re issue of loan stock	½	
	Entertaining suppliers	½	
	Entertaining employees	½	
	Lease premium – Assessable amount	1½	
	– Deduction	1	
	Income from investments	1	
	Disposal of shares	½	
	Interest payable	½	
	P & M – Main pool with WDA	1½	
	– AIA	1½	
	– Special rate pool with WDA	1½	
	– FYA @ 100%	1	
			15
(b)	Trading profit	½	
	Property business profit	2	
	Bank interest	½	
	Chargeable gain	½	
	Franked investment income	1	
	Group dividends	½	
	Corporation tax	2	
			7

			Marks
(c)	Due date	1	
	Interest	2	
			3
(d)	75% shareholding	1	
	50% effective interest	1	
			2
(e)	Time limit	1	
	Set off of capital losses	1	
	Tax rate	1	
			3
			30

(a) **Gastron Ltd – Trading profit for the year ended 31 March 2013**

	£	£
Profit before taxation		618,008
Add		
Depreciation	85,660	
Amortisation of leasehold property	6,000	
Gifts of pens to customers (N1)	1,200	
Gifts of hampers to customers (N1)	1,100	
Donation to local charity	0	
Legal fees re renewal of lease (N2)	0	
Legal fees re issue of loan stock	0	
Entertaining suppliers (N3)	1,300	
Entertaining employees (N3)	0	
		95,260
Deduct		
Lease premium (W1)	4,920	
Income from property	20,600	
Bank interest	12,400	
Dividends	54,000	
Profit on disposal of shares	80,700	
Interest payable (N4)	0	
Capital allowances (W2)	40,648	
		(213,268)
Trading profit		500,000

Notes

1   Gifts to customers are only an allowable deduction if they cost less than £50 per recipient per year, are not of food, drink, tobacco, or vouchers for exchangeable goods, and carry a conspicuous advertisement for the company making the gift.

2   The costs of renewing a short-lease (less than 50 years) and of obtaining loan finance are allowable.

3   The only exception to the non-deductibility of entertainment expenditure is when it is in respect of employees.

4   Interest on a loan used for trading purposes is deductible in calculating the trading loss on an accruals basis.

Workings

1 The office building has been used for business purposes, and so the proportion of the lease premium assessed on the landlord can be deducted, spread over the life of the lease.

The amount assessed on the landlord is £49,200 calculated as follows:

	£
Premium received	60,000
Less: £60,000 × 2% × (10 – 1)	(10,800)
	49,200

This is deductible over the life of the lease, so the deduction for the year ended 31 March 2013 is £(49,200/10) = £4,920.

2 *Plant and machinery*

	FYA @ 100% £	AIA £	Main pool £	Special rate pool £	Allowances £
TWDV b/f			16,700	18,400	
Additions qualifying for AIA					
Equipment		1,600			
Lorry		17,200			
		18,800			
AIA		(18,800)			18,800
Addition not qualifying for AIA					
Motor car			9,800		
			26,500		
Disposal					
Equipment (N)			(3,300)		
			23,200		
WDA @ 18%			(4,176)		4,176
WDA @ 8%				(1,472)	1,472
Addition qualifying for 100% FYA					
Motor car	16,200				
FYA @ 100%	(16,200)				16,200
TWDV c/f			19,024	16,928	
Total allowances					40,648

Note. The cost of the equipment sold will have originally been added to the pool, so the disposal proceeds of £3,300 are deducted from the pool.

(b) **Gastron Ltd – Corporation tax computation for the year ended 31 March 2013**

	£
Trading profit	500,000
Property business profit (W1)	12,800
Bank interest	12,400
Chargeable gain	74,800
Taxable total profits	600,000
Franked investment income £36,000 × 100/90 (N)	40,000
Augmented profits	640,000
Corporation tax £600,000 @ 24%	144,000
Marginal relief 1/100 (750,000 – 640,000) × 600,000/640,000 (W2)	(1,031)
	142,969

Note

Group dividends are not included as franked investment income.

Workings

1   The property business profit is £12,800 calculated as follows:

	£	£
Rent receivable – First tenant £1,800 × 9		16,200
– Second tenant £1,950 × 2		3,900
		20,100
Impairment loss £1,800 × 2	3,600	
Decorating	3,700	
		(7,300)
		12,800

2   Gastron Ltd has one associated company, so the upper limit is reduced to £750,000 (£1,500,000/2).

(c)   (1)   Gastron Ltd's corporation tax liability for the year ended 31 March 2013 must be paid by 1 January 2014.

       (2)   If the company does not pay its corporation tax until 31 August 2014, then interest of £142,969 @ 3% × 8/12 = <u>£2,859</u> will be charged by HM Revenue and Customs for the period between 1 January 2014 and 31 August 2014.

(d)   (1)   Companies form a capital gains group if at each level in the group structure there is a 75% shareholding.

       (2)   However, the parent company must also have an effective interest of over 50% in each group company.

(e)   (1)   Gastron Ltd and Culinary Ltd must make the election by 31 March 2015 (within two years of the end of the accounting period in the gain arose).

       (2)   The election will enable the capital gain of £74,800 to be set off against capital loss of £66,000.

       (3)   It is also beneficial for the balance of the chargeable gain of £(74,800 – 66,000) = £8,800 to arise in Culinary Ltd as it will only be taxed at the rate of 20%, instead of at the marginal rate (25%) in Gastron Ltd.

50 Lithograph Ltd

Text references. Chapters 26 and 27 deal with VAT.

Top tips. Read the question carefully to determine whether the figures you have been given include the VAT or not.

Marking scheme

		Marks
(a)	Monthly payments	½
	Based on prior year	½
	10%	½
	Months 4 to 12	½
	Calculation	1
		3

			Marks
(b)	(i)	Sales @ 20%	½
		Office equipment sale @ 20%	½
		Fuel scale charge @ 1/6	1
		Purchases	½
		Expenses	½
		Machinery	½
		Bad debt	1
		Output VAT less input VAT @ 20%	½
			5
	(ii)	Balancing payment	1
		Due date	1
			2
			10

(a) Monthly payments on account

As Lithograph Ltd uses the annual accounting scheme it will be paying monthly payments on account based on its previous year's liability.

It will make payments in months 4 to 12 of its VAT accounting period, each payment being 10% of the previous year's liability.

Lithograph Ltd will therefore have made payments of 10% x £10,200 = £1,020 from April 2012 to December 2012.

(b) (i) VAT for y/e 31 December 2012

	£		£
Output VAT			
Sales	160,000	@ 20%	32,000
Office equipment sale	8,000	@ 20%	1,600
Fuel scale charge (N1)	1,400	@ $^1/_6$	233
			33,833
Less: Input VAT			
Purchases	38,000		
Expenses			
28,000 – 3,600 (N2)	24,400		
Machinery purchase	24,000		
Impairment loss (N3)	4,800		
	91,200	@ 20%	(18,240)
VAT due			15,593

Notes

1 Fuel scale charge

As the whole of the fuel VAT expense, including private fuel, has been deducted (included in the expenses) we need to restrict by using the fuel scale charge.

As this is a VAT inclusive figure we need to adjust by multiplying by $^1/_6$

2 Expenses

Customer entertaining is never allowable for VAT purposes.

3 Impairment loss

As the liability is over 6 months old and has been written off in the company's books, it is possible to claim relief.

Balancing payment and due date

The balancing payment due would be:

	£
VAT due	15,593
Less: paid on account (9 payments)	(9,180)
Due by 28 February 2013	6,413

51 Aston Martyn

Text references. Value added tax is covered in Chapters 26 and 27.

Top tips. This question is broken down into six parts, each with a specific number of marks. These indicate how detailed your answer should be – for example, in part (c) there are two marks which required two points to be made.

Easy marks. There were easy marks for dealing with the registration of Aston Martyn, and the filing of the return and payment of VAT.

Examiner's comments. With the exception of part (b), this question was generally answered quite poorly. In part (a) most candidates did not appreciate that the zero-rated supplies had to be included when calculating taxable supplies for registration purposes. Part (b) was well answered, although many candidates wasted time by stating more than four additional pieces of information. For example, common sense should mean that the business could not possibly state the VAT registration number of the customer. Many candidates simply ignored part (c), but marks were awarded for any sensible answer such as input VAT and output VAT would contra out. In part (d) too many candidates simply reproduced the penalty table without relating it to the facts given. Again, marks were awarded for any sensible conclusion. There was little knowledge of the online filing requirement for quarterly returns in part (e), although the annual accounting scheme aspects were answered much better.

Marking scheme

				Marks
(a)		Registration limit	1	
		31 January 2013	1	
		Date of registration	1	
				3
(b)		Aston's VAT registration number	½	
		An identifying invoice number	½	
		The rate of VAT for supply	½	
		The amount of VAT payable	½	
				2
(c)		Date of acquisition	1	
		Entries on VAT return	1	
				2
(d)		No penalty if reasonable care	1	
		Treated as careless	1	
		Amount of penalty	1	
				3
(e)	(i)	Online filing	½	
		Electronic payment	½	
		Deadline	1	
				2

		Marks
(ii)	Payments on account	1
	Amount of each payment	1
	Deadline	<u>1</u>
		<u>3</u>
		<u>15</u>

(a) Aston would have been liable to compulsory value added tax (VAT) registration when his taxable supplies during any 12-month period (or the period from commencement of trade, if less) exceeded £77,000.

This happened on 31 January 2013 when taxable supplies amounted to £79,200 (2,300 + 6,400 + 21,900 + 4,800 + 11,700 + 17,100 + 13,800 + 1,200).

Registration is required from the end of the month following the month in which the limit is exceeded, so Aston will have been registered from 1 March 2013 or from an agreed earlier date.

(b) The following information is required:

- Aston's VAT registration number.
- An identifying number (invoice number).
- The rate of VAT for each supply.
- The amount of VAT payable.

(c) VAT will have to be accounted for according to the date of acquisition. This is the earlier of the date that the service is completed or the date it is paid for.

The VAT charged at the UK VAT rate should be declared on Aston's VAT return as output VAT, but will then be reclaimed as input VAT on the same VAT return.

(d) HM Revenue and Customs will not charge a penalty if Aston has taken reasonable care, provided he informs them of any errors upon subsequent discovery.

However, applying the incorrect rate of VAT is more likely to be treated as careless, since Aston would be expected to check the VAT classification of his supplies.

The maximum amount of penalty will therefore be 30% of the VAT underpaid, but this penalty could be reduced to nil as a result of a subsequent unprompted disclosure to HM Revenue and Customs.

(e) (i) Aston will have to file his VAT returns online and pay the VAT that is due electronically. The deadline for doing this is one month and seven days after the end of each quarter. For example, for the quarter ended 31 May 2013 Aston will have until 7 July 2013 to file his VAT return and pay the VAT that is due.

(ii) Aston will have to make nine payments on account of VAT commencing in month four of the annual VAT return period. These will be due electronically.

Each payment on account will be 10% of the VAT payable for the previous year, although for the first year an estimated figure will be used.

The annual VAT return, along with the balancing payment, will be due two months after the end of the annual VAT period. The VAT return will have to be filed online.

52 Ram-Rom Ltd

Marking scheme

			Marks
(a)	Goods – explanation	1	
	– inventory	½	
	– non-current assets	1½	
	Services – explanation	½	
	– calculation	1½	5
(b)	Registration number	½	
	Invoice number	½	
	Rate of VAT	½	
	VAT exclusive amount	½	
	Total VAT exclusive price	½	
	Total VAT	½	3
(c)	Charge to VAT	1	
	No change if not taken up	1	2
			10

(a) Input VAT recovery – pre registration inputs

Input VAT is recoverable on goods if they are:

- Acquired within 4 years prior to registration
- For business purposes
- Not supplied onwards or consumed prior to registration

	£
Non-current assets – January 2012 acquisition £42,000 × 20%	8,400
– August 2012 acquisition £66,600 × 20%	13,320
Inventory still held £92,000 × 20%	18,400
Input VAT on goods recoverable	40,120

Input VAT is recoverable on services if they are:

- Supplied within six months prior to registration
- For purposes of business

	£
March 2012	7,400
April 2012	6,300
May 2012	8,500
June 2012	9,000
July 2012	9,200
August 2012	8,200
	48,600

$£48,600 \times 20\% = \underline{£9,720}$

Total VAT recoverable $£(40,120 + 9,720) = \underline{£49,840}$

(b) Alterations to invoice – must include

- Registration number
- Invoice number
- Rate of VAT for each supply of goods
- VAT exclusive amount for each supply of goods
- Total Invoice price excluding VAT
- The total amount of VAT

(c) Where a discount is offered for prompt payment, VAT is chargeable on the net amount, regardless of whether the discount is taken up.

53 Sandy Brick

Text references. Chapters 26 and 27 for VAT.

Top tips. As with any question which requires a calculation, setting out the figures in a proforma will help both you and the examiner marking your paper.

Easy marks. The tax point and invoice issuing rules were easy marks.

Examiner's comments. Well answered but some candidates were penalised for not clearly showing which of their calculations were output VAT and which were input VAT.

Marking scheme

	Marks
Sales – VAT registered customers	1½
– Non-VAT registered customers	1½
Advance payment	1
Materials	1
Office equipment	2
Telephone	1
Motor repairs	1
Equipment	1
	10

VAT return

	£	£
Output VAT		
Sales to VAT registered customers		
$(£(44,000 \times 95\%) = £41,800) \times 20\%$		8,360
Sales to non-VAT registered customers		
$(£(16,920 - 5,170) = £11,750) \times 1/6$		1,958
Payment on account		
$£5,000 \times 1/6$		833
Total output VAT c/f		11,151

	£	£
Total output VAT b/f		11,151
Less: Input VAT		
Materials (£(11,200 – 800) = £10,400) × 20%	2,080	
Office equipment £120 × 9 × 20% (N1)	216	
Telephone (£(400 × 70%) = 280) × 20%	56	
Motor repairs £920 × 20% (N2)	184	
Equipment £6,000 × 20%	1,200	(3,736)
Net VAT payable		7,415

Notes

(1)   Pre-registration VAT can be recovered on services for six months before the registration date. Therefore nine months of input tax can be recovered.

(2)   If a car is used for business purposes, then any VAT charged on repairs and maintenance costs can be treated as input tax. No apportionment has to be made for private use.

54 Anne Attire

Text references. Chapters 26 and 27 for VAT.

Top tips. Make sure that you read all the information given in the question – you are given this information by the examiner for a reason so you must make use of it when answering the question.

Easy marks. The due date for payment of VAT was an easy mark.

Examiner's comments. In part (a) candidates often did not appreciate that the calculation of output VAT on credit sales had to take account of the discount for prompt payment even if it was not taken by customers. In part (b) the answers of many candidates lacked sufficient depth to gain full marks. For example, the turnover limit of £1,350,000 was usually known, but only a minority of candidates correctly stated that it applied for the following 12-month period. The same comment applies to part (c). For example, candidates generally appreciated that the taxpayer's VAT registration would be cancelled, but few stated that the reason for the cancellation was the cessation of making taxable supplies. Many candidates stated that on a sale of the business as a going concern the VAT registration could be taken over by the purchaser despite the question clearly stating that the purchaser was already registered for VAT.

Marking scheme

			Marks
(a)	Output VAT – Cash sales	1	
	– Credit sales	1½	
	Input VAT – Purchases and expenses	1	
	– Impairment loss	1½	
	Due date	1	
			6
(b)	Limit	1	
	VAT returns and VAT payments	1	
	Output VAT	1	
	Input VAT	1	
	Impairment loss relief	1	
			5
(c)	(i) *Sale of assets on a piecemeal basis*		
	Cancellation of VAT registration	1	
	Output VAT	1	
			2

(ii)   *Sale of business as a going concern*
       Cancellation of VAT registration   1
       Output VAT not due   1
                                                                          ___
                                                                           2
                                                                          ___
                                                                          15

(a)   **VAT return – Quarter ended 30 November 2012**

	£	£
Output VAT		
Cash sales £28,000 × 20%		5,600
Credit sales £12,000 × 95% × 20% (N1)		2,280
Input VAT		
Purchases and expenses £11,200 × 20%	2,240	
Impairment loss £800 × 95% × 20% (N2)	152	
	____	
		(2,392)
VAT payable		5,488

The VAT return for the quarter ended 30 November 2012 should have been submitted by 7 January 2013.

Notes

(1)   The calculation of output VAT on the credit sales takes into account the discount for prompt payment, even for those 10% of customers that did not take it.

(2)   Relief for an impairment loss is not given until six months from the time that payment is due. Therefore relief can only be claimed in respect of the invoice due for payment on 10 April 2012. Relief is based on the amount of output VAT that would originally have been paid, taking into account the discount for prompt payment.

(b)   Anne can use the cash accounting scheme if her expected taxable turnover for the next 12 months does not exceed £1,350,000. Anne must also be up-to-date with her VAT returns and VAT payments.

Output VAT on most credit sales will be accounted for up to one month later than at present since the scheme will result in the tax point becoming the date that payment is received from customers. However, the recovery of input VAT will be delayed by two months.

The scheme will provide automatic impairment loss relief should a credit sale customer default on the payment of a debt.

(c)   (i)   **Sale of assets on a piecemeal basis**

           On the cessation of trading Anne will cease to make taxable supplies, so her VAT registration will be cancelled on the date of cessation or an agreed later date.

           Output VAT will be due in respect of the value of the non-current assets at the date of deregistration on which VAT has been claimed (although output VAT is not due if it is less than £1,000).

      (ii) **Sale of business as a going concern**

           Since the purchaser is already registered for VAT, Anne's VAT registration will be cancelled as above.

           A sale of a business as a going concern (TOGC) is outside the scope of VAT and therefore output VAT will not be due.

Mock exams

ACCA

Paper F6

Taxation (United Kingdom)

Mock Examination 1

Question Paper	
Time allowed	
Reading and Planning	15 minutes
Writing	3 hours
ALL FIVE questions are compulsory and MUST be attempted.	

During reading and planning time only the question paper may be annotated.

DO NOT OPEN THIS PAPER UNTIL YOU ARE READY TO START UNDER EXAMINATION CONDITIONS

ALL FIVE questions are compulsory and MUST be attempted

1 Mark Kett (Pilot paper)

On 31 December 2012 Mark Kett ceased trading as a marketing consultant. He had been self-employed since 6 April 2006, and had always made his accounts up to 5 April. On 1 January 2013 Mark commenced employment as the marketing manager of Sleep-Easy plc. The company runs a hotel. The following information is available for the tax year 2012/13:

Self-employment

(1) Mark's tax adjusted trading profit for the nine-month period ended 31 December 2012 is £23,700. This figure is before taking account of capital allowances.

(2) The tax written down values for capital allowances purposes at 6 April 2012 were as follows:

	£
Main pool	13,800
Motor car	14,600

The motor car was used by Mark, and 40% of the mileage was for private purposes.

(3) On 15 June 2012 Mark had purchased office furniture for £1,900. All of the items included in the main pool were sold for £18,800 on 31 December 2012. On the cessation of trading Mark personally retained the motor car. Its value on 31 December 2012 was £11,800.

Employment

(1) Mark is paid a salary of £3,250 (gross) per month by Sleep-Easy plc, from which income tax of £620 per month has been deducted under PAYE.

(2) During the period from 1 January 2013 to 5 April 2013 Mark used his private motor car for business purposes. He drove 2,500 miles in the performance of his duties for Sleep-Easy plc, for which the company paid an allowance of 21 pence per mile. The relevant HM Revenue & Customs authorised mileage rate to be used as the basis of an expense claim is 45 pence per mile.

(3) On 1 January 2013 Sleep-Easy plc provided Mark with an interest free loan of £76,000 so that he could purchase a new main residence.

(4) During the period from 1 January 2013 to 5 April 2013 Mark was provided with free meals in Sleep-Easy plc's staff canteen. The total cost of these meals to the company was £400.

Property income

(1) Mark let out a furnished property throughout the tax year 2012/13. He received gross rents of £8,600, 5% of which was paid to a letting agency. During December 2012 Mark spent £540 on replacing dilapidated furniture and furnishings.

(2) From 6 April 2012 to 31 December 2012 Mark let out a spare room in his main residence, receiving rent of £350 per month.

Investment income

(1) During the tax year 2012/13 Mark received dividends of £2,880, interest from government stocks (gilts) of £500, and interest of £430 from an individual savings account (ISA). These were the actual cash amounts received.

(2) On 3 May 2012 Mark received a premium bond prize of £100.

Other information

(1) On 15 December 2012 Mark made a gift aid donation of £800 (net) to a national charity.
(2) Mark's payments on account of income tax in respect of the tax year 2012/13 totalled £11,381.

Required

(a) Compute the income tax payable by Mark for the tax year 2012/13 and the balancing payment or repayment that will be due for the year.

Note: You should indicate by the use of zero any items that are non-taxable/exempt from tax. **(22 marks)**

(b) Advise Mark as to how long he must retain the records used in preparing his tax return for the tax year 2012/13, and the potential consequences of not retaining the records for the required period. **(3 marks)**

(Total – 25 marks)

2 Scuba Ltd (Pilot paper)

(a) Scuba Ltd is a manufacturer of diving equipment. The following information is relevant for the year ended 31 March 2013:

Operating profit

The operating profit is £132,348. The expenses that have been deducted in calculating this figure include the following:

	£
Depreciation	45,200
Entertaining customers	7,050
Entertaining employees	2,470
Gifts to customers (diaries costing £25 each displaying Scuba Ltd's name)	1,350
Gifts to customers (food hampers costing £80 each)	1,600

Leasehold property

On 1 July 2012 Scuba Ltd acquired a leasehold office building that is used for business purposes. The company paid a premium of £80,000 for the grant of a twenty-year lease.

Plant and machinery

On 1 April 2012 the tax written down values of plant and machinery were as follows:

	£
Main pool	47,200
Special rate pool	22,400

The following transactions took place during the year ended 31 March 2013:

		Cost (Proceeds) £
3 July 2012	Purchased machinery	14,020
29 August 2012	Purchased a computer	1,100
4 October 2012	Purchased a motor car CO_2 emissions 135g/km	10,400
18 November 2012	Purchased machinery	7,300
15 February 2013	Sold a lorry	(12,400)

The motor car purchased on 4 October 2012 for £10,400 is used by the factory manager, and 40% of the mileage is for private journeys. The lorry sold on 15 February 2013 for £12,400 originally cost £19,800.

Property income

Scuba Ltd lets a retail shop that is surplus to requirements. The shop was let until 31 March 2012 but was then empty from 1 April 2012 to 31 July 2012. During this period Scuba Ltd spent £6,200 on decorating the shop, and £1,430 on advertising for new tenants. The shop was let from 1 August 2012 to 31 March 2013 at a quarterly rent of £7,200, payable in advance.

Interest received

Interest of £430 was received from HM Revenue & Customs on 28 February 2013 in respect of the overpayment of corporation tax for the year ended 31 March 2012.

Disposal of warehouse

Scuba Ltd disposed of a small warehouse on 31 January 2013. The proceeds of sale were £90,000. Scuba Ltd had bought the warehouse for £50,000 on 1 December 2009. Scuba Ltd bought another small warehouse on 1 April 2012 for £60,000.

The relevant retail price indexes (RPIs) are as follows:

December 2009   218.0
January 2013   245.1

Qualifying charitable donation

Scuba Ltd made a qualifying charitable donation of £1,500 on 30 November 2012.

Other information

Scuba Ltd has no associated companies, and the company has always had an accounting date of 31 March.

Required

(i)   Compute Scuba Ltd's tax adjusted trading profit for the year ended 31 March 2013. You should ignore value added tax (VAT).

        Note: Your computation should start with operating profit for the period of £132,348 and should list all of the items in the statement of profit or loss indicating by the use of a zero (0) any items that do not require adjustment;   **(11 marks)**

(ii)   Compute Scuba Ltd's corporation tax liability for the year ended 31 March 2013.   **(8 marks)**

(b)   Scuba Ltd registered for value added tax (VAT) on 1 July 2010. The company's VAT returns have been submitted as follows:

Quarter ended	VAT paid (refunded) £	Submitted
30 September 2010	18,600	One month late
31 December 2010	32,200	One month late
31 March 2011	8,800	On time
30 June 2011	3,400	Two months late
30 September 2011	(6,500)	One month late
31 December 2011	42,100	On time
31 March 2012	(2,900)	On time
30 June 2012	3,900	On time
30 September 2012	18,800	On time
31 December 2012	57,300	Two months late
31 March 2013	9,600	On time

Scuba Ltd always pays any VAT that is due at the same time that the related return is submitted.

During May 2013 Scuba Ltd discovered that a number of errors had been made when completing its VAT return for the quarter ended 31 March 2013. As a result of these errors the company will have to make an additional payment of VAT to HM Revenue & Customs.

Required

(i)   State, giving appropriate reasons, the default surcharge consequences arising from Scuba Ltd's submission of its VAT returns for the quarter ended 30 September 2010 to the quarter ended 31 March 2013 inclusive.   **(8 marks)**

(ii)   Explain how Scuba Ltd can voluntarily disclose the errors relating to the VAT return for the quarter ended 31 March 2013. You are not required to discuss penalties for errors.   **(3 marks)**

(Total = 30 marks)

3 Peter Shaw

(a)   Peter Shaw made the following disposals during the tax year 2012/13:

(1)   On 10 April 2012 he sold his sole trader business which he had operated since 2002. The net gains on sale amounted to £12,400.

(2)   He held 20,000 shares in Forum Follies plc which he purchased in May 2000 for £50,000. In March 2013, Exciting Enterprises plc acquired all the share capital of Forum Follies plc. Under the terms of the take-over for every two shares previously held in Forum Follies plc shareholders received three ordinary shares in Exciting Enterprises plc plus £2 cash. Immediately after the take-over the ordinary shares in Exciting Enterprises plc were quoted at £6 each. Peter's shareholding represented less than a 1% holding in each company.

(3)   Peter purchased shares in Dassau plc, a quoted company, as follows.

	No. of shares	Cost
		£
December 2005	1,000	2,000
April 2011 1 for 2 rights issue		£2 per share

In November 2012 he sold 1,200 shares for £20,000. Peter has never worked for Dassau plc.

Peter had capital losses brought forward from the tax year 2011/12 of £2,400. His taxable income for the tax year 2012/13 is £11,970.

Required

Calculate Peter's CGT liability for the tax year 2012/13.   **(10 marks)**

(b)   Peter's daughter Wendy has made the following cash gifts:

11 August 2012   £4,000 to her son to enable him to buy a car

21 October 2012   £12,500 to her daughter on the occasion of the daughter's marriage

These are the only gifts that Wendy has made in her lifetime.

Required

Explain the inheritance tax consequences of the gifts made by Wendy.   **(5 marks)**

(Total = 15 marks)

4 Li Fung (Pilot paper)

Li Fung commenced in self-employment on 1 October 2008. She initially prepared accounts to 30 June, but changed her accounting date to 31 March by preparing accounts for the nine-month period to 31 March 2012. Li's trading profits since she commenced self-employment have been as follows:

	£
Nine-month period ended 30 June 2009	18,600
Year ended 30 June 2010	24,900
Year ended 30 June 2011	22,200
Nine-month period ended 31 March 2012	16,800
Year ended 31 March 2013	26,400

Required

(a)   State the qualifying conditions that must be met for a change of accounting date to be valid.   **(3 marks)**

(b)   Compute Li's trading income assessments for each of the five tax years, 2008/09, 2009/10, 2010/11, 2011/12 and 2012/13.   **(9 marks)**

(c)   Advise Li of the advantages and disadvantages for tax purposes of changing her accounting date from 30 June to 31 March.   **(3 marks)**

(Total = 15 marks)

5 Andrew Zoom (TX 06/09)

Andrew Zoom is a cameraman who started working for Slick-Productions Ltd on 6 April 2012. The following information is available in respect of the year ended 5 April 2013:

(1)   Andrew received gross income of £50,000 from Slick-Productions Ltd. He works a set number of hours each week and is paid an hourly rate for the work that he does. When Andrew works more than the set number of hours he is paid overtime.

(2)   Andrew is under an obligation to accept the work offered to him by Slick-Productions Ltd, and the work is carried out under the control of the company's production manager. He is obliged to do the work personally, and this is all performed at Slick-Productions Ltd's premises.

(3)   All of the equipment that Andrew uses is provided by Slick-Productions Ltd.

Andrew has several friends who are cameramen, and they are all treated as self-employed. He therefore considers that he should be treated as self-employed as well in relation to his work for Slick-Productions Ltd.

Required

(a)   List those factors that indicate that Andrew Zoom should be treated as an employee in relation to his work for Slick-Productions Ltd rather than as self-employed.

     Note: you should confine your answer to the information given in the question.   **(4 marks)**

(b)   Calculate Andrew Zoom's income tax liability and national insurance contributions for the tax year 2012/13 if he is treated:

     (i)   As an employee in respect of his work for Slick-Productions Ltd;

     Note: You are not required to calculate employers' national insurance contributions.   **(3 marks)**

     (ii)   As self-employed in respect of his work for Slick-Productions Ltd.   **(3 marks)**

(c)   Assuming that Andrew Zoom is treated as being self-employed in respect of his work for Slick-Productions Ltd, state the date by which Andrew must notify Her Majesty's Revenue and Customs of his liability to pay income tax and outline the penalties that would be payable if Andrew's delay is deemed to be careless.

(5 marks)

(Total = 15 marks)

Answers

DO NOT TURN THIS PAGE UNTIL YOU HAVE
COMPLETED THE MOCK EXAM

A plan of attack

What's the worst thing you could be doing right now if this was the actual exam paper? Sharpening your pencil? Wondering how to celebrate the end of the exam in about three hours' time? Panicking, flapping and generally getting in a right old state?

Well, they're all pretty bad, so turn back to the paper and let's sort out a **plan of attack**!

First things first

You have fifteen minutes of reading time. Spend this looking carefully through the questions and deciding the order in which you will attempt them. As a general rule you should attempt the questions that you find easiest first and leave the hardest until last. Depending on how confident you are we recommend that you follow one of the following two options:

Option 1 (if you're thinking 'Help!')

If you're a bit worried about the paper, do the questions in the order of how well you think you can answer them. You may find the shorter questions less daunting than the longer questions. Alternatively, you may feel better prepared for questions 1 and 2 and wish to start there.

- The requirements for question 1 are broken down into parts which should help you to allocate your time. You could start with part (b) if you knew the answer to this part. Ensure you use the correct pro-forma in part (a) even of you cannot fill every number in.

- Question 2 is also broken down into parts. Make sure you make a good attempt at the corporation tax AND the VAT aspects.

- Approach question 3(a) by breaking it down into parts. Calculate each gain, deal with losses and then work out the tax due. Part 3(b) is an inheritance tax question and can be dealt with separately.

- Question 4 is change of accounting date question. If you find this topic hard, it might be worth leaving this question until last.

- Question 5 is a question comparing employment and self-employment with some tax administration. Even if you couldn't remember all of the distinctions between them for part (a), you should have been able to do the simple computations in part (b).

Lastly, what you mustn't forget is that you have to **answer all of the questions in the paper. They are all compulsory**. Do not miss out any questions or you will seriously affect your chance of passing the exam.

Option 2 (if you're thinking 'It's a doddle')

It never pays to be over confident but if you're reasonably confident about the exam then it is best to work through the questions sequentially starting with question 1.

No matter how many times we remind you....

Always, always **allocate your time** according to the marks for the question in total and then according to the parts of the question. And **always, always follow the requirements** exactly. Did you calculate the payment or repayment in Question 1, not just the income tax liability: these was an easy mark and you should make sure you get it.

You've got spare time at the end of the exam.....?

If you have allocated your time properly then you **shouldn't have time on your hands** at the end of the exam. But if you find yourself with five or ten minutes to spare, check over your work to make sure that there are no silly arithmetical errors.

Forget about it!

And don't worry if you found the paper difficult. More than likely other candidates did too. If this were the real thing you would need to **forget** the exam the minute you leave the exam hall and **think about the next one**. Or, if it's the last one, **celebrate**!

1 Mark Kett

Text references. Chapters 2, 6 to 9.

Top tips. Set out your proformas in the correct layout to assist the marker to award you maximum marks.

Easy marks. You cannot avoid administration questions in the exam so make sure you learn the rules as they gain you easy marks.

Marking scheme

			Marks
(a)	Trading profit		½
	Capital allowances – Main pool		2
	– Motor car		2
	Salary		1
	Beneficial loan		1
	Staff canteen		½
	Expense claim		1½
	Property business profit		2
	Furniture and furnishings		½
	Rent-a-room scheme (exempt)		1
	Interest from government stocks		1
	Dividends		1
	Individual savings account (exempt)		½
	Premium bond prize (exempt)		½
	Personal allowance		½
	Increase in basic rate band limit		1
	Income tax		2½
	Tax suffered at source – PAYE		1
	– Dividends		1
	Balancing repayment		1
			22
(b)	Business records		1
	Other records		1
	Penalty		1
			3
			25

(a) **Mark Kett income tax computation 2012/13**

	Non-savings income £	Savings income £	Dividend income £	Total £
Trading income (W1)	25,120			
Employment income (W3)	9,910			
Property income (W6)	7,310			
Gilt interest (received gross)		500		
ISA interest (exempt)		0		
Premium bond prize (exempt)		0		
Dividends × 100/90			3,200	
Net income	42,340	500	3,200	46,040
Less PA	(8,105)			(8,105)
Taxable income	34,235	500	3,200	37,935

Tax

	£
Tax on non-savings income	
£34,235 @ 20%	6,847
Tax on saving income	
£500 @ 20%	100
Tax on dividend income	
£635 @ 10% (W8)	63
£2,565 @ 32.5%	834
Tax liability	7,844
Less tax credits	
PAYE (3 × £620)	(1,860)
Dividends	(320)
Tax payable	5,664
Less POAs	(11,381)
Repayment due from HMRC	(5,717)

Workings

1 *Trading income*

	£
Trading profit	23,700
Balancing charge (W2)	1,420
	25,120

2 *Capital allowances*

	Main pool £	Motor car (60%) £	Allowances £
TWDV b/f	13,800	14,600	
Additions	1,900		
	15,700	14,600	
Disposal	(18,800)	(11,800)	
Balancing charge	(3,100)		(3,100)
Balancing allowance		2,800 @ 60%	1,680
No WDA in year of cessation			
Balancing charge			(1,420)

3 *Employment income*

	£
Salary (1.1.13 – 5.4.13)	9,750
Loan (W5)	760
Canteen meals – not taxable	Nil
Less mileage deduction (W4)	(600)
Employment income	9,910

4 *Mileage allowance*

	£
Company pays: 2,500 @ 21p	525
Less: mileage allowance 2,500 @ 45p	(1,125)
Deduction (expense claim)	600

5 *Loan*

£76,000 × 4% × 3/12 = £760

6   *Property income*

	£
Income	
Rent from furnished property	8,600
Rent from spare room (W7)	0
Less expenses	
letting agent fees	(430)
wear & tear (£8,600 @ 10%)	(860)
	7,310

Note. There is no relief for expenditure on furniture as wear and tear allowance is given.

7   *Rent-a-room relief*

Received: £350 × 9 = £3,150

This is below the limit of £4,250 and therefore this income will be exempt.

8   *Basic rate limit*

£34,370 increased by gift aid: £800 × 100/80 = £1,000 to £35,370

This is used up as follows:

	£
Non-savings income	34,235
Savings income	500
Dividend income	635
Basic rate band limit	35,370

(b)   **Retaining records**

(i)   As Mark has self employment and property income he must retain his records for five years and ten months from the end of the tax year ie until 31 January 2019.

(ii)   He must also retain the records for his other income until this date (even though the usual period would be one year ten months).

(iii)   If he does not retain his records for this period of time HMRC can fine him up to £3,000 (although this is usually only collected in serious cases).

2 Scuba Ltd

Text references. Calculation of taxable profits, taxable total profits and corporation tax in Chapters 19 and 20. Chapter 8 for capital allowances. Administration in Chapter 25. VAT in Chapters 26 and 27.

Top tips. When dealing with an adjustment to profits, make a brief note to the examiner about why you have treated an item in a particular way. Ensure that you comment on every item in the question to obtain maximum marks.

Most of the calculations are fairly straightforward with perhaps the lease premium being the most challenging and only possible if you have studied this topic.

The most likely trap is not reading the question carefully and missing some information. It is good to mark the question in some way when you have dealt with each item (eg tick off or highlight each item dealt with).

Easy marks. The adjustment to profit was straightforward, as was the calculation of corporation tax.

Once again using a proforma for

•   adjustments of profit
•   capital allowances
•   calculation of taxable total profits

would have helped gain marks. You can slot the appropriate item into the proformas as you read through the question in many cases.

				Marks
(a)	(i)	Trading profit		
		Operating profit	½	
		Depreciation	½	
		Entertaining (½ each)	1	
		Gifts to customers (½ each)	1	
		Lease premium – assessable amount	1½	
		– deduction	1½	
		P&M – main pool	2½	
		– special rate pool	1½	
		– AIA	1	
				11
	(ii)	Corporation tax computation		
		Trading profit	½	
		Property business profit – rent receivable	1	
		– expenses	1	
		Interest	½	
		Chargeable gain	2	
		Rollover relief	1	
		Qualifying charitable donation	1	
		Corporation tax	1	
				8
(b)	(i)	Default surcharge		
		Quarter ended 30 September 2010	1	
		Quarter ended 31 December 2010	1	
		Quarter ended 30 June 2011	2	
		Quarter ended 30 September 2011	1	
		Extension of surcharge period	1	
		Four consecutive VAT returns on time	1	
		Quarter ended 31 December 2012	1	
				8
	(ii)	Errors on VAT return		
		Limits	2	
		Notify in writing	1	
				3
				30

(a) (i) Scuba Ltd – tax adjusted trading profit year ended 31 March 2013

	£	£
Profit before tax		132,348
Add depreciation	45,200	
customer entertaining (N1)	7,050	
employee entertaining (N1)	0	
gifts to customers: diaries (N2)	0	
gifts to customers: food hampers (N2)	1,600	
		53,850
Less lease premium (W1)		(1,860)
Adjusted profits		184,338
Capital allowances (W2)		(32,348)
Taxable trading profit		151,990

Notes

(1) Customer entertaining is never an allowable expense. Staff entertaining is allowable.

(2) Expenditure on gifts to customers is only allowable if the gift (i) costs less than £50 per item, (ii) is not food, tobacco, alcohol or vouchers, and (iii) clearly advertises the business's name.

(ii) **CT liability year ended 31 March 2013**

	£
Taxable trading profit (above)	151,990
Property income (W3)	11,570
Interest (W4)	430
Chargeable gain (W5)	30,000
Total profits	193,990
Less qualifying charitable donation	(1,500)
Taxable total profits/augmented profits	192,490

Small profits rate applies (augmented profits < £300,000)

FY 2012	£192,490 × 20%	38,498

Workings

1   *Lease premium*

	£
Premium (P)	80,000
Less 2% × (n − 1) × P	
2% × (20 − 1) × 80,000	(30,400)
Taxable as Landlord's income	49,600

This amount is deductible for the company over the life of the lease:

$$\frac{£49,600}{20} = £2,480$$

Allowable on an accruals basis ie 1 July 2012 to 31 March 2013 = 9/12 × £2,480 = £1,860

2   *Capital allowances*

	AIA £	Main Pool £	Special rate pool £	Allowances £
TWDV b/f		47,200	22,400	
Additions qualifying for AIA				
3.7.12 Machinery	14,020			
29.8.12 Computer	1,100			
18.11.12 Machinery	7,300			
	22,420			
AIA	(22,420)			22,420
Additions not qualifying for AIA				
4.10.12 Car		10,400		
Disposals				
15.2.13 Lorry		(12,400)		
		45,200		
WDA @ 18%		(8,136)		8,136
WDA @ 8%			(1,792)	1,792
TWDV c/f		37,064	20,608	
Allowances				32,348

3   *Property income*

1 August 2012 to 31 March 2013 = 8m

		£
£7,200 × 4 = £28,800 × 8/12		19,200
Less expenses:		
Decorating		(6,200)
Advertising		(1,430)
Property income		11,570

4   *Interest*

Non-trading loan relationship therefore £430 is taxable as non-trading interest receivable.

5   *Chargeable gain*

	£
Disposal proceeds	90,000
Less: cost	(50,000)
	40,000
Less: indexation allowance £50,000 × $\frac{245.1 - 218.0}{218.0}$ (= 0.124)	(6,200)
Gain	33,800
Less: gain rolled over into new warehouse (balance)	(3,800)
Gain left in charge - amount not reinvested £(90,000 – 60,000)	30,000

(b)   (i)   **Default surcharge**

	Quarter ended	Circumstance	Default surcharge consequence
1	30 September 2010	Late return and payment	Surcharge liability notice (SLN) issued, ending 30 September 2011. As this is the first default there is no surcharge
2	31 December 2010	Late return and payment	SLN extended to 31 December 2011 Surcharge @ 2% = £644
3	31 March 2011	On time	SLN remains in place until 31 December 2011
4	30 June 2011	Late return and payment	SLN extended to 30 June 2012 Surcharge @ 5% = £170 Not collected as < £400
5	30 September 2011	Late return but no VAT due	SLN extended to 30 September 2012 No surcharge as no VAT due
6	31 December 2011 to 30 September 2012	On time	As returns and payments have been on time until the end of the SLN period, the SLN record is wiped clean
7	31 December 2012	Late return and payment	New SLN issued to 31 December 2013 As this is the first default there is no surcharge
8	31 March 2013	On time	SLN remains in place until 31 December 2013

(ii)   Errors can be connected on the next VAT return if they do not exceed the greater of:

- £10,000 (under-declaration minus over-declaration)
- 1% of VAT turnover for the return period (maximum £50,000)

Other errors must be notified to HMRC in writing (eg by letter).

3 Peter Shaw

Text references. Chapters 13 to 16 on CGT. Chapter 18 on IHT.

Top tips. In part (a), you only need to work out the proportionate cost that relates to the receipt of cash on the takeover. In part (b), remember that the inheritance tax annual exemption can be carried forward one tax year if unused. However, the current year exemption must be used up first, before the brought forward exemption.

Easy marks. The gains on disposals were not difficult to calculate. The treatment of potentially exempt transfers was basic knowledge.

Marking scheme

			Marks
(a)	**Sole trader**		
	Identification of entrepreneurs' relief	1	
	Takeover		
	Gain on cash received	2	
	No gain on shares	½	
	Shares		
	Share pool	2	
	Gain	1	
	Summary		
	Set off loss brought forward	1	
	Annual exempt amount	½	
	CGT liability	2	
			10
(b)	**Gift to son**		
	Annual exemption 2012/13	½	
	Annual exemption 2011/12 b/f	½	
	Gift to daughter		
	Marriage exemption	½	
	Annual exemption 2011/12 b/f	½	
	Treated as exempt in lifetime	½	
	Survive 7 years	1	
	Death within 7 years	1½	
			5
			15

(a) Summary of gains

	£
Disposal qualifying for entrepreneurs' relief	
Sole trader business net gain	12,400
Disposals not qualifying for entrepreneurs' relief	
Forum Follies plc (W1)	15,000
Dassau plc (W2)	17,600
Less losses b/f	(2,400)
Total gains	30,200
Less annual exempt amount	(10,600)
Taxable gains	19,600

		£
CGT		
£12,400 @ 10%		1,240
£(34,370 – 11,970 – 12,400) = 10,000 @ 18%		1,800
£(19,600 - 10,000) = 9,600 @ 28%		2,688
CGT liability 2012/13		5,728

Tutorial notes

1   The capital loss brought forward and the annual exempt amount are set against the gains not qualifying for entrepreneurs' relief as this saves CGT at the rates of 18% and 28%, rather than at 10%.

2   The unused basic rate tax band is set first against the gain qualifying for entrepreneurs' relief of £12,400 even though this has no effect on the 10% tax rate.

Workings

1   *The takeover of Forum Follies plc*

The elements in the takeover consideration have the following values:

	£
Ordinary shares (30,000 × £6.00)	180,000
Cash	20,000
Total consideration received	200,000

A gain only arises on the date of the takeover in respect of the cash element of the takeover consideration. The gain in respect of the shares received is deferred until those shares are sold.

	£
Cash received (above)	20,000
Cost £50,000 × 20,000/200,000	(5,000)
Gain	15,000

2   *Dassau plc shares*

   (i)   Share pool

	Shares	Cost £
December 2005	1,000	2,000
Rights issue April 2011 1:2 @ £2	500	1,000
	1,500	3,000
Disposal November 2012	(1,200)	(2,400)
	300	600

		£
(ii)	Proceeds	20,000
	Less cost	(2,400)
	Gain	17,600

(b)   **Wendy – inheritance tax in respect of gifts**

11 August 2012

The gift of £4,000 to Wendy's son to enable him to buy a car is an exempt transfer of value as £3,000 of it is covered by the 2012/13 annual exemption and the remaining £1,000 by part of the 2011/12 annual exemption (which can be carried forward one tax year).

21 October 2012

The gift of £12,500 to Wendy's daughter on the occasion of her marriage is partly an exempt transfer of value. This is the amount of the marriage exemption of £5,000 (parent to party to the marriage) and the remaining £(3,000 – 1,000) = £2,000 of the 2011/12 annual exemption.

This leaves £(12,500 – 5,000 – 2,000) = £5,500 which is a potentially exempt transfer of value. This is treated as exempt whilst Wendy is alive. If she survives until 21 October 2019, it will become exempt. If she dies before 21 October 2019, it will become chargeable. It will be charged at 0%, so no tax will be payable on this gift, but it will use up £5,500 of her nil rate band for later lifetime gifts and the death estate.

4 Li Fung

> **Text references.** Self-employment is covered in Chapters 7 to 9.
>
> **Top tips.** There are 3 marks for part (a); you should aim to state 3 conditions.

(a) **Change of accounting date conditions**

(i) Must notify HMRC by 31 January following the tax year of the change of accounting date.

(ii) The new accounts must not exceed 18 months in length.

(iii) There must not have been a change of accounting date in the previous 5 years unless there is a commercial reason for this later change.

(b) **Trading income assessments**

	£	£
2008/09		
Actual basis: 1.10.08 – 5.4.09		
6/9 × £18,600		12,400
2009/10		
<12 months therefore tax first 12 months		
9m to 30.6.09	18,600	
1.7.09 – 30.9.09: 3/12 × £24,900	6,225	
		24,825
2010/11		
CYB: y/e 30.6.10		24,900

	£	£

2011/12
Year of change (two periods ending in same tax year)
Tax both periods and relieve overlap profits

	£	£
Y/e 30.6.11	22,200	
9m to 31.3.12	16,800	
21 months worth of profit	39,000	
Less overlap relief (W) (9 months worth)	(18,625)	
12 months worth of profit		20,375

2012/13

	£
CYB: y/e 31.3.13	26,400

Working

Overlap profits are any profits that are taxed twice when a business starts (or on a change of accounting date):

		£
1.10.08 – 5.4.09	= 6m	12,400
1.7.09 – 30.9.09	= 3m	6,225
Total	= 9m	18,625

(c) **Advantages and disadvantages of changing accounting date**

Advantages	Disadvantages
All of the overlap profits will be relieved	Tax on the profits of a tax year will be due sooner
The year end will now correspond with the tax year so will make basis periods easier	The profits taxable for a tax year will not be known until after the end of the tax year.
On cessation, only the profits earned in the tax year of cessation will be taxed.	

BPP
LEARNING MEDIA

5 Andrew Zoom

Marking scheme

			Marks	
(a)		Control	½	
		Financial risk	½	
		Basis of remuneration	1	
		Sound management	½	
		Required to do the work personally	½	
		Obligation to accept work offered	½	
		Equipment	½	
				4
(b)	(i)	*Treated as an employee*		
		Employment income	½	
		Personal allowance	½	
		Income tax liability	½	
		Class 1 NIC	1½	
				3
	(ii)	*Treated as self-employed*		
		Income tax liability	½	
		Class 2 NIC	1	
		Class 4 NIC	1½	
				3
(c)		Notification date	1	
		Penalties – maximum	2	
		Penalties – minimum	2	
				5
				10

(a) **Factors for employment rather than self-employment**

- Andrew is under the control of Slick-Productions Ltd.
- Andrew is not taking any financial risk.
- Andrew works a set number of hours, is paid by the hour and is paid for overtime.
- Andrew cannot profit from sound management.
- Andrew is required to do the work personally.
- There is an obligation to accept work that is offered.
- Andrew does not provide his own equipment.

(b) (i) **Treated as an employee**

Andrew's income tax liability 2012/13

	£
Employment income/net income	50,000
Less: personal allowance	(8,105)
Taxable income	41,895

Income tax

£	
34,370 @ 20%	6,874
7,525 @ 40%	3,010
41,895	
Income tax liability	9,884

Andrew's national insurance contributions 2012/13

Class 1 NIC
£(42,475 – 7,605) = 34,870 @ 12% + £(50,000 – 42,475) = 7,525 @ 2% = £4,335.

(ii) **Treated as self-employed**

Andrew's income tax liability 2012/13
Andrew's trading profit for 2012/13 will be £50,000, so his income tax liability will be unchanged at £9,884.

Andrew's National insurance contributions 2012/13

Class 2 NIC
52 × £2.65 = £138

Class 4 NIC
£(42,475 – 7,605) = 34,870 @ 9% + £(50,000 – 42,475) = 7,525 @ 2% = £3,289.

(c) Andrew starts being self-employed in 2012/13. He must notify HMRC that he has a new source of income by 5 October 2013.

If Andrew notifies HMRC after these dates and his delay is careless, he will be liable to pay a penalty based on the potential lost revenue (PLR) as the result of his delay. This is usually the tax liability. The maximum penalty is 30% of PLR.

If Andrew notifies HMRC without prompting, the minimum penalty is 10% if the delay is more than 12 months or 0% within 12 months.

If the notification is with prompting by HMRC, the minimum penalties are 20% and 10% respectively.

ACCA
Paper F6
Taxation (United Kingdom)

Mock Examination 2

Question Paper	
Time allowed	
Reading and Planning	15 minutes
Writing	3 hours
ALL FIVE questions are compulsory and MUST be attempted.	

During the reading and planning time only the question paper may be annotated.

DO NOT OPEN THIS PAPER UNTIL YOU ARE READY TO START UNDER EXAMINATION CONDITIONS

ALL FIVE questions are compulsory and MUST be attempted
1 Noel and Liam Wall (BTX)

(a) Noel and Liam Wall are brothers, aged 38 and 40 respectively. Noel has more income than Liam, so he is surprised that for the tax year 2012/13 his total income tax liability and national insurance contributions were much lower than Liam's. The following information is available for the tax year 2012/13:

Noel Wall

(1) Noel is a self-employed musician. His statement of profit or loss for the year ended 5 April 2013 was as follows:

	£	£
Fee income		85,245
Depreciation	1,642	
Motor expenses (note 2)	5,600	
Professional fees (note 3)	2,110	
Repairs and renewals (note 4)	2,698	
Travelling and entertaining (note 5)	960	
		(13,010)
Net profit		72,235

(2) During the year ended 5 April 2013 Noel drove a total of 8,400 miles, of which 7,560 were for business journeys.

Noel's motor car has CO_2 emissions of 180 g/km and had a tax written down value of £32,800 at 6 April 2012.

(3) The figure for professional fees includes £510 for personal tax advice in respect of the tax year 2011/12.

(4) The figure for repairs and renewals consists of £2,238 for a new guitar, and £460 for repairing this guitar when it was damaged.

(5) The figure for travelling and entertaining includes £370 for entertaining clients, and £120 for parking fines.

(6) In addition to his self-employed income, Noel received dividends of £7,560 during the tax year 2012/13. This was the actual cash amount received.

Liam Wall

(1) Liam is employed as a music producer by Forever Ltd. The company runs a recording studio. During the tax year 2012/13 he was paid a gross annual salary of £65,522.

(2) Throughout the tax year 2012/13 Forever Ltd provided Liam with a diesel powered motor car which has a list price of £32,400. The official CO_2 emission rate for the motor car is 201 grams per kilometre. The company also provided Liam with fuel for private journeys.

(3) On 1 December 2012 Forever Ltd paid a golf club membership fee of £580 for the benefit of Liam.

(4) On 1 January 2013 Liam paid a professional subscription of £220 to the Guild of Producers, a HM Revenue & Customs' approved professional body.

(5) In addition to his employment income, Liam received building society interest of £6,640 during the tax year 2012/13. This was the actual cash amount received.

Required

(i) Calculate Noel's income tax liability and national insurance contributions for the tax year 2012/13.

> *Note:* your computation of Noel's trading income should start with net profit for the period of £72,235 and should list all of the items in the statement of profit or loss indicating by the use of a zero (0) any items that do not require adjustment. **(12 marks)**

(ii) Calculate Liam's income tax liability and national insurance contributions for the tax year 2012/13.

(8 marks)

(b) Denzil Dyer has been a self-employed printer since 2009. He has recently registered for value added tax (VAT).

Denzil's sales consist of printed leaflets, which are standard rated. He sells to both VAT registered customers and to non-VAT registered customers.

For a typical printing contract, Denzil receives a 10% deposit at the time that the customer makes the order. The order normally takes fourteen days to complete, and Denzil issues the sales invoice three to five days after completion. Some customers pay immediately upon receiving the sales invoice, but many do not pay for up to two months.

Customers making an order of more than £500 are given a discount of 5% from the normal selling price. Denzil also offers a discount of 2.5% of the amount payable to those customers that pay within one month of the date of the sales invoice.

All of Denzil's printing supplies are purchased from a VAT registered supplier. He pays by credit card and receives a VAT invoice. However, Denzil also purchases various office supplies by cash without receiving any invoices.

Denzil does not use the annual accounting scheme, the cash accounting scheme or the flat rate scheme.

Required

(i) Advise Denzil as to when he should account for the output VAT relating to a typical standard rated printing supply. **(4 marks)**

(ii) Explain the VAT implications of the two types of discount that Denzil gives or offers to his customers. **(3 marks)**

(iii) Advise Denzil of the conditions that will have to be met in order for him to recover input VAT. You are not expected to list those goods and services for which input VAT is non-recoverable. **(3 marks)**

(Total = 30 marks)

2 Helium Ltd

Helium Ltd is a UK resident company. Helium Ltd operates in the UK, and via two overseas branches in the countries Argon and Boron. Helium Ltd has no associated companies. The following information is available for Helium Ltd for the year ended 31 March 2013:

UK Trading income

The UK trading profit is £275,000. This figure is before taking account of capital allowances.

Plant and machinery

Helium Ltd purchased the following assets in respect of the year ended 31 March 2013:

		£
15 April 2012	Machinery	37,590
10 October 2012	Motor car	14,500
14 January 2013	Computer	2,400

The motor car was purchased for one of the company's directors who will use the car 45% for business purposes. It has 150g/km CO_2 emissions.

The computer has an expected working life of 5 years. Any relevant election will be made in respect of this purchase.

On 7 August 2012, Helium Ltd sold machinery which had originally cost £12,000. The proceeds of sale were £14,000.

The tax written down value of the main pool at 1 April 2012 was £137,365.

Property income

Helium Ltd let out an office building from 1 June 2012 on a 7 year lease. It received a premium of £10,000 on the grant of the lease. The rental payable under the lease was £600 per month.

Helium Ltd paid an insurance premium of £2,040 on 1 June 2012 for the period between 1 June 2012 and 31 May 2013.

Loan interest received

Loan interest of £7,500 was received on 30 September 2012, and £7,500 on 31 March 2013. There were no accruals at the year end. The loan was made for non-trading purposes.

Overseas branches

Helium Ltd's overseas branch in Argon generated a profit before tax of £90,000, on which tax at 22% was payable in Argon.

Helium Ltd's overseas branch in Boron generated a loss of £(25,000).

No election has been made in respect of the overseas branches.

Dividends received

The company also received dividends of £13,500 from Carbon plc, an unconnected UK company. This figure was the actual cash amount received.

Future expansion

Helium Ltd is considering expanding overseas operations. This would be achieved by buying shares in a company in the country of Xenon. Helium Ltd would expect to receive dividends from the company, which is expected to make profits.

Required

(a)   Calculate Helium Ltd's corporation tax liability for the year ended 31 March 2013.   **(18 marks)**

(b)   Show why it would not have been beneficial for Helium Ltd to have made an election in respect of the overseas branches before 1 April 2012.   **(4 marks)**

(c)   Explain briefly, without calculations, possible effects of the Xenon company on Helium Ltd's future corporation tax calculations.   **(3 marks)**

(Total = 25 marks)

3 Rotate, Spin and Turn (BTX)

You are a trainee accountant and your manager has asked for your help in advising three unconnected corporate clients that have each sold freehold factories.

Rotate Ltd

On 2 September 2012 Rotate Ltd sold a freehold factory for £470,000. The indexed cost of the factory on that date was £240,100. On 8 August 2012 Rotate Ltd had purchased a replacement freehold factory for £415,000.

Spin Ltd

On 14 November 2012 Spin Ltd sold a freehold factory for £360,000. The indexed cost of the factory on that date was £333,200. On 5 January 2013 Spin Ltd purchased a replacement leasehold factory, with a lease period of 15 years, for £394,000.

Turn Ltd

On 22 December 2012 Turn Ltd sold a freehold factory for £290,000. The indexed cost of the factory on that date was £230,000. 80% of this factory had been used in a manufacturing business run by Turn Ltd. However, the remaining 20% of this factory has never been used for business purposes. On 18 January 2013 Turn Ltd purchased a replacement freehold factory for £340,000.

Other information

Unless otherwise stated, each of the factories has always been used for business purposes. Where possible, Rotate Ltd, Spin Ltd and Turn Ltd have all elected to hold over the gain arising on the disposal of their respective freehold factories under the rollover relief (replacement of business assets) rules.

Required

(a)   State the conditions that must be complied with in order that rollover relief can be claimed. You are not expected to list the categories of asset that qualify for rollover relief.   **(3 marks)**

(b)   Advise Rotate Ltd, Spin Ltd and Turn Ltd of the rollover relief available on the disposal of their respective freehold factories. Your answer should include:

(1)   Calculations of the capital gains immediately chargeable, and

(2)   An explanation of the future tax implications arising from the gains that have been deferred.

(12 marks)

(Total = 15 marks)

4 Duke and Earl

Duke and Earl Upper-Crust, aged 44, are twin brothers.

Duke is employed by the High-Brow Bank plc as a financial adviser. During the tax year 2012/13 Duke was paid a gross salary of £120,000. He also received a bonus of £25,000 on 15 March 2013. On 31 March 2013 Duke made a contribution of £50,000 (gross) into a personal pension scheme.

Earl is self-employed as a financial consultant. His trading profit for the year ended 5 April 2013 was £34,000. On 31 March 2013 Earl made a contribution of £40,000 (gross) into a personal pension scheme.

Neither Duke nor Earl has any other income. In previous years, both Duke and Earl have made gross pension contributions of at least £50,000.

Required

(a) Calculate Duke and Earl's income tax liabilities for the tax year 2012/13, together with the actual net of tax amounts that Duke and Earl will have paid to their personal pension companies.   **(8 marks)**

(b) Advise Duke of the maximum additional amounts that he could have contributed into personal pension schemes for the tax year 2012/13, whether or not such additional contribution would have qualified for tax relief, and how the annual allowance would affect such additional contribution.

(5 marks)

(c) Explain how your answer to part (b) would have been different if Duke had made a gross pension contribution of £46,000 (instead of £50,000) in 2011/12.   **(2 marks)**

(Total = 15 marks)

5 Rahul

Rahul died on 22 December 2012. During his lifetime he made the following gifts:

Date	Gift	Recipient
15 August 2002	Quoted shares worth £288,000	Daughter
10 March 2006	House worth £290,000	Son
7 July 2008	Cash of £327,000	Trust (Rahul agreed to pay the IHT due)

The nil rate bands in previous years were as follows:

2002/03	£250,000
2005/06	£275,000
2008/09	£312,000

Rahul left the following assets in his death estate:

	£
Quoted shares	180,000
House	400,000
Life assurance policy	see below

The life assurance policy was worth £30,000 immediately before Rahul's death. The sum assured by the policy was £110,000 and this was paid to his executors on 10 March 2013.

Rahul also had the following debts at his death:

	£
Repayment mortgage secured on house	125,000
Income tax	2,400

Rahul's executors paid his funeral expenses of £5,600 on 31 January 2013.

In his Will, Rahul left the quoted shares to his wife and the remainder of his estate to his son. The executors filed an account for inheritance tax on 10 April 2013.

Required

(a) Calculate the inheritance tax payable on the lifetime gifts made by Rahul:

    (i)   during his lifetime; and

    (ii)   on his death,

    Where relevant, state the due date of payment and who is liable to pay the inheritance tax. **(10 marks)**

(b) Calculate the inheritance tax payable on Rahul's death estate. State the due date of payment and who is liable to pay the inheritance tax. **(5 marks)**

(Total = 15 marks)

Answers

**DO NOT TURN THIS PAGE UNTIL YOU HAVE
COMPLETED THE MOCK EXAM**

A plan of attack

What's the worst thing you could be doing right now if this was the actual exam paper? Sharpening your pencil? Wondering how to celebrate the end of the exam in about 3 hours time? Panicking, flapping and generally getting in a right old state?

Well, they're all pretty bad, so turn back to the paper and let's sort out a **plan of attack**!

First things first

You have fifteen minutes of reading time. Spend this looking carefully through the questions and deciding the order in which you will attempt them. As a general rule you should attempt the questions that you find easiest first and leave the hardest until last. Depending on how confident you are we recommend that you follow one of the following two options:

Option 1 (if you're thinking 'Help!')

If you're a bit worried about the paper, do the questions in the order of how well you think you can answer them. You may find the shorter questions less daunting than the longer questions. Alternatively, you may feel better prepared for questions 1 and 2 and wish to start there.

- Question 1 is on standard income tax topics. Part (b) is about VAT and you must make sure you make a good attempt at this part of the question as well.

- Question 2 is a corporation tax computation. Use the standard pro-forma in your answer and ensure that you deal with all the information given in the question.

- Question 3 dealt with capital gains for a number of companies. Work through the gains or losses systematically and don't forget to apply relevant reliefs.

- Question 4 dealt with pensions. There were easy marks on the basic income tax computations even if you were unsure about the details of the pension rules.

- Question 5 is an inheritance tax question. As well as computing inheritance tax due, you were also required to state the due dates for payment which are easy marks.

Lastly, what you mustn't forget is that you have to **answer all of the questions in the paper. They are all compulsory**. Do not miss out any questions or you will seriously affect your chance of passing the exam.

Option 2 (if you're thinking 'It's a doddle')

It never pays to be over confident but if you're reasonably confident about the exam then it is best to work through the questions sequentially starting with question 1.

No matter how many times we remind you....

Always, always **allocate your time** according to the marks for the question in total and then according to the parts of the question. And **always, always follow the requirements** exactly.

You've got spare time at the end of the exam.....?

If you have allocated your time properly then you **shouldn't have time on your hands** at the end of the exam. But if you find yourself with five or ten minutes to spare, check over your work to make sure that there are no silly arithmetical errors.

Forget about it!

And don't worry if you found the paper difficult. More than likely other candidates did too. If this were the real thing you would need to **forget** the exam the minute you leave the exam hall and **think about the next one**. Or, if it's the last one, **celebrate**!

1 Noel and Liam Wall

> **Text references.** Chapters 2 to 4, 7 to 9 and 12. VAT in Chapters 26 and 27.
>
> **Top tips.** Using familiar proformas for the adjustment to profits and computation of employment income should ensure that you present your workings in a clear and logical way.
>
> To make sure that you don't miss anything it is a good idea to mark the question in some way, eg tick off items as you deal with them.
>
> **Easy marks.** The adjustment to profits was fairly straightforward, as was the computation of the income tax liability in both cases. Make sure you allocate your time correctly to enable you to have time to calculate both liabilities.

Marking scheme

				Marks
(a)	(i)	Net profit	½	
		Depreciation	½	
		Motor expenses	1	
		Professional fees	½	
		Repairs and renewals (½ each)	1	
		Travelling and entertaining (½ each)	1	
		Capital allowances – Motor car	1	
		– Guitar	1	
		Dividends	1	
		Personal allowance	½	
		Income tax	1½	
		Class 2 NIC	1	
		Class 4 NIC	1½	
				12
	(ii)	Salary	½	
		Car benefit – relevant percentage	1	
		– calculation	½	
		Fuel benefit	1	
		Golf club membership	½	
		Professional subscription	½	
		Building society interest	1	
		Personal allowance	½	
		Income tax	1	
		Class 1 NIC	1½	
				8
(b)	(i)	VAT period	1	
		Basic tax point	1	
		Payment received	1	
		Issue of invoice within 14 days	1	
				4
	(ii)	Large order discount	1	
		Prompt payment discount	2	
				3
	(iii)	Made to taxable person	1	
		Supported by evidence	1	
		Supplied for business purposes	1	
				3
				30

(a) (i) **Noel Wall – income tax computation 2012/13**

	Non-savings income £	Dividend income £	Total £
Trading profits (W1)	73,075		
Dividends (£7,560 × 100/90)		8,400	
Net income	73,075	8,400	81,475
Less: PA	(8,105)		(8,105)
Taxable income	64,970	8,400	73,370

Tax		£
£34,370 @ 20%		6,874
£30,600 @ 40%		12,240
£8,400 @ 32.5 %		2,730
Tax liability		21,844

		£
Class 2 NIC: 52 × £2.65		138
Class 4 NIC: £(42,475 − 7,605) × 9% + (73,075 − 42,475) × 2%		3,750

Workings

1   *Trading profit*

		£
Net profit		72,235
Add: depreciation	1,642	
Motor expenses $(5,600 \times \dfrac{8,400 - 7,560}{8,400})$	560	
Professional fees: personal tax advice fees	510	
Repairs and renewals: new guitar (capital)	2,238	
Repairs and renewals: repairs to guitar	0	
Travelling and entertaining: entertaining clients	370	
Travelling and entertaining: parking fines	120	5,440
		77,675
Less: capital allowances (W2)		(4,600)
Taxable trading profit		73,075

2   *Capital allowances*

	AIA £	Trader's car (90%) £	Allowances £
TWDV b/f		32,800	
Addition – guitar	2,238		
AIA	(2,238)		2,238
WDA × 8% (N)		(2,624) × 90%	2,362
TWDV c/f		30,176	
Total allowances			4,600

Note: 90% (7,560/8,400) of the use of the car is for business purposes.

(ii) **Liam Wall – income tax computation 2012/13**

	Non-savings Income £	Savings income £	Total £
Employment income (W1)	83,766		
BSI (£6,640 × 100/80)		8,300	
Net income	83,766	8,300	92,066
Less: PA	(8,105)		(8,105)
Taxable income	75,661	8,300	83,961

Tax

	£
£34,370 @ 20%	6,874
£41,291 @ 40%	16,516
£8,300 @ 40%	3,320
Tax liability	26,710

Class 1 NIC: £(42,475 – 7,605) × 12% + £(65,522 – 42,475) × 2%   4,645

Note. Taxable employment benefits are not subject to Class 1 NIC.

Workings

1   *Employment income*

	£
Salary	65,522
Car benefit (W2)	11,016
Fuel benefit (W3)	6,868
Golf club membership	580
	83,986
Less: professional subscription	(220)
Employment income	83,766

2   *Car benefit*

Round CO_2 emissions down to nearest 5, ie 200

200 – 100 = 100 g/km

Divided by 5 = 20

Taxable % = 11 + 20 + 3 (diesel powered) = 34%

List price = £32,400

Value of benefit   £32,400 × 34% = £11,016

3   *Fuel benefit*

£20,200 × 34% = £6,868

(b) (i) **Accounting for output VAT**

Output VAT must be accounted for according to the VAT period in which the supply is treated as being made. This is determined by the tax point.

The printing contracts are supplies of services, so the basic tax point for each contract will be the date that it is completed.

Where payment is received before the basic tax point, then this date becomes the actual tax point. The tax point for each 10% deposit is therefore the date that it is received.

If an invoice is issued within 14 days of the basic tax point, the invoice date will usually replace the basic tax point outlined above. This will apply to the balance of the contract price since Denzil issues invoices within three to five days of completion.

(ii) **Discounts**

Where a discount of 5% is given for an order of more than £500 then output VAT is simply calculated on the revised, discounted, selling price.

As regards the 2.5% discount offered for prompt payment, output VAT is calculated on the selling price less the amount of discount offered.

There is no amendment to the amount of output VAT charged if the customer does not take the discount but instead pays the full selling price.

(iii) **Input VAT**

The supply must be made to Denzil since he is the taxable person making the claim.

The supply must be supported by evidence, and this will normally take the form of a VAT invoice. Denzil will therefore not be able to recover any input VAT in respect of the purchases of office supplies for cash where there is no invoice.

Denzil must use the goods or services supplied for business purposes, although an apportionment can be made where supplies are acquired partly for business purposes and partly for private purposes.

2 Helium Ltd

Text references. Chapters 19 and 20 for taxable total profits and CT calculation. Chapter 24 deals with the overseas aspects.

Top tips. Don't forget double tax relief when dealing with overseas profits.

Easy marks. Use of proformas, particularly to calculate taxable profits and capital allowances ensures you do not make mistakes and lose marks.

Marking scheme

			Marks
(a)	UK trading profit	½	
	PM – addition	½	
	– AIA	1	
	– short life asset	1	
	– disposal	1	
	– WDA	1	
	Overseas trading profit: Argon	1	
	Overseas trading loss: Boron	1	
	Property income – premium taxed as property income	2	
	– rents received	1	
	– insurance premium	1	
	Interest income	1	
	FII	1	
	CT	3	
	DTR	2	
			18
(b)	Argon profit not taxable	1	
	Boron loss not relievable	1	
	CT @ 20%	1	
	Comparison with original CT	1	
			4

(c)	Associated company	1
	Dividends exempt	1
	FII	1
		$\underline{1}$
		$\dfrac{3}{25}$

(a) **Helium Ltd – CT liability year ended 31 March 2013**

	£
UK trading profit	275,000
Less: CAs (W1)	(52,874)
	222,126
Argon branch trading profit	90,000
	312,126
Less: Boron branch loss	(25,000)
Taxable trading income	287,126
Property income (W2)	13,100
Interest income (accruals basis)	15,000
Taxable total profits	315,226
FII £13,500 × 100/90	15,000
Augmented profits	330,226
CT @ 24% on £315,226	75,654

Less marginal relief $£(1,500,000 - 330,226) \times \dfrac{315,226}{330,226} \times 1/100$ (11,166)

	64,488
Less DTR Argon branch (W3)	(18,412)
CT liability	46,076

Workings

1 *Capital allowances on plant and machinery*

	AIA	Main pool	Short life asset	Allowances
	£	£	£	£
TWDVs c/f		137,365		
Additions qualifying for AIA				
15.4.12 Machinery	37,590			
AIA	(25,000)			25,000
	12,590			
Transfer balance to pool	(12,590)	12,590		
14.1.13 Computer (N)			2,400	
Additions not qualifying for AIA				
10.10.12 Car		14,500		
		164,455		
Disposal				
7.8.12 Machinery (restricted to cost)		(12,000)		
		152,455		
WDA @ 18%		(27,442)	(432)	27,874
TWDVs c/f		125,013	1,968	
Allowances				52,874

Tutorial note

A depooling election should be made for the computer as it has an expected working life of less than eight years. Although the AIA could be set against this short life asset, it is more tax-efficient to use the allowance against main pool expenditure.

2   *Property income*

	£	£
Premium received	10,000	
Less: (7–1) × 2% × £10,000	(1,200)	
Taxable as property income		8,800
Rent received 10 × £600	6,000	
Less: insurance premium 10/12 × £2,040	(1,700)	
Net rental income		4,300
Total property income		13,100

3   *DTR on Argon branch profits*

DTR is lower of

(i)   UK tax on overseas profit £(90,000/315,226) × £64,488 = £18,412

(ii)   Overseas tax on overseas profit £90,000 × 22% = £19,800

ie £18,412

(b)   **Helium Ltd – CT liability year ended 31 March 2013 if election made**

	£
Taxable total profits from part (a)	315,226
Less Argon branch profit	(90,000)
Add Boron branch loss	25,000
Taxable trading profits	250,226
FII £13,500 × 100/90	15,000
Augmented profits	265,226
CT @ 20% on £250,226	50,045
Additional CT if election had been made £(50,045 – 46,076)	3,969

(c)   The overseas company will be an associated company, so the small profits lower and upper limits would be reduced to £150,000 and £750,000 respectively. This may increase the rate of UK corporation tax.

The dividends received from the Xenon company are exempt from UK corporation tax.

However franked investment income includes all dividends received by UK and foreign companies (other than group income). Therefore, if the holding is less than 51%, the dividends could affect the calculation of corporation tax.

Tutorial note:

The question was deliberately vague about Helium Ltd's percentage holding so that you could make all the above points without contradiction.

3 Rotate, Spin and Turn

Text references. Chapter 21 covers the rules for chargeable gains of companies.

Top tips. This question tests thoroughly the rollover relief rules. Remember that you always need to calculate the indexed gain first, before you can think about taking advantage of any reliefs.

Easy marks. The calculation of the three indexed gains were easy marks.

(a) **Conditions for rollover relief**

(i) The reinvestment must take place between one year before and three years after the date of disposal of the original asset.

(ii) The old and new assets must both be qualifying assets and be used for business purposes.

(iii) The new asset must be brought into business use at the time that it is acquired.

(b) **Rotate Ltd**

	£
Proceeds	470,000
Less: Indexed cost	(240,100)
	229,900
Less: Rollover relief (balancing figure)	(174,900)
Chargeable gain	55,000

The gain that remains chargeable is the amount of proceeds received that have not been reinvested in the purchase of the replacement asset, ie £(470,000 – 415,000) = £55,000.

When the replacement factory is ultimately disposed of the base cost will be £240,100 (415,000 – 174,900).

Spin Ltd

	£
Proceeds	360,000
Less: indexed cost	(333,200)
	26,800
Less: rollover relief	(26,800)
Chargeable gain	–

The sale proceeds are fully reinvested, and so the whole of the gain can be rolled over.

The leasehold factory is a depreciating asset, and so the base cost of this factory is not adjusted.

The gain of £26,800 will be held over until the earlier of 5 January 2023 (ten years from the date of acquisition), the date that the factory is disposed of, or the date that the factory ceases to be used for business purposes, at which point it will be chargeable.

Turn Ltd

	£
Proceeds	290,000
Less: indexed cost	(230,000)
	60,000
Less: rollover relief (balancing figure)	(48,000)
Chargeable gain	12,000

The proportion of the gain relating to non-business use is £12,000 (60,000 × 20%), and this amount does not qualify for rollover relief.

The business proportion of the sale proceeds (290,000 × 80% = 232,000) is fully reinvested, and so the balance of the gain can be rolled over.

When the replacement factory is ultimately disposed of the base cost will be £292,000 (340,000 – 48,000).

4 Duke and Earl

> **Text references.** Chapter 2 covers the income tax computation. Pension contributions are covered in Chapter 5.
>
> **Top tips.** Tax relief is available on pension contributions up to an amount of 100% of relevant earnings. Personal pension contributions are always paid net of basic rate tax; higher rate relief is given, where appropriate, by extending the basic rate band.
>
> **Easy marks.** Part (a) required two straightforward income tax computations.

Marking scheme

		Marks
(a)	**Duke Upper-Crust**	
	Employment income	1
	Personal allowance	1
	Income tax	1½
	Net contribution	1
	Earl Upper-Crust	
	Trading profit	½
	Personal allowance	½
	Income tax	1
	Net contribution	1½
		8

		Marks	
(b)	No restriction regarding contributions	1	
	Tax relief up to earnings	1	
	Annual allowance — Effective limit	1	
	— Tax charge on excess contribution	1	
	— Cancellation of relief given	1	
			5
(c)	Unused annual allowance	1	
	Additional contribution	1	
			2
			15

(a) **Duke Upper-Crust – Income tax computation 2012/13**

	£
Employment income (120,000 + 25,000)	145,000
Less personal allowance (W1)	(8,105)
Taxable income	136,895

Income tax	
£84,370 @ 20% (W2)	16,874
£52,525 @ 40%	21,010
Income tax liability	37,884

All of Duke's pension contribution of £50,000 qualifies for tax relief, so he will have paid £40,000 (80% × £50,000) to his personal pension company.

Workings

1 *Calculation of adjusted net income for restriction of personal allowance*

	£
Net income	145,000
Less personal pension contribution	(50,000)
Adjusted net income	95,000

Since the adjusted net income is less than the limit of £100,000, the personal allowance is given in full.

2 *Basic rate limit*

The basic rate limit will be increased to £(34,370 + 50,000) = £84,370.

Earl Upper-Crust – Income tax computation 2012/13

	£
Trading profit	34,000
Less personal allowance	(8,105)
Taxable income	25,895

Income tax	
£25,895 @ 20%	5,179
Income tax liability	5,179

Only £34,000 of Earl's pension contribution of £40,000 qualifies for tax relief, since relief is only available up to the amount of earnings.

The amount of tax relief is £6,800 (£34,000 at 20%), so Earl will have paid £33,200 £(40,000 – 6,800) to his personal pension company.

(b) There is no restriction regarding the amounts that Duke could have contributed into a personal pension scheme for 2012/13.

However, tax relief is only available on an amount up to earnings. Therefore, Duke would only receive tax relief on additional pension contributions of up to £95,000 £(145,000 – 50,000).

Although there is tax relief on pension contributions up to relevant earnings, the annual allowance (£50,000 in 2012/13) acts as an effective limit.

Any tax relieved contributions in excess of the annual allowance are taxed as if they were additional income, with the tax being paid under the self assessment system.

The annual allowance charge therefore cancels out the tax relief that would have been given. There is no charge where contributions have not qualified for tax relief.

(c) If Duke had made a pension contribution of £46,000 in 2011/12, he would not have used up his annual allowance of £50,000 for that year. £(50,000 – 46,000) = £4,000 would be unused.

Duke could use this to make additional gross contributions of £4,000 in 2012/13, 2013/14 or 2014/15 without incurring an excess annual allowance charge.

5 Rahul

Text references. Chapter 18 covers the inheritance tax examinable in F6.

Top tips. Remember that a potentially exempt transfer will be exempt if the donor survives seven years from making it and that it will not be part of the accumulation figure. However, if the donor does not survive seven years, the potentially exempt transfer is a chargeable transfer and will be part of the accumulation figure.

Easy marks. There were easy marks for stating the due dates for payment and who was liable to pay the tax.

Marking scheme

				Marks
(a)	(i)	*Lifetime IHT on lifetime gifts*		
		15 August 2002	PET	1
		10 March 2006	PET	1
		7 July 2008 CLT		
			AE 2008/09	½
			AE 2007/08 b/f	½
			nil rate band	½
			tax using 20/80 to gross up	½
			gross transfer	½
			due date	½
			liability	½
	(ii)	*Death IHT on lifetime gifts*		
		15 August 2002	PET exempt	½
		10 March 2006	PET chargeable	½
			within nil band so no IHT due	½
		7 July 2008 CLT		
			nil rate band available	½
			tax at 40% on balance	½
			taper relief	½
			deduct lifetime tax	½
			due date	½
			liability	½
				10

(b) *Death estate*

	Marks
Shares	½
House less mortgage	1
Life policy	½
Income tax	½
Funeral expenses	½
Spouse exemption	½
Tax at 40%	½
Due date	½
Liability	½
	5
	15

(a) (i) **Lifetime IHT on lifetime gifts**

15 August 2002

Potentially exempt transfer after annual exemptions 2002/03, 2001/02

10 March 2006

Potentially exempt transfer after annual exemptions 2005/06, 2004/05

7 July 2008

Chargeable lifetime transfer

No chargeable transfers in 7 years before this transfer, so full nil rate band of £312,000 available.

	£
Gift	327,000
Less: AE 2008/09	(3,000)
AE 2007/08 b/f	(3,000)
Net transfer of value	321,000

			£
IHT	£312,000	× 0% =	Nil
	£ 9,000	× 20/80 =	2,250
	£321,000		2,250

The gross transfer is £(321,000 + 2,250) = £323,250.

Check

IHT	£312,000	× 0% =	Nil
	£ 11,250	× 20% =	2,250
	£323,250		2,250

The tax is due on 30 April 2009 and is payable by Rahul.

(ii) **Death IHT on lifetime gifts**

15 August 2002

Potentially exempt transfer – exempt because donor survived 7 years

10 March 2006

Potentially exempt transfer - chargeable because donor did not survive 7 years

	£
Gift	290,000
Less: AE 2005/06	(3,000)
AE 2004/05 b/f	(3,000)
Gross transfer of value	284,000

No chargeable transfers in 7 years before this transfer, so full nil rate band of £325,000 available.

Transfer within nil band so no IHT payable on this transfer.

7 July 2008

Chargeable lifetime transfer

Additional tax due because donor did not survive 7 years.

There was a lifetime transfer of value of £284,000 in seven years before 7 July 2008 (transfers after 7 July 2001) so the nil rate band available is £(325,000 – 284,000) = £41,000.

	£
Gross transfer of value	323,250

			£
IHT	£41,000	× 0% =	Nil
	£282,250	× 40% =	112,900
	£323,250		112,900
Less taper relief @ 40% (death between 4 and 5 years after transfer)			(45,160)
Death IHT			67,740
Less lifetime IHT paid			(2,250)
IHT payable			65,490

The tax is due on 30 June 2013 and is payable by the trustees.

(b) **Death estate**

	£	£
Quoted shares		180,000
House (N1)	400,000	
Less: mortgage	(125,000)	
		275,000
Life policy (proceeds payable as a result of death)		110,000
		565,000
Less: income tax	2,400	
funeral expenses	5,600	
		(8,000)
		557,000
Less: spouse exemption (legacy of quoted shares)		(180,000)
Chargeable death estate		377,000

Transfers in the 7 years before death were £(284,000 + 323,250) = £607,250 so the nil rate band of £325,000 at death is used up by these lifetime transfers.

Death tax @ 40% on £377,000 is £150,800.

Due date 10 April 2013, payable by executors.

Mock exam 2: answers

ACCA

Paper F6

Taxation (United Kingdom)

Mock Examination 3
(December 2012 paper)

Question Paper	
Time allowed	
Reading and Planning	15 minutes
Writing	3 hours
ALL FIVE questions are compulsory and MUST be attempted.	

During reading and planning time only the question paper may be annotated.

DO NOT OPEN THIS PAPER UNTIL YOU ARE READY TO START UNDER EXAMINATION CONDITIONS

ALL FIVE questions are compulsory and MUST be attempted

1 Josie Jones

On 30 June 2012 Josie Jones, aged 42, ceased self-employment as a graphic designer. On 1 August 2012 she commenced employment with Typo plc as a creative director. The following information is available for the tax year 2012/13:

Self-employment

(1)   Josie's trading profits for the final two periods of trading were as follows:

	£
Year ended 30 April 2012	95,560
Two-month period ended 30 June 2012	10,440

Both these figures are before taking account of capital allowances.

(2)   There were no capital allowances for the year ended 30 April 2012 and the tax written down value of the capital allowances main pool at 1 May 2012 was nil. On 21 May 2012 Josie purchased computer equipment for £2,000. This was sold for £1,700 on 30 June 2012.

(3)   Josie has unused overlap profits brought forward of £41,700.

Employment

(1)   Josie is paid a salary of £15,100 per month by Typo plc. The salary is paid on the last day of each calendar month.

(2)   During August 2012 Typo plc paid £11,600 towards Josie's removal expenses when she permanently moved to take up her new employment with the company as she did not live within a reasonable commuting distance. The £11,600 covered both her removal expenses and the legal costs of acquiring a new main residence.

(3)   On 1 September 2012 Typo plc provided Josie with an interest free loan of £33,000 that she used to renovate her new main residence. This loan was still outstanding at 5 April 2013.

(4)   During the period from 1 August 2012 to 5 April 2013, Josie was provided with free meals in Typo plc's staff canteen. The total cost of these meals to the company was £1,340. The canteen is available to all of the company's employees.

(5)   During the period from 1 October 2012 to 5 April 2013, Typo plc provided Josie with a diesel powered motor car with an official CO_2 emission rate of 144 grams per kilometre. The motor car, which has a list price of £14,400, cost Typo plc £13,900. Typo plc does not provide Josie with any fuel for private journeys.

(6)   For the tax year 2012/13 Typo plc deducted a total of £44,043 in PAYE from Josie's earnings.   *PAYE*

Other information

(1)   Josie owns two properties, which are let out. Property one qualifies as a trade under the furnished holiday letting rules, whilst property two is let out unfurnished. The income and allowable expenditure for the two properties for the tax year 2012/13 are as follows:

	Property one	Property two
	£	£
Income	6,600	7,200
Allowable expenditure	9,700	2,100

(2)   During the tax year 2012/13 Josie received building society interest of £8,000, interest of £1,200 from a holding of £24,000 5% Treasury Stock 2025, and dividends of £6,480. These were the actual cash amounts received.

(3)   On 2 October 2012 Josie received a premium bond prize of £100.

(4)   During the tax year 2012/13 Josie made gift aid donations totalling £4,400 (net) to national charities.

(5)   Josie's payments on account of income tax in respect of the tax year 2012/13 totalled £34,400.   *PoA*

Required

(a) Calculate the income tax payable by Josie Jones for the tax year 2012/13.

Note:

You should indicate by the use of zero any items that are non-taxable/exempt from tax. **(20 marks)**

(b) (i) Calculate Josie Jones' balancing payment or repayment for the tax year 2012/13 and her payments on account for the tax year 2013/14. You should state the relevant due dates.

Notes:

1. You should assume that no claim is made to reduce the payments on account.
2. You should ignore value added tax (VAT) and national insurance contributions (NIC).

(3 marks)

(ii) Assuming that Josie Jones expects to remain employed throughout the tax year 2013/14, explain why she will probably be able to make a claim to reduce her payments on account for the tax year 2013/14. **(2 marks)**

(Total = 25 marks)

BPP note

This question has been slightly altered from that originally set under Finance Act 2011, following examiner review.

2 Clueless Ltd

(a) You are a trainee accountant and your manager has asked you to correct a corporation tax computation that has been prepared by the managing director of Clueless Ltd, a company which manufactures children's board games. The corporation tax computation is for the year ended 31 March 2013 and contains a significant number of errors:

Clueless Ltd – Corporation tax computation for the year ended 31 March 2013

	£
Trading profit (working 1)	413,438
Loan interest received (working 2)	32,100
	445,538
Dividends received (working 3)	29,462
	475,000
Corporation tax (£475,000 at 24%)	114,000

Working 1 – Trading profit

	£
Profit before taxation	345,966
Depreciation	15,740
Donations to political parties	400
Qualifying charitable donations	900
Accountancy	2,300
Legal fees in connection with the issue of loan stock (the finance was used for a trading purpose)	5,700
Repairs to warehouse following a flood	13,200
Entertaining suppliers	3,600
Entertaining employees	1,700
Gifts to customers (pens costing £40 each and displaying Clueless Ltd's name)	920
Gifts to customers (food hampers costing £45 each and displaying Clueless Ltd's name)	1,650
Capital allowances (working 4)	21,362
	413,438

Working 2 – Loan interest received

	£
Loan interest receivable	32,800
Accrued at 1 April 2012	10,600
Accrued at 31 March 2013	(11,300)
Loan interest received	32,100

The loan was made for a non-trading purpose.

Working 3 – Dividends received

	£
From unconnected UK companies	16,200
From unconnected overseas companies	4,500
From a 100% UK subsidiary company	8,762
Dividends received	29,462

These figures were the actual cash amounts received.

Working 4 – Capital allowances

	Main pool £	Motor car £	Special rate pool £	Allowances £
WDV brought forward	2,400		13,500	
Additions				
Machinery	8,300			
Motor car [1]	13,800			
Motor car [2]		11,800		
	24,500			
Annual investment allowance	(24,500)			24,500
Disposal proceeds			(9,300)	
			4,200	
Balancing allowance			(4,200)	(4,200)
WDA – 18%		(2,124)	× 50%	1,062
WDV carried forward	0	9,676		
Total allowances				21,362

(1) Motor car [1] has a CO_2 emission rate of 140 grams per kilometre.

(2) Motor car [2] has a CO_2 emission rate of 185 grams per kilometre. This motor car is used by the sales manager and 50% of the mileage is for private journeys.

(3) All of the items included in the special rate pool at 1 April 2012 were sold for £9,300 during the year ended 31 March 2013. The original cost of these items was £16,200.

Other information

From your files, you note that Clueless Ltd has one associated company (the 100% UK subsidiary company mentioned in working 3).

Required

Prepare a corrected version of Clueless Ltd's corporation tax computation for the year ended 31 March 2013.

Notes:

1. You should indicate by the use of zero any items in the computation of the trading profit for which no adjustment is required.

2. In answering this part of the question you should ignore value added tax.   **(16 marks)**

(b) The managing director of Clueless Ltd understands that for the year ended 31 March 2013 the company will have to file its self-assessment corporation tax return online, and that the supporting accounts and tax computations will have to be filed using the inline eXtensible Business Reporting Language (iXBRL). The managing director is concerned about how the company will be able to produce documents in this format.

Required

(i) State the date by which Clueless Ltd's self-assessment corporation tax return for the year ended 31 March 2013 should be filed;   **(1 mark)**

(ii) Explain the options available to Clueless Ltd regarding the production of accounts and tax computations in the iXBRL format.   **(3 marks)**

(c) Clueless Ltd is registered for value added tax (VAT), but currently does not use any of the special VAT schemes. The company has annual standard rated sales of £1,200,000 and annual standard rated expenses of £550,000. Both these figures are exclusive of VAT and are likely to remain the same for the foreseeable future. Clueless Ltd is up to date with all of its tax returns, including those for corporation tax, PAYE and VAT. It is also up to date with its corporation tax, PAYE and VAT payments. However, the company often incurs considerable overtime costs due to its employees working late in order to meet tax return filing deadlines.

Clueless Ltd pays its expenses on a cash basis, but allows customers two months credit when paying for sales. The company does not have any impairment losses.

Clueless Ltd is planning to purchase some new machinery at a cost of £22,000 (exclusive of VAT). The machinery can either be purchased from an overseas supplier situated outside the European Union, or from a VAT registered supplier situated in the European Union. Clueless Ltd is not a regular importer and so is unsure of the VAT treatment for this purchase.

Required

(i) Explain why Clueless Ltd is entitled to use both the VAT cash accounting scheme and the VAT annual accounting scheme, and why it will probably be beneficial for the company to use both schemes;

          (6 marks)

(ii) Explain when and how Clueless Ltd will have to account for VAT in respect of the new machinery if it is purchased from (1) a supplier situated outside the European Union, or (2) a VAT registered supplier situated elsewhere within the European Union.   **(4 marks)**

          (Total = 30 marks)

3 Acebook Ltd

(a) Explain how limited companies can obtain relief for capital losses. **(3 marks)**

Note: You are not expected to explain how groups of companies can obtain relief for capital losses.

(b) Acebook Ltd sold the following assets during the year ended 31 December 2012:

(1) On 10 March 2012 Acebook Ltd sold its entire shareholding of 50p ordinary shares in Oogle plc for £3.20 per share. The company had originally purchased 8,000 shares in Oogle plc on 28 June 2003 for £25,200. On 31 October 2006 Oogle plc made a 2 for 1 bonus issue. Then, on 14 February 2008, Oogle plc made a 1 for 5 rights issue. Acebook Ltd took up its allocation under the rights issue in full, paying £4.30 for each new share issued.

Indexation factors are as follows:

June 2003 to October 2006	0.104
June 2003 to February 2008	0.166
June 2003 to March 2012	0.326
October 2006 to February 2008	0.055
October 2006 to March 2012	0.201
February 2008 to March 2012	0.138

(2) On 30 June 2012 three acres of land were sold for £192,000. Acebook Ltd had originally purchased four acres of land, and the indexed cost of the four acres on 30 June 2012 was £196,000. The market value of the unsold acre of land as at 30 June 2012 was £53,000. During June 2012 Acebook Ltd spent £29,400 clearing and levelling all four acres of land. The land has never been used for business purposes.

(3) On 1 October 2012 an investment property owned by Acebook Ltd was destroyed in a fire. The indexed cost of the property on that date was £138,400. Acebook Ltd received insurance proceeds of £189,000 on 20 October 2012, and on 31 October 2012 the company paid £172,400 for a replacement investment property. Acebook Ltd has made a claim to defer the gain arising from the receipt of the insurance proceeds.

Required

Calculate Acebook Ltd's chargeable gains for the year ended 31 December 2012. **(12 marks)**

(Total = 15 marks)

4 Sophia Wong

You should assume that today's date is 15 March 2012.

(a) Sophia Wong is self-employed as a lawyer. For the year ended 5 April 2013 Sophia has forecast that her tax adjusted trading profit will be £80,000. This will be her only income for the tax year 2012/13, and Sophia's total income tax liability and national insurance contributions (NIC) for this year if she continues to trade on a self-employed basis will be £25,910 as follows:

	£
Income tax	21,884
Class 2 NIC	138
Class 4 NIC	3,888
	25,910

Sophia understands that she could save tax and NIC if she instead traded as a limited company, and she is therefore considering incorporating her business on 6 April 2012. The forecast taxable total profits of the new limited company for the year ended 5 April 2013 are unchanged at £80,000 (before taking account of any director's remuneration).

Required

Assuming that Sophia Wong incorporates her business on 6 April 2012, advise her whether or not there will be an overall saving of tax and national insurance contributions (NIC) for the tax year 2012/13 if she withdraws all of the profits from the new company as:

(i) director's remuneration (after allowing for employer's class 1 NIC, gross director's remuneration will be £71,207); or **(6 marks)**

(ii) dividends (after allowing for corporation tax, net dividends will be £64,000). **(5 marks)**

Notes:

1. For both alternatives, you are expected to calculate the corporation tax liability (if any) of the new limited company for the year ended 5 April 2013, the income tax payable by Sophia Wong, and the class 1 NIC (if any) payable by Sophia and the new company.

2. You should assume that the rates of corporation tax remain unchanged.

(b) The only chargeable asset of Sophia Wong's business is goodwill and this is valued at £150,000. The goodwill has a nil cost.

Sophia will not make any other disposals during the tax year 2012/13. She has unused capital losses of £39,400 brought forward from the tax year 2011/12.

Required

(i) State the capital gains tax consequences for the tax year 2012/13 if Sophia Wong transfers her business to a new limited company on 6 April 2012 in exchange for ordinary shares; **(2 marks)**

(ii) Explain why it would be beneficial if the consideration for the transfer of Sophia Wong's business instead consisted of £50,000 in cash and £100,000 in £1 ordinary shares. **(2 marks)**

(Total = 15 marks)

5 Rosie Rohan, Sam Shire and Tom Tirith

You should assume that today's date is 15 February 2013.

(a)   Rosie Rohan, aged 48, is the managing director of Hornburg plc. During the tax year 2012/13 Rosie was paid gross director's remuneration of £220,000. She has made the following gross personal pension contributions:

Tax year	Pension contribution £
2008/09	33,000
2009/10	41,000
2010/11	26,000
2011/12	Nil

Rosie was a member of a pension scheme for the tax year 2011/12.

Required

Advise Rosie Rohan of the total amount of pension scheme annual allowances that she has available for the tax year 2012/13, the method by which tax relief will be given for any personal pension contributions that she makes during that year, and the tax implications if she makes contributions in excess of the available annual allowances.

Notes:

1.   You are not expected to calculate Rosie Rohan's income tax liability.
2.   You are not expected to consider the situation where pension contributions do not attract tax relief.

(6 marks)

(b)   Sam Shire, aged 32, has already invested £4,000 into a cash individual savings account (ISA) during the tax year 2012/13. He now wants to invest into a stocks and shares ISA.

Required

Advise Sam Shire of the maximum possible amount that he can invest into a stocks and shares ISA for the tax year 2012/13, and the tax advantages of holding stocks and shares within an ISA.   **(2 marks)**

(c)   Tom Tirith, aged 76, made a cash gift of £200,000 to his daughter on 20 December 2011. He is now going to make a cash gift of £450,000 to a trust on 20 February 2013.

The nil rate band for the tax year 2011/12 is £325,000.

Required

(i)   Calculate the lifetime inheritance tax that will be payable in respect of Tom Tirith's gift of £450,000 to a trust if:

(1)   the trust pays the tax arising from the gift; or
(2)   Tom pays the tax arising from the gift.

The total marks will be split equally between each part.   **(3 marks)**

(ii)   Assuming that Tom Tirith pays the tax arising from the gift of £450,000, calculate the additional inheritance tax that would be payable in respect of the gift if Tom were to die on 30 June 2017.

Note: You should assume that the nil rate band of £325,000 remains unchanged.   **(4 marks)**

(Total = 15 marks)

Answers

**DO NOT TURN THIS PAGE UNTIL YOU HAVE
COMPLETED THE MOCK EXAM**

A plan of attack

What's the worst thing you could be doing right now if this was the actual exam paper? Sharpening your pencil? Wondering how to celebrate the end of the exam in about 3 hours time? Panicking, flapping and generally getting in a right old state?

Well, they're all pretty bad, so turn back to the paper and let's sort out a **plan of attack**!

First things first

You have fifteen minutes of reading time. Spend this looking carefully through the questions and deciding the order in which you will attempt them. As a general rule you should attempt the questions that you find easiest first and leave the hardest until last. Depending on how confident you are we recommend that you follow one of the following two options:

Option 1 (if you're thinking 'Help!')

If you're a bit worried about the paper, do the questions in the order of how well you think you can answer them. You may find the shorter questions less daunting than the longer questions. Alternatively, you may feel better prepared for questions 1 and 2 and wish to start there.

- Question 1 is an income tax question. There are plenty of easy marks available in this question but there is a lot of information to deal with so make sure you mark off each item as you include it in your answer.

- Question 2 is a slightly unusual corporation tax question in which you are given a computation that contains lots of errors which you need to spot and correct.

- Question 3 is on corporate chargeable gains including shares in a share pool. Using the correct pro forma for computing the cost of the shares sold is key to getting good marks on this question.

- Question 4 is about withdrawing income from a company either as salary or as dividend. Although this looks a bit complicated, the actual computations are quite straightforward. There is also some basic CGT planning.

- Question 5 is a three part question on pensions, individual savings accounts and inheritance tax. It is very important that you attempt all three parts of the question to obtain a reasonable number of marks.

Lastly, what you mustn't forget is that you have to **answer all of the questions in the paper. They are all compulsory**. Do not miss out any questions or you will seriously affect your chance of passing the exam.

Option 2 (if you're thinking 'It's a doddle')

It never pays to be over confident but if you're reasonably confident about the exam then it is best to work through the questions sequentially starting with question 1.

No matter how many times we remind you....

Always, always **allocate your time** according to the marks for the question in total and then according to the parts of the question. And **always, always follow the requirements** exactly.

You've got spare time at the end of the exam.....?

If you have allocated your time properly then you **shouldn't have time on your hands** at the end of the exam. But if you find yourself with five or ten minutes to spare, check over your work to make sure that there are no silly arithmetical errors.

Forget about it!

And don't worry if you found the paper difficult. More than likely other candidates did too. If this were the real thing you would need to **forget** the exam the minute you leave the exam hall and **think about the next one**. Or, if it's the last one, **celebrate!**

1 Josie Jones

Marking scheme

			Marks
(a)	*Trading income*		
	Profit for year ended 30 April 2012		½
	Profit for period ended 30 June 2012		½
	Overlap profits		1
	Capital allowances		
	Period ended 30 June 2012	- Addition	½
		- Proceeds	½
		- Balancing allowance	½
	Employment income		
	Salary		1
	Removal expenses		1
	Beneficial loan		1½
	Staff canteen		½
	Car benefit - Percentage		1½
	- Benefit		1
	Property income		
	Property one		1
	Property two		1
	Investment income		
	Building society interest		½
	Gilt interest		1
	Premium bond prize (exempt)		½
	Dividends		½
	Taxable income		
	Personal allowance not available		1
	Tax payable		
	Increase in limits for gift aid donations		1
	Tax liability		2
	Tax credits/tax deducted at source		1½
			20

(b)	(i)	Balancing payment	1½
		Payment on account	1½
			3
	(ii)	PAYE	1
		Reduced to cover other income	1
			2
			25

(a) **Josie Jones – Income tax computation 2012/13**

	Non-savings income	Savings income	Dividend income	Total
	£	£	£	£
Trading income (W1)	64,000			
Employment income (W3)	126,754			
Property business income (W5)	5,100			
BSI £8,000 × 100/80		10,000		
Gilt interest (received gross)		1,200		
Premium bond prize (exempt)		0		
Dividends £6,480 × 100/90			7,200	
Net income	195,854	11,200	7,200	214,254
Less PA (N)	(0)			(0)
Taxable income	195,854	11,200	7,200	214,254

Tax

	£	£
On non-savings income		
£39,870 (W6) @ 20%		7,974
£115,630 @ 40%		46,252
£155,500 (W6)		
£40,354 @ 50%		20,177
£195,854		
On savings income		
£11,200 @ 50%		5,600
On dividend income		
£7,200 @ 42.5%		3,060
Income tax liability		83,063
Less: dividend tax credit £7,200 × 10%	720	
PAYE	44,043	
BSI tax deducted at source £10,000 × 20%	2,000	
		(46,763)
Income tax payable		36,300

Tutorial notes:

1 Only £8,000 of the relocation costs is exempt.

2 The provision of meals in a staff canteen does not give rise to a taxable benefit.

3 The furnished holiday letting loss from property one can only be carried forward against future furnished holiday letting profits.

4 Premium bond prizes are exempt from income tax.

5 No personal allowance is available as Josie's adjusted net income of £(214,254 – 5,500) = £208,754 exceeds £116,210.

Workings

1　*Trading income*

	£	£
Year ended 30 April 2012		
Trading profit		95,560
Period ended 30 June 2012		
Trading profit	10,440	
Less capital allowances (W2)	(300)	
		10,140
Less　overlap profits		(41,700)
Trading income		64,000

2　*Capital allowances*

	Main pool £	Allowances £
Period ended 30 June 2012		
WDV b/f	nil	
Addition	2,000	
Proceeds	(1,700)	
	300	
Balancing allowance	(300)	300

3　*Employment income*

	£
Salary £15,100 × 8	120,800
Removal expenses £(11,600 – 8,000)	3,600
Loan £33,000 @ 4% × 7/12	770
Staff canteen (exempt)	0
Car benefit (W4)	1,584
Employment income	126,754

4　*Car benefit*

Amount by which CO_2 emissions exceed base level: (140 (rounded down) – 100) = 40 ÷ 5 = 8.
Car benefit percentage is 8 + 11 + 3 (diesel supplement) = 22%.
Car available from October 2012 to 5 April 2013 = 6 months.
Car benefit is £14,400 (list price) × 22% × 6/12 = £1,584.

5　*Property business income*

	£
Property one	
£(6,600 – 9,700) = £(3,100) loss c/f against FHL income	0
Property two	
£(7,200 – 2,100)	5,100
	5,100

6　*Tax rate limits*

Josie's basic and higher rate tax limits are increased by (£4,400 × 100/80) = £5,500 to £(34,370 + 5,500) = £39,870 and £(150,000 + 5,500) = £155,500.

(b)　(i)　Josie's balancing payment for 2012/13 due on 31 January 2014 is £(36,300 – 34,400) = £1,900.

Her payments on account for 2013/14 will be £(36,300 × 50%) = £18,150. These will be due on 31 January and 31 July 2014.

(ii)　For 2013/14 the tax on Josie's employment income will be collected under PAYE.

Therefore a claim can be made to reduce the payments on account so that they just cover any remaining income tax that is payable, such as that on the property business profit.

2 Clueless Ltd

> **Text references.** Computing taxable total profits is covered in Chapter 19 and computing the corporation tax liability in chapter 20. Overseas matters for companies are dealt with in Chapter 24. Self-assessment for companies will be found in Chapter 25. Special schemes for VAT and overseas aspects of VAT are in Chapter 27.
>
> **Top tips.** You might have started with parts (b) and (c) of this question, rather than part (a). These should have yielded marks quickly if you knew the relevant points.
>
> **Easy marks.** There were some easy marks for standard items of adjustment to profit and computation of corporation tax in part (a).
>
> **Examiner's comments.** Well answered with the exception of parts (b)(ii) and (c)(ii).

Marking scheme

		Marks
(a)	*Trading profit*	
	Depreciation	½
	Donations to political parties	½
	Qualifying charitable donations	½
	Accountancy	½
	Legal fees	½
	Repairs	½
	Entertaining suppliers	½
	Entertaining customers	½
	Gifts to customers - pens	½
	Gifts to customers – food hampers	½
	Capital allowances	½
	Capital allowances computation	
	WDV b/f	1
	AIA	1
	Motor car [1] addition to main pool	½
	Motor car [2] addition to special rate pool	½
	Disposal proceeds	½
	WDA @ 18%	1
	WDA @ 8%	½
	Loan interest	1
	Qualifying charitable donation	½
	Franked investment income	
	Grossed up dividends	1½
	Group dividend	½
	Upper limit	½
	Corporation tax	
	Main rate on taxable total profits	½
	Marginal relief	1
		16

				Marks
(b)	(i)	Tax return submission date		1
	(ii)	Using HMRC software	1	
		Use of other software	1	
		Tagging	1	
				3
(c)	(i)	Eligible for both schemes on turnover	1½	
		Up to date with payments for both schemes	1	
		Up to date with returns for cash accounting scheme	1½	
		Output tax under cash accounting scheme	1	
		Input tax under cash accounting scheme	1	
		Annual accounting scheme – one return	1	
				6
	(ii)	(1) Payment on importation	1	
		Input tax recovery	1	
		(2) Output tax on date of acquisition	1	
		Input tax recovery	1	
				4
				30

(a) **Clueless Ltd – Corporation tax computation for the year ended 31 March 2013**

	£
Taxable trading profit (W1)	355,760
Loan interest receivable	32,800
Total profits	388,560
Less qualifying charitable donations	(900)
Taxable total profits	387,660
Add franked investment income (W3)	23,000
	410,660

Marginal relief applies (W4)

	£
£387,660 @ 24%	93,038
Less marginal relief 1/100 (750,000 – 410,660) × 387,660/410,660	(3,203)
Corporation tax liability	89,835

Workings

1   *Taxable trading profit for the year ended 31 March 2013*

		£
Profit before taxation		345,966
Add:	Depreciation	15,740
	Donations to political parties	400
	Qualifying charitable donations	900
	Accountancy	0
	Legal fees	0
	Repairs	0
	Entertaining suppliers	3,600
	Entertaining employees	0
	Gifts to customers (pens)	0
	Gifts to customers (food hampers)	1,650
		368,256
Less:	Capital allowances (W2)	(12,496)
	Taxable trading profit	355,760

1   The only exception to the non-deductibility of entertainment expenditure is when it is in respect of employees.

2   Gifts to customers are an allowable deduction if they cost less than £50 per recipient per year, are not of food, drink, tobacco or vouchers for exchangeable goods, and carry a conspicuous advertisement for the company making the gift.

2   *Capital allowances*

	AIA £	Main pool £	Special rate pool £	Allowances £
WDV brought forward		2,400	13,500	
Addition qualifying for AIA				
Machinery	8,300			
Annual investment allowance	(8,300)			8,300
Additions not qualifying for AIA				
Motor car [1]		13,800		
Motor car [2]			11,800	
Disposal proceeds			(9,300)	
		16,200	16,000	
WDA – 18%		(2,916)		2,916
WDA – 8%			(1,280)	1,280
WDV carried forward		13,284	14,720	
Total allowances				12,496

Tutorial notes:

1   Motor car [1] has CO_2 emissions between 111 and 160 grams per kilometre and therefore qualifies for writing down allowances at the rate of 18%.

2   Motor car [2] has CO_2 emissions over 160 grams per kilometre and therefore qualifies for writing down allowances at the rate of 8%. The private use of a motor car is irrelevant, since such usage will be assessed on the employee as a benefit.

3   *Franked investment income*

Franked investment income is £([16,200 + 4,500 = 20,700] × 100/90) = £23,000.

The dividends from the 100% subsidiary company are not franked investment income as they are group dividends.

Tutorial note:

As far as paper F6(UK) is concerned, all overseas dividends are exempt from UK corporation tax. They are included as franked investment income when calculating a company's augmented profits in exactly the same way as UK dividends.

4   *Upper limit*

Clueless Ltd has one associated company, so the upper limit is reduced to £(1,500,000/2) = £750,000

(b)   (i)   Clueless Ltd's self-assessment tax return for the year ended 31 March 2013 must be submitted by 31 March 2014.

(ii)   If Clueless Ltd has straightforward accounts, it could use the software provided by HM Revenue and Customs. This automatically produces accounts and tax computations in the iXBRL format.

Alternatively, other software that automatically produces iXBRL accounts and computations could be used.

A tagging service could be used to apply the appropriate tags to the accounts and tax computations, or Clueless Ltd could use software to tag documents itself.

(c) (i) Clueless Ltd can use both schemes because its expected taxable turnover for the next 12 months does not exceed £1,350,000 exclusive of VAT.

In addition, for both schemes the company is up to date with its VAT payments, and for the cash accounting scheme it is up to date with its VAT returns.

With the cash accounting scheme, output VAT will be accounted for two months later than at present as the date of the cash receipt determines the return in which the transaction is dealt with rather than the invoice date.

The recovery of input VAT on expenses will not be affected as these are dealt with on a cash basis.

With the annual accounting scheme, the reduced administration in only having to file one VAT return each year should save on overtime costs.

(ii) (1) **Supplier situated outside the European Union**

Clueless Ltd will have to pay VAT of £22,000 @ 20% = <u>£4,400</u> to HM Revenue and Customs at the time of importation.

This will then be reclaimed as input VAT on the VAT return for the period during which the machinery is imported.

(2) **Supplier situated elsewhere within the European Union**

VAT will have to be accounted for according to the date of acquisition. This will be the earlier of the date that a VAT invoice is issued or the 15th day of the month following the month in which the machinery comes into the UK.

The VAT charged of <u>£4,400</u> will be declared on Clueless Ltd's VAT return as output VAT, but will then be reclaimed as input VAT on the same VAT return.

3 Acebook Ltd

Text references. Capital losses are included in Chapter 22. Chargeable gains for companies are covered in Chapter 21. Part disposals and compensation are dealt with in Chapter 13.

Top tips. Use the three column pro forma for the company's share pool and take care to add the indexation allowance to the cost in the pool to obtain the indexed cost.

Easy marks. Part (a) was a straightforward statement of the use of capital losses for companies. The part disposal in part (b) was not difficult, in particular as the indexed cost was given.

Examiner's comments. Surprisingly, a number of students had problems with part (a), often explaining relief for a trading loss, covering the rules for individuals, or discussing groups. Time was wasted calculating the CGT liability. Indexation was often applied prior to the bonus issue. Otherwise very well answered.

Marking scheme

		Marks
(a)	Set off against gains in same accounting period	1½
	Carry forward against first available gains	1½
		3

		Marks
(b)	**Oogle plc shares**	
	Purchase June 2003	½
	Bonus issue October 2006	1
	Indexation to February 2008	1
	Rights issue February 2008	1½
	Indexation to March 2012	1
	Disposal proceeds	1
	Indexed cost	1
	Land	
	Disposal proceeds	½
	Indexed cost	1½
	Enhancement expenditure	1
	Investment property	
	Gain immediately chargeable	2
		12
		15

(a) When a limited company has a capital loss, it is first set off against any chargeable gains arising in the same accounting period.

Any remaining capital loss is then carried forward and set off against the first available chargeable gains of future accounting periods.

(b) **Acebook Ltd – Chargeable gains for the year ended 31 December 2012**

Oogle plc

	No of shares	Cost £	Indexed cost £
Purchase June 2003	8,000	25,200	25,200
Bonus issue October 2006 2: 1	16,000		
	24,000		
Indexed rise to February 2008 0.166 × £25,200			4,183
Rights issue February 2008 1:5 @ £4.30	4,800	20,640	20,640
	28,800	45,840	50,023
Indexed rise to March 2012 0.138 × £50,023			6,903
			56,926
Disposal	(28,800)	(45,840)	(56,926)

The gain is computed as follows:

	£
Proceeds 28,800 × £3.20	92,160
Less indexed cost	(56,926)
Indexed gain	35,234

Land

	£
Proceeds	192,000
Less cost $\dfrac{192,000}{192,000+53,000} \times £196,000$	(153,600)
enhancement expenditure (clearing and levelling land)	
$\dfrac{192,000}{192,000+53,000} \times £29,400$	(23,040)
Indexed gain	15,360

Investment property

An amount equal to the insurance proceeds not reinvested of £(189,000 – 172,400) = £16,600 is an immediate chargeable gain for the year ended 31 December 2012.

Tutorial note:

The balance of the gain of £([189,000 – 138,400 = 50,600] – 16,600) =£34,000 is deferred by deducting it from the cost of the replacement property.

4 Sophia Wong

Text references. Computation of income tax is covered in Chapter 2. Employment income is in Chapter 3. National insurance contributions are the subject of Chapter 12. Incorporation relief is dealt with in Chapter 15.

Top tips. Lay out your computations clearly so the marker knows which scenario you are dealing with. Make sure that you use these computations to answer the question in part (a) which is to advise on whether or not there will be an overall saving of tax and national insurance contributions.

Easy marks. There were some easy marks in this question for basic computations of income tax and national insurance contributions.

Examiner's comments. Many left this question until the end, and it was generally badly answered. Students often refused to accept that they had been given some of the information (employer's NIC, corporation tax) and wasted time trying to calculate the figures themselves. Even worse, a few students calculated the tax and NIC for the self-employed basis.

Marking scheme

			Marks	
(a)	(i)	Employer's NICs	1	
		No corporation tax liability	1	
		Personal allowance	½	
		Income tax: basic rate	½	
		higher rate	½	
		Employee's NICs	1½	
		Total tax and NICs compared with sole trader	1	
				6
	(ii)	No Class 1 NICs	½	
		Corporation tax	1	
		Grossed up dividends	½	
		Personal allowance	½	
		Income tax: basic rate	½	
		higher rate	½	
		Tax credit	½	
		Total tax and NICs compared with sole trader	1	
				5
(b)	(i)	No CGT on incorporation	1	
		Deduction from cost of shares	1	
				2
	(ii)	Chargeable gain if cash consideration	1	
		Explanation why beneficial	1	
				2
				15

(a) (i) **Profits withdrawn as director's remuneration**

Employer's class 1 NIC will be £(80,000 – 71,207) = £8,793.

There is no corporation tax liability for the new company as taxable total profits are nil as a result of the payment of director's remuneration and associated employer's class 1 NIC which are deductible expenses.

Tax and NIC implications for Sophia

Sophia's income tax liability for 2012/13 will be:

	£
Director's remuneration	71,207
Less personal allowance	(8,105)
Taxable income	63,102

Income tax

	£
£34,370 × 20%	6,874
£28,732 × 40%	11,493
£63,102	
Income tax liability/income tax payable	18,367

Sophia's employee class 1 NICs for 2012/13 will be:

	£
£(42,475 – 7,605) = 34,870 × 12%	4,184
£(71,207 – 42,475) = 28,732 × 2%	575
Employee class 1 NICs	4,759

The total tax and NIC cost if all of the new company's profits are withdrawn as directors remuneration is £(8,793 + 18,367 + 4,759) = £31,919.

This is £(31,919 – 25,910) = £6,009 more than the cost on a self-employed basis.

(ii) **Profits withdrawn as dividends**

There will be no class 1 NICs.

The corporation tax liability of the new company ended 5 April 2013 will be £(80,000 – 64,000) = £16,000.

Sophia's income tax liability for 2012/13 will be:

	£
Dividends £64,000 × 100/90	71,111
Less personal allowance	(8,105)
Taxable income	63,006

	£
Income tax	
£34,370 ×10%	3,437
£28,636 × 32.5%	9,307
£63,006	
Income tax liability	12,744
Less tax credit £63,006 × 10%	(6,301)
Income tax payable	6,443

The total tax and NIC cost if all of the new company's profits are withdrawn as dividends is £(16,000 + 6,443) = £22,443.

This is £(25,910 – 22,443) = £3,467 less than the cost on a self-employed basis.

(b) (i) If £50,000 of the consideration is in the form of cash, then £(150,000 × 50,000/150,000 (100,000 + 50,000)) = £50,000 of the gain will be chargeable during 2012/13.

(ii)   The chargeable gain of £50,000 will fully utilise Sophia's annual exempt amount of £10,600 for 2012/13, and the brought forward capital losses of £39,400. This means that £50,000 of the consideration has been taken without incurring a charge to capital gains tax.

5 Rosie Rohan, Sam Shire and Tom Tirith

Text references. Personal pensions are covered in Chapter 5. Individual savings accounts are dealt with in Chapter 2. Inheritance tax is the subject of Chapter 18.

Top tips. Remember that there is useful information contained in the Tax Tables provided in the examination. In this question, the annual allowance amount, the ISA limits and the taper relief percentages were vital and could be found in the Tax Tables.

Easy marks. There were easy marks in all three parts of the question, for example, a description of the tax relief on personal pensions, the ISA tax exemptions and the calculation of inheritance tax on cash lifetime transfers. It was important to keep your answer brief and to the point in part (b) which was only worth 2 marks.

Examiner's comments. Generally well answered. The PET was sometimes included in part (c)(i) – losing marks but also complicating the otherwise straightforward calculations.

Marking scheme

					Marks
(a)			Annual allowance 2008/09	½	
			Annual allowance 2011/12	½	
			Unused allowances	2	
			Basic rate tax relief	½	
			Higher and additional rate tax relief	1	
			Identification of annual allowance charge	½	
			Annual allowance charge at marginal rates of income tax	1	
					6
(b)			Maximum investment into stocks and shares ISA	1	
			Tax exemptions for ISAs	1	
					2
(c)	(i)	(1)	Annual exemption 2012/13	½	
			IHT liability at 20%	1	
		(2)	IHT liability at 20/80	½	
			Gross chargeable transfer	1	
					3
	(ii)		Gross chargeable transfer (from (i) (2) above)	½	
			Available nil rate band potentially exempt transfer	1	
			amount available for CLT	½	
			IHT liability at 40%	½	
			Taper relief	1	
			Lifetime tax paid	½	
					4
					15

(a) **Rosie Rohan**

Annual allowances

The unused annual allowance for 2008/09 cannot be brought forward as this is more than three years prior to 2012/13.

Rosie was a member of a pension scheme for 2011/12, so the full annual allowance for that year is available.

She has unused allowances of £(50,000 – 41,000) = £9,000 from 2009/10, £(50,000 – 26,000) = £24,000 from 2010/11, and £50,000 from 2011/12, so the available annual allowances for 2012/13 are therefore £(50,000 + 9,000 + 24,000 + 50,000) = £133,000.

Tax relief

Personal pension contributions are made net of basic rate tax.

Higher and additional rate tax relief is given by increasing Rosie's basic and higher rate tax limits for 2012/13 by the gross amount of the pension contributions.

Excess contributions

If pension contributions are made in excess of the available annual allowances, then there will be an annual allowance charge.

This charge will be subject to income tax at Rosie's marginal rate(s) of income tax by treating the excess contributions as an extra amount of non-savings income received by Rosie.

(b) **Sam Shire**

Since Sam has already invested £4,000 into a cash ISA, he can invest a maximum of £(11,280 – 4,000) = £7,280 into a stocks and shares ISA for 2012/13.

Dividend income received within a stocks and shares ISA is exempt from income tax and chargeable gains are exempt from capital gains tax.

(c) **Tom Tirith**

(i) (1) *Inheritance tax (IHT) paid by donee (the trustees)*

			£
Gift (value transferred)			450,000
Less annual exemption 2012/13			(3,000)
Gross transfer of value			447,000
IHT	£325,000	× 0%	Nil
	£122,000	× 20%	24,400
	£447,000		24,400

(2) *Inheritance tax (IHT) paid by donor (Tom)*

			£
Gift (value transferred)			450,000
Less annual exemption 2012/13			(3,000)
Net transfer of value			447,000
IHI	£325,000	× 0%	NIl
	£122,000	× 20/80	30,500
	£447,000		30,500
Gross transfer of value £(447,000 + 30,500)			477,500

Tutorial note

The gift made on 20 December 2011 utilises the annual exemption for 2011/12.

(ii)   *Additional liability arising on death if donor (Tom) pays the tax*

		£
Gross transfer of value (from (i) (2) above		477,500

IHT	£131,000 (W) × 0%	Nil
	£346,500 × 40%	138,600
	£477,500	138,600
Less taper relief @ 40% (death between 4 and 5 years after transfer)		(55,440)
Death tax		83,160
Less lifetime tax paid		(30,500)
Additional liability		52,660

Working

The potentially exempt transfer made on 20 December 2011 will utilise £(200,000 – 6,000 [annual exemptions for 2011/12 and 2010/11]) = £194,000 of the nil rate band of £325,000 for 2017/18.

Therefore only £(325,000 – 194,000) = £131,000 is available against the chargeable lifetime transfer to the trust.

Tax tables

SUPPLEMENTARY INFORMATION

1. Calculations and workings need only be made to the nearest £.
2. All apportionments may be made to the nearest month.
3. All workings should be shown.

TAX RATES AND ALLOWANCES

The following tax rates and allowances are to be used in answering the questions.

Income tax

		Normal rates	Dividend rates
		%	%
Basic rate	£1 – £34,370	20	10
Higher rate	£34,371 – £150,000	40	32.5
Additional rate	£150,001 and over	50	42.5

A starting rate of 10% applies to savings income where it falls within the first £2,710 of taxable income.

Personal allowances

		£
Personal allowance	standard	8,105
Personal allowance	65 – 74	10,500
Personal allowance	75 and over	10,660
Income limit for age-related allowances		25,400
Income limit for standard personal allowance		100,000

Car benefit percentage

The base level of CO_2 emissions is 100 grams per kilometre.

The percentage rates applying to petrol cars with CO_2 emissions up to this level are:

	%
75 grams per kilometre or less	5
76 grams to 99 grams per kilometre	10
100 grams per kilometre	11

Car fuel benefit

The base figure for calculating the car fuel benefit is £20,200.

Individual savings accounts (ISAs)

The overall investment limit is £11,280, of which £5,640 can be invested in a cash ISA.

Pension scheme limits

Annual allowance	£50,000

The maximum contribution that can qualify for tax relief without any earnings is £3,600.

Authorised mileage allowances: cars

Up to 10,000 miles	45p
Over 10,000 miles	25p

Capital allowances

Plant and machinery %
Main pool 18
Special rate pool 8

Motor cars
New cars with CO_2 emissions up to 110 grams per kilometre 100
CO_2 emissions between 111 and 160 grams per kilometre 18
CO_2 emissions over 160 grams per kilometre 8

Annual investment allowance
First £25,000 of expenditure 100

Corporation tax

Financial year	2010	2011	2012
Small profits rate	21%	21%	20%
Main rate	28%	26%	24%
Lower limit	300,000	300,000	300,000
Upper limit	1,500,000	1,500,000	1,500,000
Standard fraction	7/400	3/200	1/100

Marginal relief

Standard fraction $\times$ (U – A) $\times$ N/A

Value Added Tax

Standard rate 20.0%
Registration limit £77,000
Deregistration limit £75,000

Inheritance tax: tax rates

£1 – £325,000 Nil
Excess – Death rate 40%
– Lifetime rate 20%

Inheritance tax: taper relief

Years before death	% reduction
Over 3 but less than 4 years	20
Over 4 but less than 5 years	40
Over 5 but less than 6 years	60
Over 6 but less than 7 years	80

Capital gains tax

Rates of tax – Lower rate 18%
– Higher rate 28%
Annual exempt amount £10,600
Entrepreneurs' relief – Lifetime limit £10,000,000
– Rate of tax 10%

National insurance contributions
(not contracted-out rates)

		%
Class 1 Employee	£1 – £7,605 per year	Nil
	£7,606 – £42,475 per year	12.0
	£42,476 and above per year	2.0
Class 1 Employer	£1 – £7,488 per year	Nil
	£7,489 and above per year	13.8
Class 1A		13.8
Class 2	£2.65 per week	
	Small earnings exception	£5,595
Class 4	£1 – £7,605 per year	Nil
	£7,606 – £42,475 per year	9.0
	£42,476 and above per year	2.0

Rates of Interest (assumed)

Official rate of interest	4.0%
Rate of interest on underpaid tax	3.0%
Rate of interest on overpaid tax	0.5%

Review Form – Paper F6 Taxation (UK) (01/13)

Name: _____   Address: _____
_____
_____

How have you used this Kit?
(Tick one box only)

☐ Home study (book only)

☐ On a course: college _____

☐ With 'correspondence' package

☐ Other _____

Why did you decide to purchase this Kit?
(Tick one box only)

☐ Have used the complementary Study text

☐ Have used other BPP products in the past

☐ Recommendation by friend/colleague

☐ Recommendation by a lecturer at college

☐ Saw advertising

☐ Other _____

During the past six months do you recall seeing/receiving any of the following?
(Tick as many boxes as are relevant)

☐ Our advertisement in *Student Accountant*

☐ Our advertisement in *Pass*

☐ Our advertisement in *PQ*

☐ Our brochure with a letter through the post

☐ Our website www.bpp.com

Which (if any) aspects of our advertising do you find useful?
(Tick as many boxes as are relevant)

☐ Prices and publication dates of new editions

☐ Information on product content

☐ Facility to order books off-the-page

☐ None of the above

Which BPP products have you used?

Text	☐	Success CD	☐	i-Learn	☐
Kit	☑	i-Pass	☐	Home Study Package	☐
Passcards	☐				

Your ratings, comments and suggestions would be appreciated on the following areas.

	Very useful	Useful	Not useful
Passing F6	☐	☐	☐
Planning your question practice	☐	☐	☐
Questions	☐	☐	☐
Top Tips etc in answers	☐	☐	☐
Content and structure of answers	☐	☐	☐
Mock exam answers	☐	☐	☐

Overall opinion of this Kit   Excellent ☐   Good ☐   Adequate ☐   Poor ☐

Do you intend to continue using BPP products?   Yes ☐   No ☐

The BPP author of this edition can be e-mailed at: AlisonPriest@bpp.com

Please return this form to: Ian Blackmore, ACCA Publishing Manager (Fundamentals papers), BPP Learning Media Ltd, FREEPOST, London, W12 8BR

Review Form (continued)

TELL US WHAT YOU THINK

Please note any further comments and suggestions/errors below.